9/06

2

the full
spectrum

the full spectrum

a new generation
of writing about
gay, lesbian, bisexual,
transgender, questioning,
and other identities

edited by
david levithan
&
billy merrell

Alfred A. Knopf

New York

THIS IS A BORZOI BOOK PUBLISHED BY ALFRED A. KNOPF

Compilation copyright © 2006 by Alfred A. Knopf, an imprint of Random House Children's Books, a division of Random House, Inc.
Owing to space limitations, page 273 constitutes an extension of this copyright page.

www.randomhouse.com/teens

Educators and librarians, for a variety of teaching tools, visit us at www.randomhouse.com/teachers

Library of Congress Cataloging-in-Publication Data
The full spectrum : a new generation of writing about gay, lesbian, bisexual, transgender, questioning, and other identities / edited by David Levithan and Billy Merrell. — 1st ed.
  p. cm.
ISBN-13: 978-0-375-83290-1 (trade) — ISBN-13: 978-0-375-93290-8 (lib. bdg.)
ISBN-10: 0-375-83290-4 (trade) — ISBN-10: 0-375-93290-9 (lib. bdg.)
1. Gay youth. 2. Sexual minority youth. 3. Sexual orientation. 4. Gender identity.
5. Gay youths' writings. I. Levithan, David. II. Merrell, Billy. III. Title.
HQ76.27.Y68F85 2006
306.76'6'0835—dc22
2005023435

Printed in the United States of America

10 9 8 7 6 5 4 3 2 1

First Edition
May 2006

contents

O.K. by Courtney Gillette   1

A Gay Grammar by Gabe Bloomfield   9

It's Not Confidential, I've Got Potential by Eugenides Fico   12

Snow and Hot Asphalt by Benjamin Zumsteg   21

When You're a Gay Boy in America by Danny Zaccagnino   31

I Smell the Gas of My Father's Fishing Boat by Adam K. Boehmer   37

Fourth of July by Lauren Rile Smith   39

MY DIARY: DOCUMENTED. DONE. by L. Canale   41

Crying Wolfe by Jack Lienke   55

Trans-ventures of an F2M by Alexzander Colin Rasmussen   70

Queer: Five Letters by Kat Wilson   78

Falling Off My Bike and Riding into the Sunset by Christopher Wilcox   87

The Night Marc Hall Went to the Prom by J. J. Deogracias   97

Don't Tell Me That I'm Overly Sensitive and Paranoid by Alex Weissman   101

My poems by Isaac Oliver   105

Sacagawea by Laura Heston   107

A Fairy's Tale by Travis Stanton   108

A Boy in the Girls' Bathroom by Dylan Forest   121

Our Space by Jovencio de la Paz   125

Four Photos by Justin Levesque   129

Break-up in Slow Motion by Joshua Dalton   138

A Story Called "Her" by Alison Young   146

Moment: This Could've Been Me by Evin Hunter   156

A Quietly Queer Revolution by Laci Lee Adams   159

Hatchback by Kaitlyn Tierney Duggan   170

Walking the Tracks by Eric Knudsen   185

The Most Important Letter of Our Life by JoSelle Vanderhooft 189

Without a Trace by Anthony Rella 195

body isn't this by Zara Iris 209

Nice Ass by Jesse Cameron Alick 214

"Girl + Faggots" by Caspian Gray 215

Something for the Ladies by Danny Thanh 218

Click and Drag by Joel de Vera Moncada 224

Jill Sobule and Four Other Torture Devices by Ella Pye 227

Gaydar by Jesse Bernstein 234

The Short Version by Grover Wehman 245

All You Need Is Love by Stefanie Davis 254

That Night by Matthew Mayo 256

Continuation of the Life by Tyrell Pough 260

Three Sunsets by Robert Brittain 263

Notes to the Reader

I have a confession to make.

As much as I hate to admit it, and as weird as it sounds for me to introduce these pieces by acknowledging I made a mistake while first reading them, it's true—and in a collection such as this, in which truth and honesty are being celebrated as each of these young writers reveals to us, bravely but sometimes painfully, their individual takes on the world we're all living in, it seems important to write this so that you may be less likely to make the same mistake as me.

It may be obvious to you that the queer experience has changed severely over the past decade. It may also be obvious that things are still changing, I would like to think for the better. But as obvious as this is, I'm still surprised when I talk to older friends about their experiences in high school and college, especially when, while sharing coming-out stories, I'm told that someone didn't even know they were gay until they were much older.

Having realized relatively young that I was queer, and having come out to a few friends shortly after, the idea of going through adolescence and partway through adulthood before figuring oneself out seems foreign to me, almost impossible, though I know it isn't.

I had heard of people being gay and not wanting anyone else to know. Even if from the moment I knew at least a few other people did, too, I can relate to those who kept it hidden. But keeping sexuality hidden isn't as easy as it once was. We live in a society that labels people, for better or for worse. Long before I started being attracted to guys, I was aware of the fact that other men were. I've come to understand that a big part of my being comfortable with my sexuality so early on was due to my having understood this to be a possibility. I was forced to defend my sexuality long before I had a firm grasp of what any of it meant. I had no clue if I was gay or not, but after spending years having to think about it and having to explain myself when, at sixteen, I started being attracted to men, I knew immediately.

This isn't to say that I expect it is the same with everyone else. All of my friends seem to have different sets of experiences. Some knew younger than I did and waited to tell; others still aren't sure or don't think it's as important as everyone seems to think. But one thing that most people have in common is an ability to say, even if only to themselves, where in the spectrum they fall at any particular moment.

Which is why, when I made a friend recently who wasn't willing to state his sexuality, it made me uneasy. Even if people don't think sexuality is important, they usually still told me where they stood, individually. Even if people preached that labeling another is wrong, they were usually willing to label themselves. I hadn't realized how much I relied on knowing how people categorize themselves as a way of better understanding them.

When after a year of coffee talks and lunches, poem critiques and class gossip, my friend finally talked about, for lack of a better term, his sex life, I found myself instantly more comfortable with him. This really made me think about the sexual politics I preach. How can I agree that labeling people is destructive, that sexuality is fluid and doesn't fit into neat categories, and still expect people to label themselves in order for me to be comfortable? How can I stand behind queer theorists who advocate acceptance and rail against the concept of "normality" and still expect this friend of mine to out himself in order for me to feel close to him? And, most of all, how can I be compiling an anthology of voices and in fact giving voice to the various queer people of my generation if I'm not able to practice the acceptance I preach?

Which brings me to my confession. Only after my realization did I further realize the mistake I had made reading the hundreds of pieces that were sent in for consideration: I didn't only have this expectation of my friend, it turns out; I had the same expectation for each of our writers.

Because the selection process was anonymous and I didn't know the name, age, or gender of each speaker as I was reading his or her work, I found myself reading initially to figure out what category of "queer" the entrant was. Is this one a guy or a girl, an F2M or an M2F? Is she gay, bi, curious? Is he still questioning or is he certain? And only after I found that information out could I enjoy the important part of each piece, which was never the *revealed* sexuality but the *revelation* of what sexuality means.

I invite you to read on, with all of this in mind. What you'll find is a sampling of voices not unlike your own, voices tense with longing but rich with experience. They each have their own individual truths to tell, though rarely are they looking to confess. So be patient and accepting, and they will tell you in their own time what they've seen or felt to be real.

But keep my mistake in mind. In the end, I don't think I would have chosen the pieces differently, so perhaps my apology is unnecessary. Still, it isn't enough to say that society labels people or that expecting labels from one another isn't productive. Society, after all, is made up of each of us. The theory I had preached turned out only to be theory, meaning that unless we make our ideals a reality, they're only words on paper.

—Billy Merrell, October 2005

This book would have been very different if it had been compiled fifteen years ago, when I was in high school. It would have been different ten years ago, or even five years ago. I have faith that in five years, times will have changed enough to alter our snapshot here. And in ten years. And in fifteen years. This is a remarkable time to be young and queer in America. There is progress, and there is backlash. There is love, and there is hate. There is hope, and there is despair. Things are changing fast, and they're not changing fast enough. We know who we are, our friends know who we are, our families (for the most part) know who we are, and we are all able to look our identities in the eye. It's the rest of the culture, the rest of society, that hasn't quite gotten it yet. We still don't have equal rights. We still can't walk most streets holding hands without that fear creeping in. We are still seen by our protestors more for what we are rather than who we are. But a change is going to come. Maybe in five years. Maybe in ten. Maybe longer. Maybe sooner.

One way to effect change is to share truths. To tell our stories. To make our hearts and minds heard.

This anthology started in many places at once. It started in the lives of the writers contained within its pages. It started because Billy Merrell and I wanted more LGBTQ voices than just our own and those of our author friends to be a part of teen literature. It started because our editor, Nancy Hinkel, heard a LGBTQ teen panel moderated by Robert Lipsyte and wondered why there hadn't been a major-publisher anthology of young queer voices.

Billy and I set up a Web site—www.queerthology.com—to accept submissions. All the writers had to be under twenty-three, and all the writing had to be nonfiction. (Some of the names within the stories have been changed to protect the identities of the people being written about, but all of the stories are true and all of the writers' names are real.) We spread the word through our author friends, our own Web sites, and good old-fashioned word of mouth. Then we had the good fortune of partnering with GLSEN (Gay, Lesbian and Straight Education Network), the leading national education organization focused on ensuring safe schools for all students. Proceeds from the sale of this book will go to GLSEN to support what they do.

Of course, there is no way for a single anthology to encompass the fullest spectrum of today's young LGBTQ experience—to do that, we'd have to have essays from every single LGBTQ individual, since every story has its own unique place on the spectrum. We've aimed to present as wide a range as possible within the confines of the book's length; some parts of the spectrum are better represented than others, and there are still voices to be heard from. We view this as a start, not an end.

There are a number of people we have to thank—many of whom we don't know yet. Thank you to all of the contributors. Thank you to everyone who submitted their stories. Thank you to everyone—authors, teachers, friends, librarians, editors—who spread the word. Thank you to everyone at Knopf, especially Nancy (for her amazing dedication), Allison Wortche (for her incredible support), and Melissa Nelson (for her fantastic design). Thank you to everyone at GLSEN and all the other organizations that have supported this project, its contributors, and LGBTQ youth. Happily, there are more of them than we could possibly list. Thank you to all of the students, LGBTQ and straight, who are allying for equal rights. Billy and I have been lucky to visit towns and cities where communities are coming together to make a safe, tolerant, encouraging space for all people. We hope, in its own small way, this book helps.

One of my favorite e-mails ever came from a seventy-year-old who, looking at LGBTQ youth now, said, "Things sure have changed since I was a teenager in the 1940s." Well, I'm happy I can say, "Things sure have changed since I was a teenager in the late 1980s and early 1990s." May they continue to change. For the better of us all.

—David Levithan, October 2005

For more, check out www.queerthology.com

O.K.

by Courtney Gillette

My first kiss was a girl.

It was almost like a pity kiss, a kiss to get me through that rite of passage, the way I wanted it. Rose was the only person who knew I liked girls, she was the only one I trusted enough to tell. We went to junior high together in a small town in Pennsylvania. She had frizzy hair and a mother who took Prozac and yelled a lot. Rose lived on this surreal plane of reality, allowing the world to be as dramatic as it was at the age of fifteen, and I loved her for that.

We were in color guard together. While marching band appeared to be lowest rung on the ladder of popularity, color guard managed to go even below that, to a subterranean territory of uncoolness. I don't really remember what we were doing there. I had played the trumpet but was always last chair, so when they told me I had to join marching band, that I had to go out in those stupid costumes under those bright football-game lights, I opted for color guard instead. As if wearing costumes of yellow spandex and glitter while tossing six-foot metal poles with red flags was a better option. It seemed like a good idea at the time.

Rose and I were ugly, misfits. Most of the girls in color guard were social outcasts: frumpy girls too fat or too awkward for cheerleading. They became flag twirlers, "chicks with sticks." I remember how much the bus would stink with our sweat and girl smells, the odor of panty hose and too much eye shadow, coming home from cavalcades in the fall. The seats were made of a sticky material, and Rose and I would be squished in the small space, sitting beside each other. We would each have a headphone from my Walkman on, listening to Björk and trying to drown out the chatter of thirty girls talking about the new cute boy in the trombone section. The other girls knew we were weird and kind of left it at that. They didn't like me because I refused to wear makeup. The captain of the squad, a short, fat girl with greasy brown hair, would yell at me as she wielded red Maybelline lipstick. "It's part of the costume," she'd hiss. "You *have* to wear it." I finally conceded and let them smear the cheap colors on my face, only to get back at them the next week when I came to practice with my hair dyed blue with Manic Panic. It was the week before championships, and our coach cried when she saw me. "What are we going to do?" she sobbed, pointing at me like I had lost an appendage, as if I was completely incapable of spinning a flag now that my hair was blue. We borrowed a scratchy brown wig from the theater department and I had to be very careful not to turn my head too fast, lest the synthetic locks go flying off my head and land on the fifty-yard line as I marched past, performing a flag routine to some Gershwin song. Rose and I came to enjoy being the social outcasts of color guard. It was an extra badge of strangeness for us.

Besides, Rose and I were *deep*, much deeper than those other girls who read *YM* and wore sweaters from the Gap. Rose and I were into poetry, we would read e. e. cummings to each other over the phone, part of long marathon conversations about the meaning of life. We were fifteen, we were invincible, we were enlightened. I would get off the yellow school bus and run home, dropping my schoolbag and picking up the phone as soon as I came in. I would always lie on the gray carpet in the family room as we talked for hours. My brother would play Nintendo and sometimes scowl at the weird things I said about true love and art and suffering. Rose had spent a few months in a mental hospital when she was younger, so she was my idol as far as real-life drama went. She never really told me why, kept the story mysterious, only saying that one day in the car with her mother she said something about death that caused her mother to drive her straight to the psychiatric ward of the local state hospital. I was fascinated. Rose was my Sylvia Plath, my muse and my heroine. As we trundled through the muddy waters of adolescence, I could tell Rose anything I felt, and she would agree, validating my virgin emotions. It was in all this intensity that I fell in love with her.

Rose had a boyfriend. He was kind of pudgy and had a really annoying laugh. They would hold hands as we walked around the mall, drinking milk shakes from the Dairy Queen. I didn't like it when they held hands. Her boyfriend couldn't understand how deep Rose and I were. I humored him because Rose did.

"Do you love him?" I would ask on the phone, watching the blocks of sunlight that came in through the window make patterns on the carpet. Rose would sigh dramatically.

"Yes, but I don't think he knows. I don't think he understands love like I do."

I nodded emphatically. I understood love. Rose and I had charted the entire emotion out in terms of desire, affection, and completion. Solitude was to be savored, but being in love was a privilege.

It was this concept of affection that stalled our philosophies on love and intimacy, because I hadn't been kissed before. Once a boy at the roller rink in the seventh grade tried to kiss me, but I turned my face away and mumbled something about having a cold. There was something about boys I just didn't want. I would act like I wanted them, imagine that somewhere in the world there was a sensitive boy with long hair who played guitar and read books on feminism, and he would be my boyfriend. Then I would kiss boys. But at a high school where the homecoming football games were so big the whole town shut down for the occasion, I wasn't holding my breath on finding a sensitive, artistic boyfriend anytime soon.

In the ninth grade Rose's boyfriend went away to Bible camp for the summer and came back deciding Rose was just too weird. He thought he should be spending his adolescence having romances with good Christian girls, not with a girl who was obsessed with death and the color black. I was secretly relieved that he was gone. Now maybe I could hold hands with Rose at the mall. If we both knew so much about love, couldn't we be in love? I pondered it for weeks, listening to Tori Amos, lying in bed and staring at the trees outside, desperate for an answer. I finally asked Rose one day, during our afternoon phone conversation. "I have a question," I posed formally, my body sweating with anticipation.

"Okay," Rose said. I could hear her breathing softly, probably lying on her bed, in the room with the lavender curtains her mother had decorated the whole house with.

I thought I was going to puke with the anxiety of what I was about to say. I took a deep breath and said very slowly, "If I kissed you, would you kiss me back?"

Rose didn't say anything. I wanted to crawl under the gray carpet and die. I heard her clear her throat and then say, carefully, "Yes. But not with that tongue thing. I never liked that."

I don't remember what we said after that.

That weekend Rose came over to spend the night. We did what we did every time we had a sleepover—we looked up lyrics to Björk songs on the Internet, we read comic books, we watched *Saturday Night Live* and ate ice cream sundaes. Turning off the TV, we went upstairs to my room to hang out. Rose had bought new incense at the mall, so we burned it by the window and lit a bunch of candles, too, sitting on the bed with the lights turned out. My room was a circus of *Sailor Moon* posters, dried flowers, and books spilling off the shelves, piles of paperbacks and journals in stacks on the floor. She sat across from me, looking at me with a sly grin. "I dare you," she said.

"What?" I could only hear the sound of my heart crashing against my breastbone, a deafening noise inside of me.

She laughed a little, drumming her fingernails on her thigh. "I dare you," she repeated. "I dare you to kiss me."

I couldn't feel my body. The room seemed ridiculously hot, and the pungent smell of the incense was making me dizzy. In between tracks I could hear the CD skipping in the stereo. I was frozen, my hands dead weights on the bedspread, and Rose just sat there and looked at me. Finally I lunged forward, put my lips on hers, and felt the heat of her breath on my face. We kissed slowly, timidly, my eyes squeezed shut. It hurt how much I wanted it, how much I wanted Rose. I found myself slipping my tongue out of my mouth, pushing it into the warmth of hers. I thought I would explode. Rose pulled back slightly, gave a small smile before shifting away from me, standing up and going to the CD player, changing the album. I sat on the bed, not sure whether to cry or to thank her. She turned on the lights, a cue that the moment was over. I suggested we watch more TV and she shrugged. Downstairs we channel-surfed through the infomercials and B-movies of late-night television. She was detached and cold. I wanted to scream. I sat on the couch in the living room next to her, sometimes munching leftover popcorn from the bowl we had made earlier. The cold kernels tasted stupid on my tongue. We finally gave up on the TV and decided to go to bed. Upstairs, Rose rolled her sleeping bag out on the floor, but instead of changing in my bedroom like we always did, she took her pajamas out of her schoolbag and went into the bathroom. I stood awkwardly next to my bed, wondering what I had done wrong.

The next Monday Rose didn't come to school. I ran home from the bus and dialed her number before I had even put down my backpack. Her mother answered.

"Hi, is Rose there?"

"Is this Courtney?" her mother asked in a sharp voice.

"Yeah," I said.

Her mother coughed a little. "Rose can't come to the phone. She's indisposed."

Indisposed. She pronounced the word long and hard. I had to go to the big dictionary on the shelf in the living room and look it up. *Indisposed. To be averse, disinclined. To be or feel ill, sickened. To be rendered unfit, disqualified.* I blinked, shut the book, and slid it back into place, next to the encyclopedias and the anthologies of Shakespeare. I hoped Rose was okay.

When Rose stopped talking to me, I just kind of accepted it. I didn't know what else to do. Our other friends were curious. Did something happen? Did we have a fight? I would shake my head madly or shrug my shoulders, trying to look aloof. They would shrug back, talk about how strange she was. Maybe she was having her period. I swallowed all the confusion and regret deep inside me, and nodded at their conclusions. Strange.

I thought I would be able to finish out the school year avoiding Rose as it seemed she wanted me to, but there was the marching band trip to Ocean City, Maryland, for a parade. We had been preparing for it all year. It was an overnight trip, and we would be staying in a hotel. I had signed up to share a room with Rose and our two friends Patricia and Julie. I panicked. One day after practice I went to the parent in charge of arranging the trip. "Is it too late to change room assignments?" I asked, making a pleading, desperate face. The woman had a perm and was wearing a sweatshirt with our high school's emblem on the front.

"No can do!" she said cheerily. "All the rooms are packed. If I switched you I'd have to switch other girls' rooms around, too. It's only two nights, dear. I'm sure you can work things out."

The day before the trip I acted sick, told my mother I was vomiting and couldn't go. She took my temperature and patted my head when it read the normal 98 degrees. "Just nerves," she told me with a smile. "It's such an exciting trip, you'll have so much fun." That night I cried so hard into my pillow that my brother banged on the wall from his room, yelling for me to shut up.

On the trip I just stayed quiet. I figured if I didn't say anything it would look okay, normal. I listened to my headphones constantly and stayed in the room watching television while other kids played Ping-Pong and went in the swimming pool. Rose stayed out of the room, hanging out with some of the boys from the drum section.

They smoked cigarettes outside by the Dumpster and she would come back reeking of Newports. Julie thought Rose had a crush on the guy who played snare. I sat stone-faced on the bed and said nothing. It rained the day of the parade and our flags drooped sadly; they made us march because it was only drizzling when we started. "Just a little spritz," our coach encouraged us merrily. Our costumes were so cheap that the orange sashes bled onto our leotards, looked like rashes up and down our legs and arms. It was our last night in the hotel. We had some free time before we were scheduled to go out to dinner at some seafood restaurant on the boardwalk. I went into the room to get my headphones, thinking everyone was downstairs. When I came in, the bathroom door was slightly ajar. I saw Rose coming out of the shower, naked. *"What are you doing?"* she screamed. Her eyes became daggers and she slammed the door hard. I started to shake and walked out of the room, started walking down the hall, half running. At the end of the hall I collapsed into a heap in the corner by some fake plant and sobbed, burying my head between my knees. I heard the ding of the elevator opening. Soon Patricia and Julie were by me.

"I kissed her!" I yelled. *"I kissed Rose! That's why she hates me! I kissed her!"*

I was gulping for air. Patricia and Julie were staring at me. I thought about how I was losing more and more friends, about how stupid that kiss had been, how it had ruined everything. Patricia leaned forward and hugged me. "It's okay," she said quietly. "It's really okay."

The next week at school Patricia must have said something to Rose. She came over to me one morning before homeroom and asked me to talk. I picked up my book bag and walked down the hall with her. She looked at the ground when she spoke. "I'm just not like that, okay?" she said in an angry rush of words. She glanced at my face and then looked back at the ground again. "I just don't want people to think I'm like that. You can be whatever you want, but I'm not . . . I'm just not."

I was fiddling with the strap of my book bag, the one that was frayed and dangling. I shrugged. "Okay," I said, my voice hollow. I wanted to go back to my friends, I wanted Rose to be something that never happened. She mumbled something about being late and walked down the stairs, lost in the crowd of teenagers going to first period. I walked back to my locker and tried not to think about it. I consoled myself with the idea of college, that I could move far away to some city and have a girlfriend and be queer and make out with her whenever and wherever I wanted. I tried not to think of Rose anymore. I told myself that a kiss was all I had wanted.

A Gay Grammar
by Gabe Bloomfield

This is not a story in which a helpless teenager is beaten. This is not a story about sexual repression. This is not a story about rape.

It doesn't involve confusion, it doesn't have any major breakdowns.

Nobody attempts to commit suicide in this story.

This may be an uncommon story. The main character is happy. The main character rarely feels pressured, except when it's by schoolwork. The main character is gay. But he is not gay-bashed; in fact, his sexual orientation barely feels part of him anymore, because he and his family and friends have so easily accepted it into their lives.

The main character does not feel gay. He just feels like himself.

The main character is I.

If you think that the last sentence of the previous section looks odd, or even wrong, you're probably not alone. The vast majority of English speakers would actually have said "The main character is me" (or, to avoid the conundrum altogether, "I am the main character"). This is grammatically incorrect; however, this type of grammatically taboo construction has been used so often that it has been practically accepted into English grammar as what is right.

You see, the verb *to be* does not take an object; it takes a predicate nominative, which is why you have to use *I* (the nominative) instead of *me* (the accusative). But that hardly matters. What matters is that if I said that sentence while talking to a crowd of people, I would get a lot of odd looks. Many people think that it's wrong, although most would not voice their opinion. My friends and parents would look at me and turn to one another and sigh, because they know that I'm a nut for grammar and that I say it the right way rather than the way that sounds right to most of the people in the room.

This is oddly like being gay. My friends and parents know it too well to notice, or if they do, they just smile. Just another one of my quirks, part of who I am. Other people notice it, too. It's not that hard to tell. Somebody could even say that it sticks out. But they may be confused, unsure, even frightened. Some people know the grammar and are comfortable with my gayness. Some people would have said "The main character is me," and they do not know how to react to my strangely worded pronouncement.

To my gay self.

I inherited—yes, inherited—my grammar habit from my father. He was a stickler for grammar, too, and he often corrected my speech when I was younger. It worked—my grammar became flawless. However, I also inherited his tendency to correct other people's grammar. If, in the middle of telling a story, somebody says "Me and Kate went to the store," I'll shove in "Kate and I" without missing a beat. The people around me will glance in my direction and then turn back toward the person telling the story, realizing that it was just Gabe, correcting grammar again. The storyteller will give me an evil look, then go on with the story. Sometimes he or she will repeat my correction and finish telling the story. Other times he or she will ignore it completely. Sometimes the speaker will deliberately repeat "Kate and me," just to make me mad. I've learned to ignore it.

So that's what I do, I correct grammar. Do I like that I do it? No. Can I help it? No, it's just part of who I am. I deal with it.

If grammar is my gayness, then my correction of other people's grammar is my coming out, my "flaunting." The first few times I did it, people started arguments about it. Why did I have to do that? Couldn't I just leave the grammar alone? Why did I have to shove the fact that I knew grammar well into other people's faces?

The first few times I did it, people were surprised. They didn't know what to say. I corrected grammar? I'm gay? What does this mean??

How are homosexuality and grammar even remotely alike?

People got used to it. People dealt. Now when I say that I think a guy is hot to one of my friends, the only argument I get is about my taste in guys. In fact, my gayness goes over much better than my grammar correction, which still garners a few evil looks every time I do it.

However, just as "Kate and me" or "The main character is me" have been accepted as part of our language despite the fact that they're obviously incorrect, so has it become okay to spit upon a culture, a lifestyle, a sexuality, whatever you want to call it, simply because what is right has been forgotten for what is easy. Being gay is difficult in a world that begins its sentences with conjunctions and allows participles to dangle unchecked.

Despite the wandering dependent clauses, despite the fragments passing themselves off as sentences, we're not going away.

We're here for the fight.

It's Not Confidential, I've Got Potential
by Eugenides Fico

A couple of days before my appointment, a friend and I were talking about how stuck we are in our roles as "men." When people say we are "men," we can hear the quotation marks in their derisive voices. What people don't seem to understand is that I'm not trying to be a man, and I'm not trying to be a "man." I just haven't found the place between my half-man and my half-self that feels more right than this does.

My appointment was for 5:20. I was nineteen, but I hadn't had a pap test yet. Going for a pap smear is not in line with my idea of myself. It's not even in line with my idea of my half-self. But after being berated by my doctor for an entire summer, I resolved to do it. After all, pap smears are, by nature and definition, a feminine thing to do. At that point, I had spent sixteen years trying to stamp out anything that was feminine in me, and an additional three years trying to build up anything masculine. I wasn't ready to go off into the downtown of Cedar Rapids, Iowa, and have someone verify, by all accounts, that there's no way I'm not a girl. Getting reminded once a month is quite enough for me.

My problem is that I don't want this "girl-thing" hanging over me. I'm caught between the effort of being a guy and the struggle to not forget where I'm from. After nineteen years of being told that I'm a girl—sixteen years of trying to equalize society's goals with my own—I can't forget that part of me. I told my friend about my appointment, about how it was a slap in the face to any alternate gender I try to create. Shim replied by saying, "The first step to recovery is admitting you have a problem." Shim has the same problem.

We like to wear girly clothes sometimes. It's a rare occurrence, but it happens. On days like that, people invariably make "comments," thinly veiled questions asking why the sudden change in demeanor, the change in self-expression. We invariably fall back on excuses—"I have to do my laundry." "This was the only blue thing I could find, and I felt like blue." "I have to meet someone's parents later." It's not like any of these are reasons. They're almost always true, but that doesn't mean we don't enjoy the girl in us sometimes. My friend was wearing a skirt as we talked about pap tests and society and people we date and college classes. I was wearing baggy jeans and a T-shirt. It's not that we dress like men because we think we're men. We simply recognize the fact that certain parts of us are not feminine. And once we recognized this, we wanted the world to recognize it as well.

The walk over to the appointment was full of distractions. It was one of those not-quite-cool days that the Midwest seems to be full of during the fall. I had on my patched pants—pants I had spent hours sewing together after my mom serged the cloth for me. And even though the walk made me a little warm, I had worn a button-down shirt, long-sleeved and plaid. Whenever I wear that shirt, I think of the boy in *Where the Red Fern Grows,* and I think of Jess from *Bridge to Terabithia.* I pretend that I'm some kid who grew up on a farm in the Midwest and went to college just a few hours from my hometown, rather than a girl who grew up less than a mile from the Delaware River, going to Trenton, New Jersey, for church every Sunday and driving to Philadelphia to attend folk concerts in the summer.

I never imagine that Cedar Rapids is my hometown. Growing up, we called Trenton the toxic-waste dump of the East. I make fun of Trenton with the knowledge that Trenton is a part of me. It's like when Minnesotans make fun of their own accents, or Iowans make fun of themselves for falsely being known as the Potato State. The fact that Trenton is so shitty is exactly why I love it.

Which is why Cedar Rapids can't be my hometown. It's too close to Trenton. It's like when you fall in love with someone but then break up. And then you meet someone so much like that first person that all you can do is see the differences between them. You can't love the second person in the same way or for the same reasons; you can only love them for the reasons that are different. Cedar Rapids and Trenton are the same city, which is why I always know how they're unalike. They went through the same industrial boom. They went through the same industrial desertion. There are the same ghettos and the same areas you avoid at night.

As I walked down Second Ave., a dusty old man stepped out of the brickwork, his friend having asked for some change for a phone call. Her eyes were drugged over, but I didn't see that until I was close enough to give her the money.

"How you doin'?" the guy asked me as his friend floundered for change for my bill. I fought the urge to step back as he moved closer to me. Behind me, a couple cars drove past. I answered that I was okay, that I was stressed about midterms, but whatever. I did not mention that I didn't actually have any midterms, and I was more worried about my appointment today than anything else I had coming up in the next week. "You need some weed," he told me. I glanced at his friend, still counting change. There was a wide open space behind me, and neither of them was in a condition to chase me down. "No, I'm okay, really," I said, thinking that maybe I shouldn't have stopped, that maybe I really did need to get to my appointment on time. "Naw, you need some *weed.*" He gave me that look, that look that says "You know what I mean, and you know that I'm right." The friend finally finished counting. "I'm really okay," I told him as his friend held out a palm full of coins. "It's a couple cents short. Is that okay?" I nodded. "It's fine," I said as she handed me change with a nickel more than I deserved. I didn't bother mentioning her mistake and instead just got out of there.

I thought about who they thought I was. There's a small

dilemma every time I am in a situation where I don't feel safe. My feminine training kicks in, cataloging exits and escape routes. But my masculine enforcement tries to compensate for my lack of confidence by putting on more bravado than I can hope to defend. I wonder if they noticed my giveaways. My voice is high, though it's not all that noticeable until I sing. Over the years, I've developed a slight rasp, due to hours of attempting to lower my crystalline soprano. I would take a tenor, or a countertenor. That's not asking for much. I don't need a bass or a baritone. Instead, I ended up with a high-pitched laugh and a smoker's soprano rather than a liquid-cool alto.

Walking along, I thought about how to talk at the appointment. When you lower your voice too much, people can always tell. They can tell by how fake it sounds and by the face you make as you try to do it. I was thinking that I could create an image of myself in my mind so strongly that my appointment wouldn't break me down. I just had to resolve myself. Gender is an act. All gender is an act. There's just a very big difference in people's minds about when that act is "right" and when that act is a "lie."

I got to the right intersection, Second Ave. and Fifteenth St. I couldn't remember the address, and I couldn't tell which side of the intersection Planned Parenthood was on. I looked at both of the possible buildings. Neither looked promising. One had a sign out front concerning realty, the other had a sign about Mount Mercy Hospital. Planned Parenthood isn't connected with the hospital, but I figured that was a better bet.

I walked in the door, hoping I didn't look like too much of an ass. There was a woman behind the desk. She was maybe forty-five, with short hair cut very feminine and glasses low on her nose. Her hand held a bunch of papers. She gave me one of those looks, that over-the-glasses, who-the-fuck-are-you look. I wondered if she wore her glasses low in order to perfect that look. "Can I *help* you?" Like it was the last thing in the world she wanted to do. My mind froze a little, thinking about the fact that she probably didn't like college kids who invaded her town and walked around in grungy, patched-up pants. Thinking that she might suspect I wasn't the guy I was trying to make her think I was. I made my voice as low as possible without straining it. "I'm looking for Planned Parenthood." She looked back at her papers. "Across the street and around the back." There was no sincerity in my voice when I said thanks and walked back out. The defiant teenager part of me hoped she'd make assumptions about me while I wasn't there to defend myself, just because I knew she was wrong. The transgendered part of me hoped those assumptions would involve me having a pregnant girlfriend.

There was a canopy hanging out behind the realty building. I walked under it and opened one of the glass double doors. I found another set of doors around a corner, clearly labeled *Planned Parenthood of East Central Iowa*. I walked in and stopped, surveying the scene. Women sat in chairs, comfortable in this waiting room. Some children played with toys that had been provided. The women and children stared at me. I lost my focus and glanced around the rest of the room. There's a difference between glancing and surveying, although most people don't notice it. There's a difference between looking nervous and looking like you're used to being in control; people always notice that. Glancing never implies control.

I told a friend of mine about it later, how everyone stared at me when I walked in. He's a farmboy from Charles City. "That's Iowa," he said. "That's what we do. When someone walks into the room, we look at them to see if there's any way we know them." In Pennsylvania, a glance is customary, but nothing more. For men, a swift perusal is what is required. In that look, we assess whether we know the person or not, and we make our initial judgments. And one of the most important judgments is whether the person is a guy or a girl. With nine pairs of women's and children's eyes staring at me, they must surely have realized the physical fact I was trying to hide.

I walked up to the counter, trying to regain my control. I told the receptionist why I was there, trying not to let everyone else in the room know as well.

Half an hour later, having completed page after page of paperwork, I was in a private room, sitting in one of those mass-produced chairs that still manages to be semi-comfortable. A woman came in. I made a conscious effort to keep my head up and not fidget. She had papers in front of her, the ones I had filled out minutes before. As she looked them over, she asked me questions, clarifying where my words had been insufficient.

"You're on birth control?"

"I went on because I got my period for five and a half weeks out of eight," I said.

She winced sympathetically and asked what kind of birth control it was. Reaching into my backpack, I handed her the package. She nodded and handed me a prescription, saying she had prescribed me for one year.

"You've had sexual relations with both men and women?" I was impressed by how nonjudgmental she sounded. Iowa has gotten me on my toes.

"Yeah, but the last person I dated was a girl, and we didn't have sex." She wrote something down.

"Have you had sex?"

I paused, unsure how to proceed. I had known this would come up. But I had just forced myself to come to the appointment without thinking. If I don't think about things, I can't get scared enough to back out.

"Well," I said, "see, when I was younger, there was this older boy in my neighborhood." I was looking at a picture on the wall; it reminded me of the teeth pictures I always see at the dentist, the ones that show gingivitis. "I don't think I've ever had sex, but I kind of blocked out some of what happened." I wasn't looking at her; the picture on the wall depicted a cervix. "So I'm not exactly sure." I should have stopped talking there, but I kept going. "That was actually part of why I wanted to come. Because I don't think I have AIDS or anything, but there's always a chance." She nodded, looking at me. Maybe I didn't actually say those last thoughts. I tend to misremember things, imagining I've said something I thought about. I can't remember the rest of our conversation. I just remember thinking to myself, *She's the fourth person to know.*

I have a habit of being unaffected by things, but I think things must affect me more than I know. It's just a question of what I'm willing to admit to myself. When I think about having sex with a guy, it weirds me out. I can't imagine trusting someone that much. But thinking about having sex with a girl makes sense, like I was vaguely meant to play that role. Philosophers have this theory called Compatibility Theory. It's the idea that a man and a woman are meant for each other because they complement each other. The theory states that men and women are opposite, and opposites attract. Maybe the theory is right. Maybe I'm an opposite of women because I was born one, the same way Cedar Rapids is Trenton's opposite because of the differences they have, differences I only notice because of their similarities.

The woman sitting with me, maybe her name was Susan, didn't seem interested in whether or not I was compatible with The Boy, and she didn't seem to care whether or not I was compatible with either of my girlfriends. She was more interested in whether I was at risk for AIDS and whether my siblings had genetic-related diseases. I appreciated how she did that.

I didn't think much during the examination. Susan explained everything before she did it, warning me of what was coming. Despite this, I wasn't ready. I had spent the past two weeks thinking I knew what a pap smear would be like, but the actuality was nothing like my preconceived notions.

I left half an hour later, the feeling of invasion making me wince a little with every other step. It didn't hurt to walk, but rather it hurt to know someone had known parts of me even I didn't know directly. Susan had asked me to take off my clothes and put on the paper gown, shutting the door behind her. The gown was pink. It was strangely warm against my skin. It reminded me of when I learned how much heat newspapers can hold. When she came back, her professional hands took over, the same as her professional words had taken control during our discussion. I've based so much of my gender identity on my body. My identity is fundamentally related to the idea that, because of how I was born, people don't treat me the way I would like to be treated. The pap smear touched where I had hidden my identity, breaking the barrier I had tried to create on my walk. It wasn't so much the invasion of my vagina as the invasion of my self.

People often assume I hate my vagina, that I would rather have been born male and be done with it. They're all wrong. I remember when I was younger, I suffered from the same syndrome Pinocchio did. I thought I could grow up and have a sex-change and become a "real" boy. Now that I'm older, I can't have a sex-change because that would mean sacrificing the personalities I've tried to become. People who move from one sex to the other are required to destroy their previous lives. There's a home video of my family at Christmas when I was nine years old. I got makeup from my grandmother, and I ran around the house excited to have it. I don't remember this, but it's important to me that it happened. It's central to my idea of myself, the fact that I found makeup important when I was that age. I can't have a sex-change because sex isn't the problem. The problem is that people are too intent to categorize me as a person who enjoys shopping and makeup and boys, simply because I look a certain way.

At this point, the stereotypes people hold for me don't include shopping or boys. They hold the opposite. It's assumed that I know about sports teams and cars and that I only want to date girls. My gender is an act, but acting is open to interpretation. People see me the way they are comfortable seeing people. I'm "the gay girl" on campus because that's who people can handle me being. On the rare day that I wear girly clothes, people do a double take. They say, "Gen! You look good." Other days, I simply look like the person they've learned to see me as. I don't say I have to do my laundry because I'm embarrassed that I sometimes like tight shirts and flare pants. I say it because, in their minds, by admitting that I sometimes enjoy the girl in me, I admit that I'm not a man.

A couple months after the pap, I went to a different town,

where no one knew me. I wore a beard, applied with spirit gum and my own hair. People asked a friend about me, seeing me for the "man" I was trying to hide. I try to be a man for the same reasons I say I have to do my laundry. By taking anything less, I take on the role of not-man. And the only other role society will recognize is woman.

Snow and Hot Asphalt
by Benjamin Zumsteg

Conversations about where I grew up can go one of two ways. When pressed for time, I say I grew up in Chicago. Mostly.

I do this on purpose, hoping that I don't have to explain. If I do, I have to involve my arms in back-and-forth movements, explaining the two points in my life in which I lived in Utah. When that comes up, I get the usual response. They ask, "How did you survive that?" or "Isn't it boring?" or "What about those crazy Mormons?"

I explain what I can, trying to keep things short and simple. And each time, the same image comes to my mind in a flash of hot light.

In that image, it is late August and I am stepping out of my mother's forest-green minivan. I am in the middle of a Brigham Young University parking lot in Provo, Utah, waiting for my mother to finish some meetings. It is the week before her first year of teaching. The car is not on, but I leave the key in the ignition and let my music play in the tape player loudly, speaking my mind to the rows of baking sheet metal. *I'm gonna do my best swan dive,* the speakers sing, *into shark-infested waters. . . .*

I step out of the car for some fresh air, though "fresh" is a relative term. It is stiflingly hot outside. My lips crack as I squint into the sun. I have just begun the drying-out process that comes with moving to a desert.

I look down at the newish black asphalt, marked with winding strips of tar. I squish my flip-flop down into it with one foot, turning it inward, twisting the tar around. I release the pressure and it pops back into place as it unsticks itself from the ball of my foot.

I look up, facing east. I am met with a towering wall of mountains. From my current vantage point I am forced to look up to get the full, panoramic view. Directly ahead of me, still technically in the foothills, brush and trees dot the dull khaki-colored grasses with shades of olive. My eyes move upward, along the slithering grooves in the hillsides, as the packs of trees become thicker and thicker, coated in a deep, rich green.

My view reaches the tops of a few of the highest mountains and I see that there is still snow. It is an observation I have often taken for granted; the illustrated image of a mountain always consists of that tiny, squiggly line drawn across the top.

The whites of these caps throb in the light. This snow lives on in the hot months. It stays cool at that altitude, even as the sun beats down on it. Small glaciers in the mountain valleys keep their poise and move slowly, steadily, as they carve out their paths behind the mountain faces. Small pools dot the places where the glaciers once squatted on the landscape. Dense fields of wildflowers in orange, purple, blue, and yellow surround the pools, tucked into small valleys within the mountains.

I see none of that. I am down on the sticky asphalt while the snow shines on.

I don't ever tell anyone about that image, though. It is only what flashes through my mind as I tell them bits and pieces, as I tell them that no, I couldn't have eighteen boyfriends in Utah and that the beer really isn't weaker. But that image is permanent, burned into my eyes as I tell them the small details.

If they have time, and if I feel up to it, I tell them a little more.

I arrived in Utah from Chicago, where I had grown up. I was born in Utah sixteen years previously, but I called myself a Chicagoan. The flat, sometimes rolling land of Illinois was home to me, the way Lake Michigan taught me which way was east. The tight suburban roads of Chicago were comfortable. Utah's mountains had always been a backdrop for Christmas and summer vacations, a reason to say "I miss the mountains," but otherwise they'd remained a distant, lofty memory.

Though everyone in Chicago knew I was Mormon, I had ways of escaping it, especially as I came to terms with the fact that I was gay. I could confide in small groups of friends at school; I escaped for several hours a day at figure skating practice and for weeks on end at competitions. I could go days without seeing another Mormon except for my mother, and she was enough.

The unraveling of our relationship as mother and son, which had taken place two summers earlier, was somewhat distant at the time of our move. The secrecy of my first gay friendships, the subsequent tearful confession, and the hard-nosed surveillance that entrenched us in battle was something we didn't often speak about. However, my mother couldn't shake the feeling that I had betrayed her. In some ways, the news that I had consistently lied to her about my life was worse than the actual "problem" of my homosexuality.

Despite all this, I felt the need to keep going in this new life I was seeking out. I would still sneak off to meet gay friends while my mother worked at a library and taught her students and performed freelance gigs. Sometimes she dragged me with her to wherever she was going because she didn't trust me. She had every right not to. We could go long stretches of time without saying anything about it, but who I had become or the "choice" I was making managed to put a damper on any interaction we had.

In moving us back to Utah, my mother had new hope. She was returning to a position she had held at BYU when I was born. It was a full-time position that she actually wanted instead of working a day job to support her real passion. It was a secure, larger income in a state with a lower cost of living.

My mother held out hope that a return to the physical center of Mormon culture would influence my life. I would be going to a predominantly Mormon high school, going to church only with people who lived within two blocks of me, and living only minutes from a university that was home to over 20,000 Mormons. They were everywhere, and she thought this was a good thing.

I dreaded it. My mother accepted the position six months before it started and bought a house, sight unseen, five months before we even moved. I prepared to say goodbye to friendships that had just begun to develop in all my worlds: high school, skating, and the gay world my mother forbade me from existing in. That world, the one I still knew the least, was the hardest for me to leave behind.

I had been warned about Utah and about Provo, where I'd be living, in particular. The place was 80 percent Mormon, but strong percentages didn't necessarily mean strong faith. The bishop of my congregation before I left Chicago warned me of this, telling me that I'd see more hypocrisy amongst kids my age there than I ever did here. This was news to me, considering that one of the guys my age in my congregation had been flirting with me for about two years and several more were heavy drinkers.

After a long goodbye to Chicago, I was on that hot pavement in a parking lot at BYU, waiting for my mother to finish with her obligations. It was a scene I would repeat countless times over the course of my time in Provo; I'd sit in the car, music blaring, until she would walk out, cello usually in hand, and I would turn the music down, get out of the car, and help her with the instrument's bulky case. At her concerts in Chicago, I hauled her cello everywhere. She called me her roadie. My dutiful position had not ended with the move.

A year after I arrived in Utah, I was invited to go on a hiking trip with my congregation's youth group. I was less than thrilled, especially because it meant waking at five in the morning. We had to get an early start because it was still August and the days got very hot very quickly. We were to climb Mt. Timpanogos, the highest peak in Utah Valley at just over 11,000 feet. We would not climb to the summit, however, but to a point called Emerald Lake, which was a few hundred feet below the steep ascent to the top.

Local Indian legend (as I read on a plaque in a local Mexican restaurant) told of how "Timp" is shaped like a dead maiden, lying flat on her funeral bed, with the jagged peaks forming her feet, clasped hands, chest, and disproportionately large nose. The steep slope bridging Timp with the other mountains to the south tumbles down into a canyon and is said to be the warrior who grieves her death, clasping his hands against her head, his cape dropping to the valley floor.

I didn't mind the hike so much once we got going. What annoyed me most were the occasional stops to read an inspiring scripture passage to keep us going. The day continued to get warmer as we ascended, stopping for inspiring thought after inspiring thought. During those times, I either looked down at the ground below us or at how impossibly high the ascent looked above us, not paying attention to what was being said. We continued upward; we walked up through switchbacks in the massive wall behind the mountain as the day wore on, stopping to let others catch up. I stayed at the front of the pack, not caring to look back.

Adjusting to my new high school, Timpview High, was not unlike adjusting to a climb. It was just as bothersome and persistent as the dry, cracked skin I was constantly trying to hydrate. It left me as exhausted as the altitude did. In Provo, even a short run, every quick burst of energy, left me nearly breathless.

There were aspects of my new school that I was prepared for, just as I could have prepared myself for the drying-out process by drinking lots of water or carrying a tub of lip balm around with me. I knew that kids in my congregation would be in my classes. I knew they had been going to church with one another for years, and saw one another more than the typical five times a week required by schools. They saw one another on the weekend at church, on weeknights during church activities. They went to Boy Scouts together, they were in the Young Women's groups together. They lived across the street from one another. By junior year of high school, many of them had become inseparable in some form or another.

I knew how closely linked church life would be to school—how, during a free time-release period from school, we would trek ourselves up Timpview's sloping parking lot onto a separate property.

There, in a large, two-story church building, we would spend one hour in a protected environment governed by different rules, attendance policies, and teachers. The teachers were Brother This and Sister That, not Mr. or Mrs., and were called to these positions by the Church.

We opened with church hymns, we prayed, we studied various parts of scripture. Many students would talk about what a blessing it was to be able to come to this environment for an hour a day to avoid the evils of everyday high school. Some of these same students would end up down in the Commons area of the actual high school later in the day, swearing and flirting heavily with their latest conquests.

I was prepared for the hypocrisy, though it began to grate on me as time wore on. I would stop going to seminary consistently about halfway through my junior year, retreating into the computer lab used by the high school newspaper staff, which I joined on a whim. I could escape in my own way for that hour in the day, though my newspaper advisor occasionally poked her head in, telling me that I really should go to seminary.

Other things took me by surprise. There were dances every month, each having its own set of guidelines. Invitations were elaborate and responses were expected to be just as impressive. I had been raised with the knowledge of Homecoming, Winter Formal, Prom. But now I had new names to consider: Spring Fling, Sadie Hawkins (in which the girls asked the boys), and others, on top of the monthly Stag dances. I went to the first few dances my junior year, trying to act the part that I should play, but the dances too fell by the wayside as I continued to separate myself from normal high school activity.

I had begun to find and make friends outside of school, the kind my mom would refer to simply as *friends,* with pursed lips and a nice helping of verbal disdain. I met other gay Mormons: high school students who had barely come out to themselves, BYU students hiding their sexuality from everyone on campus because they could be kicked out, returned missionaries who told me horror stories of how they were treated during and after their two years abroad.

I made immediate bonds with those who were in these situations, but even having friendships in this place was difficult. At restaurants, going to movies, we were always watching behind our backs, hoping that we wouldn't run into people from our congregations or schools. If we did, we would think up excuses in advance. My friend Jeff and I agreed that if someone saw us together, we wouldn't explain that we had actually met each other online. We would claim that we had a mutual friend, named Jen. At one point, I was on a date with a guy who passed me off as his cousin when a couple of his college buddies saw us eating at a restaurant.

After they left, all I could say to him was, "Yup, we're definitely family."

By the end of junior year, what had become clear to me was that I could never escape it—the judgment, the constant watching. In this valley, the very center of Mormon culture, I was immersed in what I was raised to be. I knew that was the point; I had been brought here partly to be saved from what tempted me in Chicago. What taunted me was the constant presence of something higher up and far away, those small snow-capped peaks that stayed on during the hot months. In some ways, I felt like I was constantly sinking lower into the valley floor. The longer I was here, the more I was surrounded by the culture.

But the more I was surrounded by it, the easier it became to reject.

Back on Timp, the climb continued through switchbacks on the rocky slopes and up into the flat, wild fields that I remember so well. It was 90 degrees and sunny on the valley floor that day, but the fields were enshrouded in a dense, 50-degree fog. The fog would appear from the valley as a small puff of cloud, a wisp of condensation in the dry heat, but in the midst of all of it the purples and blues and oranges and yellows of the field did their best to bleed through the thick haze of the chilly mountain air.

Trekking through the richly colored expanses, we came to Emerald Lake. It looked more like a pond to me, as my definition of the term "lake" had been formed by the much more expansive Lake Michigan. Regardless of its classification, it gathered at the base of the final ascent to Timp's peak, looking up the maiden's nostrils. Snow was close now, and it took only a slight look up to see the rocky glacier that fed the lake. Hikers who had time enough to get to the top were careening down the glacier, which functioned as a giant, bumpy slide for those who didn't want to walk down. Where the glacier ended, a small river formed and opened into Emerald Lake's basin. The edge of the water was at my feet, and though we intended to turn back for home soon, I had no desire to leave the dense, cool air.

It was hot on the ground in early fall of my senior year, a perfect Indian summer day. On this Sunday, though, I sat in my bishop's office after church had ended. It looked like any other bishop's office I had been in before, with white-painted brick walls and matching upholstered furniture. In this case, it was lavender. Bishop Holmes adjusted the air-conditioning unit next to his desk, tucked his red tie into his navy suit jacket, and sat down behind his desk.

"Not such a pleasant conversation," he said as he eased into his leather chair.

He went on to explain what I already knew. A BYU student I had dated late in my junior year had had a change of heart about his sexuality. After dating for a few weeks, he'd cut off communication with me and decided to speak to his own bishop about his problem.

My bishop then explained that he knew because this student, Taylor, had told his own bishop who I was, what we had done, and where I lived. Though bishops and members were bound by something similar to doctor–patient confidentiality, he explained that special cases such as mine required communication between bishops so that the "process of repentance" could be expedited.

As I sank into my chair and blood rushed to my head, all I could think was that I had been ratted out. Taylor had been kicked out of BYU for violating its honor code and I was to blame.

"I contemplated telling your mother about this," the bishop said.

It would have been easy for him to do so. He was a musician on faculty with my mother at BYU and worked down the hall from her. It would have been so easy for him to knock on her office door and ask to speak with her for a second—

"But I decided that wasn't the best course of action," he said, and I nodded. "She has her recital coming up. I wouldn't want to upset her."

I nodded my head again, knowing that my mother was deep in practice for a debut performance at the university in a week. I, however, thought there would be better reasons to keep this from her until he spoke to me.

For an hour, I recounted what had happened between Taylor and me—how we met, what we did, what we did sexually, why it ended. I knew why it had ended because Taylor had explained it very plainly in an e-mail; there was no call, no request to meet in person and say good-bye. Just an e-mail.

I told my bishop I would cooperate. I would continue to see him and try to resolve this problem on the condition he never spoke to my mother about it, even after the pressure of her recital was over. If he even so much as told her, I said, I would never come to church again.

He handed me a few pamphlets and a book. He told me that he would tell my mother that I had come to him about this, that I wanted to resolve my problems. He said that the book and pamphlets would give me guidance from other ex-gay Mormons who had successfully walked down the right path.

I walked home on the warm fall day along a road behind my house, flipping through the success stories. I thought of Taylor's e-mail, and how he so desperately wanted to find a wonderful woman to marry and have children with so he could live a happy life.

I returned to the book in my hands. I flipped through the story of a man who kicked the gay habit, rejected his choice to become a homosexual, married a woman, and wrote a book about it under a pseudonym.

I stopped on the road next to the empty field below my house and let all the words go. With the afternoon sun setting below the mountains to the west, I threw the book and pamphlets into the field and erased Taylor's e-mail from my memory, knowing that the choice I had just made had nothing to do with my sexuality.

Years later, after I've returned to Chicago for college and am asked about my time in Utah, I place myself back in that image in the parking lot, looking east toward the peaks. I can feel the heat against my back, I can feel it come up through my flip-flops. My eyes dart about at the grooves running down the hillsides, imagining water racing down them from the peaks, invisible to the naked eye. The clumps of trees and brush are fine; they will survive the heat and impending brush fires that the dryness brings. The melting snow is close enough to them to bring sustenance.

I look down again. There is no water here on the asphalt. I twist the tar around more, noticing how it winds on along the parking lot, merging with other, smaller rivers of tar. They are the closest thing to flowing water that could survive here. I imagine that a drop of water, careening in a dive toward the asphalt, would hit the pavement in a sizzle, evaporating into the dry air.

I then remember myself up on Emerald Lake, watching as the rocky glacier sits stoically, hikers scuttling down its surface. Relief is up there: a cool breeze, a cold mass holding endless gallons of frozen water, keeping to itself. I could travel up through the brush and trees again and stay by the lake and fields. Even now, I can imagine myself up there. Looking down on the land below, I am enclosed in a thick layer of fog, taking in the scenery, never needing to see the hot valley floor again.

When You're a Gay Boy in America
by Danny Zaccagnino

When you're a gay boy in America, you quickly learn you need to develop a thick skin. This protects us from all the hateful words and unjust treatment we face every day. Our method of survival does have its flaws, however. Sometimes our armor is just not quite thick enough. Sometimes the pain can go so deep that it cuts through our skin and touches us. When it does, it leaves us with a scar. Gay boys are full of scars. There are the scars we can't see but still feel. These are our emotional scars. I carry an emotional scar given me by a Scout leader who once said I wasn't boy enough to be in the Boy Scouts. Then there are our physical scars. Each holds a memory and tells a story. They tell of battles, weakness, pain, recovery, and accidents. Some scars we wear with pride and celebrate their stories. Other scars we attempt to cover up and pretend they don't exist.

Some scars can be intentional. I spent ninety minutes straddling a leather chair while a stranger dug into my flesh with an electric needle and black ink. It was the moment every suburban punk waits his whole life for: the day I got my very first tattoo. It was a gift from my parents on my eighteenth birthday. I had only been legal for a few hours when I eagerly went under the needle. When the rebellious act was over, I was left with a black dragon between my shoulder blades with the initials E.M. next to it. I had planned this day many years in advance. I wanted to make sure I had the perfect tattoo. There would be no cheesy tribal bands for me. I chose a dragon because they are protectors. I placed it on my back so I would always have someone watching my back. I wanted a tattoo that had meaning and told a story.

My tattoo tells the story of a very dark time in my family history. My grandfather's initials were added to my tattoo because his death marked the beginning of an eight-month period in my life when there was nothing but death around me. I was only twelve and had never had anyone close to me die before. My grandfather's death was quickly followed by the death of my uncle. Then a good friend of mine's mother passed away from cancer. Shortly after that my other grandfather died. Right before Christmas my close neighbor's infant baby fell out of her crib and died. Then the series of tragic events ended with the death of my grandmother. They say she died of cancer but really she died of a broken heart. I attended a funeral once a month.

This was such a horrible time for my family to live through. I felt like we were cursed. I thought we must have done something wrong and that's why we were being put through all this sorrow. I remember feeling like death was stalking me and my family. I don't know if it was an Italian thing or a Catholic thing, or maybe it was just a pothead thing, but I was constantly paranoid and scared that at any moment death would take me or someone I loved. I thought I could never be truly happy again, because if I was, that meant I or a family member would die. It took me a long time to get past it but eventually I did. I wanted my tattoo to depict this hard time I lived through. I wanted my dragon to protect me from the curse I felt lingered in my life. I took an emotional scar and made it a physical one.

That was me at eighteen. I was a boy who lived through a family curse and was slowly inching out of the closet. I had never been in a relationship. I had experienced only one sexual encounter with a man, and that had left me somewhat disturbed and traumatized. I discovered him in an Internet chat room. If you're a gay person living in a suburban or rural area, the Internet may be your only outlet to the gay community. You are able to look up support groups, get health information, and get a boyfriend. The computer is popular among gay people because it provides one vital feature: ambiguity. You can do, say, and look at whatever you want, secretly and safely in your own living room, without anyone else knowing. The Internet protects you from the dirty looks given to you by a Barnes & Noble clerk while you discreetly try to buy a copy of *The Advocate*. The Internet saves you the embarrassment of having a childhood friend spot you running out of a gay bar. You are safe there because you have no identity. You have no face. You are only a screen name and nothing more.

The Internet was a place of sexual exploration for me. I didn't even know how gay people had sex until I looked it up on the computer. This was something they never taught me at the Catholic school I attended. At first I would only talk in chat rooms and look at pictures. Eventually I graduated to the phone. I would call strangers I met online but usually got freaked out and hung up on them mid-conversation. One St. Patrick's Day, when I was sixteen, I decided to take the ultimate plunge. I was going to meet a man from the computer in person. I'd talked to him for several hours and he'd described himself as very good-looking and only in his early thirties. He seemed nice, and early thirties wasn't really that old. He kept asking me to meet him. I declined numerous times but my curiosity got the best of me and I finally agreed.

We decided to meet at a park near my house. This was the same park where I'd attended arts camp and tried mushrooms for the first time. It had always been a place of exploration and danger for me. I slowly entered the park and nervously lit a Parliament Light. In the distance I spotted a man in a gray suit. I knew right away he was my secret date. We made eye contact but I quickly looked away and continued to stroll. We both circled the park, far away from each other, for several minutes. One of us would occasionally stop to see if the other was watching or following. This awkward dance carried on for some time. I was strangely excited by the whole scene. Anxious to see what would happen next, I took a seat on a bench and waited for him to pick up on my signal. He slowly approached and took a seat next to me. I was so nervous I thought I was going to vomit right on the park's freshly mowed grass. He must have been my father's age and looked nothing like the way he described himself on the computer. I was not attracted to him at all. I wanted to run away right then but something kept me glued to that bench. I guess I was just so desperate for this kind of attention from a man. I guess I was just curious to see how far we could take this.

He asked me if I wanted to take a walk while we spoke. I agreed, and we aimlessly circled the park while we discussed music and *South Park*. He seemed to know a lot about adolescent topics for a middle-aged man. The whole time I kept looking over my shoulder to make sure there were no neighbors or past elementary school teachers visiting the park that day. After a long conversation about nothing in particular, we reached an uncomfortable pause. It was a perfect opportunity for me to run but once again something kept me there. I was attracted to the darkness and the novelty of this whole meeting. I was in way over my head, though, and should have said my good-byes right then. I still can't clearly remember how it happened, but he cornered me and touched me the way no one had touched me before in my life. I just froze and closed my eyes. I didn't really want it to happen but I didn't stop him. I guess I didn't know how much I was craving this until I got it. The whole incident lasted a matter of seconds. I was easily excited. Once it was over I quickly snapped back to reality. This enormous feeling of guilt and total disgust came over me. I couldn't believe what I had just let happen. I frantically pulled up my pants and ran away, not saying a word to him. I got home, avoided my mother's questions, and immediately hopped in the shower. I rubbed the bar of soap violently over my body, trying to wash the filth and guilt off of me. I could still smell the man's cologne on me. I grabbed the T-shirt I was wearing and threw it out in the garbage. I thought it held too many memories of my actions that day and wearing it again would just make me sick to my stomach. Then I locked myself in my room and quietly fought back my tears.

Being a product of the eighties, I unfortunately believed the prejudice that all gay people had AIDS. I immediately thought I was going to get AIDS because of what I had done. I used to spend hours in front of the mirror examining every new pimple or mark on my body. I thought every new mark was a lesion and a sign of impending doom. I was sure I had AIDS and was going to die soon. I looked up symptoms online and convinced myself that I possessed every single one. Every cough, sneeze, headache, or feeling of fatigue I believed to be a sign of my illness. I used to watch all the other kids my age with jealous eyes because they had their whole lives ahead of them and I was dying from a fatal disease for being gay. I thought my family's curse had finally reached me. I didn't tell anyone this because I was too ashamed to admit that I'd had a sexual encounter with a man. I lived with this stress and secret for months, until I educated myself a little more and learned it was scientifically impossible for AIDS to be transmitted through the sexual act I had participated in. My first experience as a gay man had not been an encouraging one. I thought all gay people were just creepy old perverts lurking in the shadows of neighborhood parks. I believed there was no love in this world for me and I would never find someone normal.

At age eighteen I was a confused and isolated gay youth with a fresh tattoo on my back. I was sure I would spend my life alone. I thought I could never find happiness being gay. On one particularly lonely afternoon I made a desperate prayer. I needed a miracle and I needed it fast. I needed someone to end my sorrow. I closed my eyes and spoke to my grandparents who had passed on. I asked them to please send me my angel. I asked them to please send me love. I finished my plea and headed out to visit the college campus I would be attending the following fall. While examining a sculpture of an eighteen-foot metal bear on campus, I met a cute freshman from Pennsylvania who was studying dance. He was a tall, gorgeous boy who smelled like Dial soap and Versace cologne. He was a little too preppy for my punk-rock attitude but I let that one pass. We had matching blue eyes and got along right away. He showed me around the campus and gave me the lowdown on the various social classes at the school. We were discussing modern dance when two photo majors approached us and asked to take our picture. We enthusiastically sat side by side on a bench and posed together for the budding artists. While the photograph was being taken I knew it would become a great piece of journalistic history in the story of my life. This picture would depict the day I met the love of my life. I had only known him for five minutes but I had a strong feeling. During our conversation the subject of tattoos came up. He informed me that he had just gotten a tattoo recently. I asked him if I could see it and he obliged. I slowly pulled down the neck of his shirt. There it was staring right back at me. He had a tattoo of a black dragon between his shoulder blades. My angel had been sent to me.

I Smell the Gas of My Father's Fishing Boat
by Adam K. Boehmer

Setting up nothing but points for yourself,
you work in the syncopation of things,

wandering from the house to the streets,
the bars, watching the men trickle in,

the strong wave of cologne covering
up the scent of in-heat.

You stop in medians
and sit under trees, wonder how all these lights

would be seen by babies.
Red doesn't mean *Stop* yet;

white outlines of teeth do not mean *Dentist*.
Your feet keep you walking. This isn't DC,

your shoes aren't big enough yet.
This isn't that other place you'll be soon.

The midwest perhaps, with its dog-spot skies
and cornfield vanishing points?

God cranks the handle on an old filmstrip,
pretends to know the ending. Some clumsy

saint has put the strip in upside-down and
the finale flashes too soon:

You, tied to the tracks and screaming,
HELP spelled out ornate and slithery.

Then, in reverse,
to some stranger with a rope behind his back

shaking your hand so much like your father
you'll sleep with him just this once.

Fourth of July
by Lauren Rile Smith

I.

I walked home along the parkway, watched the lights of fireflies and passing halogen headlights. Purposefully mistaking them for fireworks: letting myself be startled.

Catharsis: I bought cigarettes today for the first time in months. I've never smoked inside before. I'm renting movies she wouldn't watch with me and eating voluptuous cherries, with abstraction and little pleasure, staining my fingers. Characters kiss on the screen.

II.

I remember walking down to the park with her last August, late-night, seeing Venus. The streetlights painting everything six shades of subdued orange; the man who stopped his truck to stare at the sky, and waved to us, and told us what we were looking at.

III.

I want someone to lie next to me on the bed, touch my chest above my heart, tell me things about myself I don't know: my posture when I'm self-conscious; the expression I make when I'm lying; how my hair looks from the back; the high girlish pitch of my voice on the phone.

IV.

Little curls of ash all over my floor dissolve into fine powder and are ground into the carpet as soon as I touch.

The neighbor next door lets off a string of cherry firecrackers. All the dogs in the neighborhood are howling.

MY DIARY: DOCUMENTED. DONE.
by L. Canale

"Dad found out"
Wednesday, January 15, 2003

Today has been shit. Pure shit. My dad found out I'm gay. Isn't it funny how, like, last week I was thinking about coming out to him and then BAM! he finds out. Oh God. This fucking sucks. The tension here is so much right now. We're all trying to act like everything's all right. It is, I hope, but deep down I really don't think it is.

So how'd he find out? Eeeeehhhh. Fuck. I was talking to my Hero (the girl I'm in love with, Carol) today, like I normally do. I'm not saying much because my throat hurts so bad because I'm still sick. So I'm just listening and eating ice cream and drinking water so that the pain doesn't completely annoy me. She asks a question, I answer it, she says something, I laugh, tell her I love her, and it's fine. A few minutes later I hear my dad moving in his room and I look and his door is crazy open but I don't really think too much about it because I ALWAYS say stuff about being gay while talking to my sister Tina and he's always close enough to hear but never does. So I'm like, eh, whatever. Then he goes downstairs and gets on the other line in the kitchen and tells me that he needs the phone and that freaks me out because how rude is that to interrupt a convo like that? So I get off the phone and go downstairs to fill my water bottle and my mom's waiting at the bottom of the staircase and whispers, "Your father heard you say some stuff, he's in shock, he was asking me and your sister questions. She left because she's worried." And I was like, holy FUCKING hell. Oh hell no, this can't be happening, it can't be fucking happening. So I start crying and he walks in and says all this stuff about how it's a mortal sin to be gay, how I'm just confused, how I don't know anything. How I'm too young to understand, how I've never dated before. How this and how that, and we go back and forth for an hour. Me telling him that I do know, how I know me better than anyone else knows me. How I don't want him to make me feel wrong because I'm not wrong, dammit. I've been through that shit, feeling wrong and whatever, and I don't want to go through it again. He uses all these examples. Like how his heroes are all men, but he's not gay. And I'm like "Well that's you" and he's like "No, you don't know" and I ask him if he was ever attracted to them and he says no and I have to explain what being gay is about and it's uncomfortable and shitty and scary. Then he says that it isn't allowed under his house, that he's going to change me because he doesn't want to lose me, and I'm like "Damn, Dad, if you keep saying stuff like that you ARE going to lose me. I can't control this. I'm not going to change. I know what I am."

Ahhhhhhhhhhhhhhhhhh. HE FOUND OUT. I didn't tell him, he found out. I at least kinda knew I was in the process of coming out while I was telling my mom a few years ago. This came out of nowhere and bit me in the ass. Completely out of nowhere. Oh God. So . . . anyway, after a couple hours he cooled down a bit and told me that I could think I was whatever, but he won't allow me to act on it. Oh okay, sure. Kiss my ass. I'm so mad at him. Why was he listening to my conversation? Why'd he have to bring the Bible and religion into it, it's shit like that that turns me off of it. I mean, I'm Christian. I go to church and I pray all the time; I have religion, but when people throw bullshit in my face like "God loves you less because you date girls" I wonder, do I really want to be a part of this? That's why I'm mad at him. He wants me to go to a Catholic church and talk to a priest and I'm thinking it's none of his fucking business what the hell I am. He doesn't give a shit about me, and

I care less about him. A priest. I told my dad it wasn't going to do anything, but I'll go to his church and I'll talk to his priest. It's not going to change me.

I want to leave this place. I fucking hate it here now. I'm gonna go crazy. My dad's such a good guy sometimes, when you get past all the bullshit. He told me all this stuff about what he went through as a teenager and he was real brave for telling me. I could tell it made him unbelievably uncomfortable, but I'm glad he did, not just because that's how he made me feel today, unbelievably uncomfortable, but because it made him real. He's been through some fucked up shit and now I understand why he thinks the way he does. He's been through a lot so I can't really hate him. I don't hate him, even though I want to.

After, I guess it hit him that maybe, just maybe, I might know what I'm talking about. All he kept saying was that he wanted to be back in my life. That he wasn't going to let THEM take me away, and I was like "Them . . ."—that fucking hurt. So I told him to stop saying "them." I *am* them. He's so scared for me, he doesn't want me to be different, but I don't get it, why some parents and phobics say they don't want us to be different when it's them, their fear, that's making us different. We'd be just fine and dandy if everyone would *just let us be.* I'm so numb right now, I've cried so much, this sucked. Today sucked. Well, not the first hour of my day. Haha, I woke up real late and then Carol called. My sister Tina talked with her for a little bit because I was in the bathroom. It was cool, T says she likes her. I was like "You know? Me, too." Haha. I'm glad I got to talk to her. I don't think we can talk when he's home anymore, though. I'm scared he'd say something if she calls and he picks up. He's been picking up the phone all day, which he normally doesn't do. Usually he lets the machine get it. I think he was hoping it'd be her. I'm like what the hell? What are you going to say? I'm still gonna talk to her. Bloody hell. Fear's a bitch. I hate it.

You know it's funny, though, one of my friends just came out to her mom and her mom didn't really take it too well and I've just been like "Well, give it time, blahblahblah. She'll come around." And with all my heart I meant it, but damn, it's hard to believe when you're going crazy and want it so bad, everything to be okay, I mean. I'm doubting he'll ever really come around.

I don't even have the reward of being brave to look back on. I didn't come out to him, *he found out*. I'm gonna go.

"Oh, it's killing me"
Thursday, January 16, 2003

I woke up early today because I have to watch my brother. The poor kid, his voice sounds like he sucked on a balloon. Hahaha. He sounds a little bit better, though. It was so cute a couple of nights ago, he was playing Nintendo and I was in the living room watching TV and he walks in dragging his big-ass blanket and he's holding a Brylane home catalog. It's chock full of boring house shit, no toys or anything, just towels and stuff like that. So anyway, he sits right next to me and starts looking at the catalog. It was so cute. Plus, I'm the only person he lets sit that close to him.

So yeah, things suck, but I got to talk to Cort last night. She's my best friend. That was nice. I e-mailed her yesterday telling her that Tina's "surprise" party is Friday at 3:20 and then at the end I was like "Oh, and guess what? My dad found out, love you—Lo." Yup, she said her heart stopped beating when she read it. I was like, "Yeah, my heart's been doing that a lot today, too," to say the least. Oh well, right? I'm so happy I got to talk to her, though, I was going crazy! I'm still going crazy, actually, even more so today because everything from yesterday is sinking in and I heard my parents talking this morning. My dad's gonna try to change me. He doesn't want me to talk to anyone, 'specially Carol. And he doesn't want me to have feelings for anyone. He just wants me to be, I dunno, a nun or something. He can kiss my ass, he can kiss it twice. I'll talk to his fucking priest, dammit, but I'm not changing and I'm not becoming a nun and I am going to find a girl one day and I'm gonna have a family with that girl and he's either going to be happy for me and be a part of our lives or he's not. I'm not afraid of him. I'm scared as shit right now, but not of him. I have a sick feeling this is going to tear my perfect family apart. I heard him talking about how he's not going to lose this fight, how if he doesn't win, we're going to lose him. How he's not going to make it through the year because he can't take it, it's too much for him to handle. There was already too much going on in his life and this just made it too much for him. We're going to kill each other. I'm going to end up killing him because I'm not going to change, and he's killing me because I'm not going to change. He's trying to change my mom, too. He speaks very well. If you're naive, he'll convince you that he's right because there's a lot of confidence in his voice. I know he's not really confident, though. Tina knows he's not. I hope my mom knows he's not, but she's all about keeping quiet. I'm going to have to tell her that this isn't a time to keep quiet because if I have to fight this shit alone . . . dude, I can't. I won't be able to do it. I won't, it's that simple, I won't be able to do it. Last week I thought I was down and there was no way it could get worse, I was asking for help because I was at war with MYSELF. Fuck that. I'd do anything to go back to that. Now it's not Me vs. Me. It's me vs. forty-five years of my dad's beliefs. I need help, I'm going crazy. I can't believe this happened. My God, it's nothing like how I planned. I'm so scared. I have no idea of what's going to happen, stuff just comes out of NOWHERE now. Stuff comes out of nowhere and I'm supposed to handle it. Either way I fucking lose. I don't change, I ruin my family. I change, I ruin myself. My dad's killing me, he doesn't know it, but he is.

"F-That"

Friday, January 17, 2003

OH MAN. My dad is full of SO MUCH SHIT. It's funny as hell, my God. Well, I'm feeling better, yay, I'm still not feeling good. It's okay, that will come soon enough. Feeling good, I mean. It's fucking cold here. My dad sucks. I love him, but I LOATHE HIM. And the only reason why I love him is because I have to. Okay, so here's what's so funny:

1. He keeps saying he wants to be a part of my life—haha.
2. He wants me to read a book written by the Pope—hahaha.

3. He wants my mom to talk me into being "normal"—haha-haha.

4. He wants the family to say the rosary every night—hahaha-haha.

5. He doesn't want me going on the computer, because it "introduced" me to "their" world—hahahahahaha.

And last but not least, brace yourself, it's golden:

6. He doesn't want me talking to my Hero—HAAAAAAAAA HAHAHAHAAAAAAAAAAAAAAAAAAAAAAAA HAHHAHAHAAAAA-AAAAAAAA HAHAHHAAAAA HAHAHAAA HAHAAHHHAAA.

Oh fuck, my rib, it's cramping. The pain. Oh boy . . . like hell I'm not talking to Carol! HHHHAAAAAAAAAAAAAAAAAA HAHH-HAAAAAAAAAAAAAAAA HA. So yeah, he can kiss my ass. He can kiss hers, too, he can kiss everyone's ass because if he keeps pulling shit like that, I'm out. Don't know where the hell I'll go, but I will leave his sorry ass. I'm sorry, the man's gotta learn. No person controls my life except ME. It's that simple. NO. ONE. CON-TROLS. MY. LIFE. EXCEPT. ME. I told Carol that calling after five or six would be kinda . . . you know . . . and if my dad ever picked up I told her to just hang up because I don't want him to freak her out. I don't want this to hurt anything with us. If anything really bad comes from this, like really, *anything*, whether it be with my mom or brother or sister or my Hero . . . I will never forgive him. And he'll lose one of the only good things he's got in his miserable life.

Right now, honestly, I don't want him in my life. I don't want him dead or anything, 'cause one day, when I'm out and about living on my own, when I'm gone, maybe I'll want to . . . whatever, be his daughter, play the daughter role, but right now I'm tired of him. It's not just because of yesterday and today, it's everything leading up to yesterday. It's my childhood and everything he did to ruin it. I BLAME HIM. I love all people because of my mom, she's taught me that people are beautiful, but I'm scared of those same people because of him.

Well, its almost eleven here. It takes me two hours to fall asleep, and I have to wake up early tomorrow.

"Day 3"

Saturday, January 18, 2003

My dad left the book *Catechism of the Catholic Church* on my computer desk for me to read. Yup, I threw it across the room 'cause it was in the way. It's a heavy book. It's on the dining room table now because I felt bad. In it was this note: "Lourdes—please as a favor to me, please read. Love Dad" and there's, like, a little stick figure guy next to it. Ha, I'm like what the hell, but I have to admit it was cute. I don't know why I care, I don't know why I actually flipped through that damn book. I'm not Catholic, I'll never be Catholic. I'm Christian. Is it so hard? He thinks that I'm gay, or thinks I think I'm gay, because I have no religion. Mhmm . . . riiight. That's it. I heard my parents arguing again this morning. My dad was calling my mom crazy for not seeing eye to eye with him. No shit, asshole, she gets it, you don't. Anyway, so basically he thinks I'm this sad, depressed, lonely, lazy little girl who had it rough in high school and is afraid of her future. Funny how that's a stereotype for shy people. The truth is, he knows nothing about me. Up until just a short while ago I was a normal, happy, corny, life-loving dork who actually enjoyed most of high school because I participated in shit and was successful with it. I had friends and everyone pretty much liked me and I pretty much liked them back. But the biggest thing he's got wrong, man, is I'm not a little girl anymore. I know so much more than he thinks. It's painful to hear him say stuff like that. I haven't been a kid since Cort's mom died in . . . oh my God . . . today's the anniversary of when her mom had her brain aneurysm . . . oh my God I forgot. Too much shit's been running through my head. Wow, well, basically, my kidhood ended six years ago today. That's when the roller coaster started. I can't believe I forgot. Damn, she was a great woman, she really was. Always laughing and joking around and buying us stuff. We'd have fun if she was still around. I think she'd like me. OH MY GOD! and there's snow on the ground! She LOVED snow! She absolutely loved it. She'd just sit out on her porch, sometimes with Cort, but usually alone or with her neighbor and watch it. She loved it so much. God, wow.

My dad gave me a kiss on my forehead before he left for work. Aw. No. Whatever. I was like don't trip over your ignorance on your way OUT of my room, a thank-you. He's trying too hard, dammit, he wants back in me and T's life . . . but he should know that he was getting there without doing anything. Now . . . there's no way, not while we're living under the same roof. Hell no. He told my sister that she can't go to her church. That's the worst thing he could ever say to her. I'll take her. She's so out of here when she turns eighteen. Damn, dude, she'd be out now if she could. My mom's taking me job-searching tomorrow. Yeah, whoohoo. At least I'll be out of the house, right? Right. So . . . wow, yeah, I gotta get out of here. Moving on . . . my brother is SO sick, the poor guy can't eat or drink anything without throwing it up. He just had some Gatorade and five seconds later threw it up. He's losing too much weight. He doesn't look right at all. It's kind of scaring me. I like him chubby. Oh God, what's happening here! Three weeks ago we were all healthy and happy and fine, now we're in the shits. Damn. Hmm . . . well, T's party is today, don't know what I'm wearing. Some repair guy's coming whenever to fix the dryer. I'm gonna go because if I don't, I'll just start writing about my dad again. I still can't believe he knows. My God.

"He's kicking me out"
Sunday, January 19, 2003

Yeah . . . today hasn't been so good. It's probably been the worst day of my life, actually. I went to church with Dad and T. That was fine. We took Sampson. I love my car. Anyway, so on our way back my sister said something, nothing out of line, I didn't think so, at least. Something about how the Bible is the only book we should be reading, not a book written by some man because the Bible is God's word and that's what we should go by. Anyway, he slapped her across the face for saying that, so I said something and he told me to shut up and then he says something about how I have to give up this gay shit and I just drove and told him that he lost me. That he lost a good thing because I wasn't going back to him. So then we get home, T runs in the house, Dad follows, I sit in Sampson for a little and then I hear yelling so I run out, slip on some ice that's on the walkway to my house, and totally bust my knees and my left palm, it's ugly looking. So I'm out there searching for my glasses and car keys because they went flying when I fell. He comes out to help me and says that he loves me more than anything and I start crying and tell him that he has to love me for everything and he says he won't so I find my glasses, run inside, yell for my mom. When I see her, she's crying so much. I've never seen her cry so much, my mom is so strong, she never cries like that. It breaks my heart, it really does. I keep saying he lost me, I have to get out, Mom, help me. Then my dad comes in and my mom starts SCREAMING at him, I mean really calling him crazy, saying that I'm his daughter, that she loves me no matter what, that he should, too, and he says stuff about how religion is number one to him, that he'll kill me before I live my life in mortal sin and all this stuff. I yell and say I have no father, that if he was my dad he'd love me no matter what, and he runs over to me, right in my face, and is yelling shit, I don't even remember what, but he is spitting as he speaks and he's right there, in my face, I've never had someone in my face like that before. I just stare at him and take it and then he says something about how I'm not his daughter, how he doesn't want me under his roof, I'm getting kicked out, I should go pack up my shit because I have to find somewhere else to go . . . and that he is going to kill me and I dare him to. Well fuck. So I run upstairs, Tina follows, my mom and he talk/argue. I punch the wall, which I think broke my knuckle. I'm totally screaming "You fucking bastard!" at the top of my lungs because I can't believe it. It's like a Lifetime movie gone terribly wrong. So more shit happens, I don't remember but then my mom comes upstairs to check on my poor brother who's just lying on his bed. THEN my dad starts yelling "EVIL MEN, GAYS AND LESBIANS UNITE! MEN ARE BAD! GAY POWER! MEN ARE BAD, LESBIANS UNITE!" and I'm like WHAT THE FUCK IS GOING ON HERE? and I can hear that he's marching around the downstairs so I run into my mom's room and I'm like "He's gone fucking crazy, Mom! Do something! Get him out!" so she goes downstairs and stops short on the bottom stair and all I hear is "Put it down, Joe, put it down. She's your daughter, you've gone crazy, put it down" and me and T are like what the fuck is going on? So we're yelling for mom to just get him out and then we hear "I have to save her soul, even if it kills her" and I'm like "What the fuck is this? The fucking *Exorcist*?" and then my mom's like "Joe, put down the knife." WHAT?!? **NO LIE.** So I start screaming, I fucking start screaming for my mom to do something. For her to get him out, that he's crazy, that it's him or me, that this, that that. I run down the stairs, grab my jacket, tell my parents that Dad is a fucking lunatic and I run out of the house and to the bridge.

I have nowhere to go. I have to leave, though. He kicked me out. I think my mom's going to do something. She's not letting me leave. I can't stand him. I hate him. I called my old coach because I had no idea who else to call. We talked for a little. It was nice talking to her. I'm not blaming myself, I did for five seconds but my sister was like "Lo, you're a chosen one, you're here to help people with your writing. God chose you, he made you this way so that you could open people's eyes with your words. Your life, your story, is going to help someone one day. You're chosen." And I believe her. I believe we're all chosen for something and I believe this and my writing is how I'm going to help people. So that's my motivation to get through this shit. One day, it's all going to be great and make so much sense. I'm gonna look back and laugh because that's what I always do. Everything's changing, but nothing's going to change *me*, you know? I'm still the same. I'm going to get through this. I'm scared, but I'll be okay. I'm thinking I might go to Richie's . . . or something. I don't know. I might be sleeping over at Cort's tonight. Maybe, I don't know. I can't look ahead past my foot anymore, shit comes out of nowhere. Wherever I go, that's where I'll go.

"Hi, I'm M.S."
Monday, January 20, 2003

Since yesterday morning was shit, I left with Tina to go to the mall and watch a movie last night. We didn't go to a movie. After walking around the mall and showing her GoodyGirl (the cute girl that works at Sam Goody), we went to Red Bank to walk around and find Cort's work. We walked for an hour in the freezing cold last night because we couldn't find it but it was kind of fun, except for when these guys said "Hey baby" to us as they walked by. That hurt my ego. I was upset because they weren't intimidated by me. I really was sad. Haha. So we finally found where she worked and stayed there until closing. After, we went back home to get our stuff to sleep over at Cort's. I met her new dog and we looked at pictures. Well, T and Cort did, I was kinda just lying there trying not to think of anything but of course a wave of memories would just hit me out of nowhere. We joked about how people say "hurr" now instead of "here." "Get over hurr . . . Are those straight-leg or flurr? . . . You're mean, that's not furr . . ." and it went like that for fifteen minutes straight.

While T was in the bathroom, Cort showed me a naked picture of Mark. My God. I'm sure straight girls would like it but EW. Uuuuh, we went to a diner for breakfast and the waitress was real nice. After that we went back to her place to get our shit and talked about how everything sucks on our drive back. I showed her Sampson when we got home. She loved Sampson. And then we said goodbye. I stayed away from my dad, took a nap, woke up, haven't seen my dad, don't want to see my dad. Tina says he apologized to her, I told my mom to tell him not to talk to me because I don't want to hear it. Yes, I'm bitter. I'm not in a good mood, I'm achy as hell. My hand's real ugly from yesterday and I think I hurt my ankle when I fell, too. I feel useless. I'm trying not to give up but it's getting real hard. I want to cry. I want to get away from everyone because I don't trust anyone anymore except Cort. I'm gonna go.

Oh, and all yesterday my dad wouldn't call me by my name, he'd say "the Mortal Sin." So me and Cort were joking that I'd go by M.S.

"Finally"
Tuesday, January 21, 2003
My dad's at work, bloody hell, finally! My GOD! Last night was corny. I'm having so much trouble sleeping now. I keep waking up, and when I wake up I'm afraid to open my eyes because I always

feel as if he's there watching me. He almost fucked out this morning on my mom because he asked her a question about Joe's medicine and it took her a while to answer him. He's going to crack again, he's exaggerating little-little things now. Like my brother has a lot of phlegm because he's sick, so my dad yelled at him and told him to spit it out in the bathroom 'cause he was coughing too much. So he spits it out and was like "I spit, are you happy now?" and he wasn't rude at all, it sounds like it could be rude but his tone was just, "Dad, are you happy?" Jody just wants my dad to be happy. Seriously, that's all he wants. So my dad's like "Are you being wise with me, too?" and Jody's just like "No, Daddy" and he sounded so sad and stuff. I wanted to cry, he said it so sad. So then the bastard goes downstairs and I hear him just walking around and stuff, pacing back and forth in the kitchen.

What have I done? I feel as though I'm losing everything and everyone. And even the people I haven't lost yet, I'm calling them scared and shit and giving them a reason to just fuck me over. I deserve it, I'm being an ass to some people, like Carol I think. What has she done to me? Nothing. So I deserve it if she wants to just . . . hurt me. But then I think to myself, well, I think you've had enough pain, Lo, but I don't think it will end until I'm out of here. Then I'll just meet someone else to hurt me. Haha, oh God. It's never gonna end. Yeeeeah, I think I'm gonna go listen to music or something. I need to stop thinking about things.

"On my side?"
Friday, January 24, 2003

My dad talked to the priest! And believe it or not, brace yourself, the priest was on my side. So since my dad doesn't have a backbone, he believes the priest even though the priest said the same things I said. "They can't control it. They're born that way. They're not to be hated. All they want is love and support. . . ." Yeah, so the priest asked my dad if I was a good person and he said yes and the priest told him not to worry about it. It could be so much worse. I'm like, no duh. I'm not a whore, I don't smoke, I don't do any sort of drug, I'm here every night, I'm here ALL THE TIME, BASTARD, I don't lie or steal or do anything, I'm fucking boring as hell. Seriously. But yeah, he's gonna leave me alone! Yaaaay, that's all I want. I'm still mad at him. He said everything I had feared hearing, seriously. I still go off into dazes where everything just comes back and I get scared and angry and sad and pissed and everything. And I'm having trouble sleeping and concentrating, well . . . that's not new, never mind. Ha, anyway, yeah, I can't just forgive that quickly, not him. I usually do, but he FUCKED UP big-time. Sadly, though, he has to live knowing what he did and said, so I'm not rubbing it in. I'm pretending to be okay with him. Whatever. He's there, I'm here, we have to live together. I'm not going to do anything to hurt the rest of the family any more than he already has. Damn. All right. But yeah, the priest was on my side. Dad said sorry. He's leaving me alone. Wishes do come true. Nightmares come true, too, but so do dreams and they make it all worthwhile. I'm sure one day I'm gonna realize why this all happened and its gonna be worth it. I know it is.

"20 months later . . ."
Monday, September 2, 2004

It's funny how things change. Here I am rereading what I wrote almost two years ago and patting myself on the back. How'd I get through it? How alone was I REALLY? Was I ever really alone, though? I don't think I was but I felt so alone at times. During that period, my mom and sister even asked me to pretend. They wanted me to tell my dad that yes, I was confused. Yes, there was hope for me. Yes, I was normal.

There is no normal. I knew that before my dad found out about me. I knew that before I ever came out to anyone. THERE. IS. NO. NORMAL. And being different isn't wrong. We are not wrong for falling in love with who we fall in love with. The girl I wrote about in my entries, Carol, is an amazing woman. We were in contact for a few years and during that crazy period in my life she was one of only a handful of people who kept me sane. She was thousands of miles away from me, but closer than most. My sister, Tina, Cortney, Carol, my mom, Jody, and a handful of online friends helped me though it. Of course God did too and the priest who was kind enough to kick my dad's ass with words. It doesn't seem like much, but it was enough. So, to all of those I just named, thanks. And Dad, I don't hate you, I wonder if I ever really did. . . .

So, though it could have ended up being a traumatizing experience, in the end, everything that happened ended up making my family tighter and me a stronger person. I've changed, no surprise, but that's not necessarily a bad thing. Change isn't something to be afraid of. Everything that comes at you comes for a reason. Finding the silver lining is a hard thing to do sometimes. . . . You want to give up, you want to hide. You feel alone but you're not, you're not alone and things will eventually get better. Self-worth and love are always worth it. Whatever "it" ends up being, hell yeah.

What makes you different makes you beautiful.

Crying Wolfe
by Jack Lienke

I first met Wolfe Reed in my ninth-grade geometry class. He was a short boy with a round face (betraying the pudgy past of his now slender frame), large, darting dark eyes, and a shoulder-length black ponytail. The pitch-tinted locks framed cedar skin—a result, I think, of a mix of Mexican and Native American heritage, though Wolfe never talked much about his family, so I never knew for sure. In truth, there was very little I knew about Wolfe's life outside of school. I knew his dad wasn't around. I knew his mom had spent some time in jail for drug-related reasons and now worked alternately as a freelance antique dealer and a poodle groomer. I knew his house wasn't far from my own—less than ten blocks, in fact. Mostly, I just knew I wanted to know more. But I also knew that was unlikely. Wolfe didn't answer questions; he belittled them. He greeted inquiry with insult, deflecting even the most banal query with some profanity-laced non sequitur. To illustrate:

Me: Do you get along with your mom?
Him: Do you get along with your dick?
Me: Why didn't you do the assignment?
Him: Why didn't you shut your ass face?

And so on.

Yet there was something about Wolfe's insults. He mimicked and cursed and swaggered and spat, but he never seemed hurtful, never felt unkind. Instead, I found his abuse strangely endearing, almost cute. Those chubby cheeks, that fragile frame—there was no question in my mind that, deep down, he was harmless.

And I guess that was one big reason we became friends, or a big reason we became whatever it is we were: he didn't scare me.

All the other boys did. It wasn't that anyone ever attacked me or threatened bodily harm. They didn't even tease me half as much as Wolfe did. But they were frightening all the same. There was a sort of fundamental violence in the way they behaved, the way they talked—loud and aggressive, their conversations heavily peppered with all the words that never failed to make me cringe. Cunt. Pussy. Faggot. Wolfe's speech may have been crass, but theirs was cruel. Negativity and disrespect seemed knee-jerk to them, with teachers, with girls, with each other. I hated it, hated being around it. That was the true menace of those boys for me—not physical pain, but spatial abuse, atmospheric contamination. With girls, I thrived. I joked, laughed, sang at the top of my lungs: I could dominate a room. But the second a boy entered the picture, I clammed up. In an instant, the territory was rendered hostile.

Middle school had been different. I'd had guy friends there. Unpopular ones, sure, but friends nonetheless. They'd been old pals, though, childhood buddies, leftovers from third and fourth grade, the days when we'd played superheroes in my living room with pillowcase-and-safety-pin capes. As we'd progressed through sixth, seventh, and eighth, I'd felt myself constantly pushed more and more to the fringes. Sleepovers and birthday parties became a chore, trying to share their interest in rollerblading and video games and Internet porn and petty vandalism. Aside from the rollerblading, it wasn't painful, just tiring. Suddenly, having fun with my friends had become hard work. And, try as I might, I couldn't make it look effortless. The reality was clear: I just didn't fit.

When I chose to abandon our little private school after eighth-grade graduation for the comparably gigantic Clarkson High, there were no tears or heartfelt goodbyes, not even disingenuous promises to keep in touch. We all knew better. Our bond was tenuous at best, and without the insulation of shared experience, a common landscape, it simply dissolved. If we couldn't groan together about Ms. Andrew's math class, what was there to talk about?

The Oklahoma State Department of Education officially considers Clarkson High an inner-city school, a moniker that never ceases to amuse its students. "Inner city," after all, conjures up any number of clichéd mental images: a claustrophobic jumble of glass, steel, and concrete; graffitied storefronts and towering apartment blocks; aggressive street vendors and even more aggressive pigeons. More fundamentally, "inner city" implies the existence of a separate and distinct "outer city," distinguishing a bustling urban center from the various residential suburbs clustered around it. Oklahoma City, in whose inner circle Clarkson is supposedly located, provides no such contrast between industrial clutter and residential sprawl. Missing is the archetypal maze of cracked and stained sidewalks punctuated by the occasional scraggly maple. This is not an asphalt jungle, but an asphalt desert: a sprawling web of gigantic parking lots and double-wide driveways connected by great tracts of sun-bleached expressway and eight-lane interstate. With a population one-sixteenth the size of New York City's spread over a land area two times as large, OKC gives the impression of one mammoth housing development mistakenly dropped in the middle of a prairie, a giant "sub" that has misplaced its "urb."

For kids whose most compelling example of urban life came from prime-time cop shows and medical dramas, the idea of our thousand-student high school, a magnet institution for the performing and visual arts nestled cozily between a supermarket and an ice cream parlor, as "inner city" just seemed ludicrous. Sure, our student body offered an economic and racial diversity conspicuously lacking in the white-flight suburbs, but *Dangerous Minds* we were not.

We were theater geeks and cello players, brooding photographers and mural painters. Hell, we made the sassy choir members in *Sister Act 2* look edgy.

Despite all of this, when I entered the front door of Clarkson on that first day of freshman year, it felt like Times Square at rush hour. I had, after all, spent my entire educational career up to now in a twelve-room building only two blocks from my house, passing every weekday with the same fifty-eight kids I'd known my whole life—mostly white, mostly wealthy, all exceedingly familiar. Stepping through the metal detector (one of Clarkson's few district-mandated nods to its inner-city status) into the school's cavernous front hallway where dozens of strange voices rocketed off fluorescent light fixtures and off-white linoleum tiles, I found myself longing for the cozy corridors of my old school, the pre-established cliques, the near-scripted conversations. But, of course, I'd come to Clarkson precisely to escape all that. I wanted diversity. I wanted to stop feeling like a middle-class kid in an upper-class world. I wanted a new start.

And at eight o'clock that morning, I got one. I walked into history class and slid into a desk amidst a cluster of guys in the back. I said nothing, just listened to them joke with a tight-lipped smile—not presumptuous enough to expect inclusion, but hoping at least for silent acceptance, tolerance. I wasn't so lucky. A boy with closely cropped red hair and buggy blue eyes stopped mid-punchline to shoot me a glare. "That's Robert's seat," he spat. I flushed to match his buzz cut, apologized a bit too eagerly, and began to shift my books to the next desk over. He and the rest of the crew behind him kept glaring. "That's Chris's seat." I blushed still deeper and looked at him, helpless. I didn't get it. I hadn't even spoken. How could I already be unwanted?

Then a girl's voice piped up from the opposite end of the room: "Ignore them." And another: "Come sit with us." I turned and spotted a pair of smiling blondes in the corner. Still aware of the red-haired boy's gaze chilly against my spine, I shuffled over. After mumbling a flustered thanks to the girls and at last settling into a truly available desk, my discomfort melted quickly away. Riley and Alice, my rescuers, were warm and talkative and, I soon learned, shared my love of WB teen dramas. I felt instantly at home.

At lunch Riley and Alice introduced me to their friends, all of whom proved equally welcoming. Before long, I found myself almost constantly in the company of a pack of girls—my "harem," as Mom called it. And so it was that I carved out my unique spot in the social hierarchy of Clarkson High. Not a lowly place, exactly, but not entirely desirable either. In middle school, I'd been a definite nerd, with a regular spot at the nerd table full of similarly nerdy boys. However internally aloof I'd felt from my fellow undesirables, to the outside world I was a firm member of the pack, just another slimy chunk of the socially awkward blob. Here I found myself higher up the ladder, but on a much more precarious rung. I sat at the right table, but on the wrong side. I was invited to the right parties, but by the wrong people. At any social event my conversation was limited entirely to those present who did not possess genitalia similar to my own. In this high school aristocracy I was the genteel poor.

Wolfe and I had a few classes together, and, in most, he treated me just like all the others, which is to say he didn't treat me much at all. Geometry, though, was different. In geometry, we were the only two boys in the entire class, and so, I guess, in this testosterone vacuum I was rendered masculine enough for interaction.

For the first few days he simply sat in the desk next to mine (I say *simply*, but this move was downright intimate compared to the behavior of other boys). He said nothing directly to me, but occasionally mumbled a complaint about the teacher under his breath. At these I would offer a suitably manly grin or throat-clearing, but otherwise I matched his reticence, spending most of class doodling on the cover of my spiral notebook.

It was the doodles that really caught his attention. Or, rather, the doodle, singular, since I really only drew one thing over and over—an image that had been indelibly pressed into my brain ever since my first harrowing exposure the previous summer.

"So, you a total nutjob, or do you just really like *Scream*?" he asked one morning, pointing to the dizzying array of blood-dripping ghost masks with which I had spiced up my notes on the proper uses of sine, cosine, and tangent.

Horror movies were an unlikely obsession for me, considering I was a paranoid wimp of a fifteen-year-old who had yet to outgrow an unreasonable fear of the dark. And yet, ever since completely losing it after being dragged to a midnight screening of *Scream* by my eighth-grade girlfriend, I'd been totally, utterly, wholeheartedly infatuated, trekking to the video store every Saturday without fail to pick up a new stack of trashy eighties slashers—*Prom Night, Pet Semetary, Hellraiser I, II,* and *III*. Even the bad ones never failed to scare the hell out of me—my pulse pounded at the slightest of shocks, my palms spewed sweat at the first hint of blood—but I loved them nonetheless. Or, rather, all the more. My intent wasn't masochism but liberation, a chance for much-needed release. Because when watching horror movies, fear was totally normal; it was, for once, the appropriate reaction and socially acceptable behavior. Needing a night-light in high school, on the other hand . . .

Of course, I wasn't going to explain all this to Wolfe—not if I wanted him to ever sit by me again. Instead, I simply replied: "Both, I guess."

He laughed. Well, he smiled and gave a slight grunt; I took it as a good sign.

"What about you?"

"*Scream* didn't scare me at all; I'm a bigger fan of Krueger."

Now this was getting exciting. "I own all seven!"

"No shit?"

And so it was that Wolfe Reed came to my house at ten in the morning that Saturday for a *Nightmare on Elm Street* marathon. Not just came, but came bearing a gift: a limited edition, pristinely preserved Freddy Kreuger board game (his mom had picked it up at a flea market a year or so earlier). I was beyond touched, even though we quickly discovered that the game managed to be at once ludicrously complicated and profoundly boring. Fourteen nonstop hours of increasingly spectacular (if decreasingly frightening) maiming, murder, and mayhem later, we emerged from my living room bleary-eyed, vaguely nauseated, and utterly brain-dead. Traumatic experiences, though, have a way of bringing people together, and the marathon was no exception. It may have taken a thoroughly desensitizing round of gratuitous violence to forge, but Wolfe and I shared a connection now, a bond every bit as thick as the fluorescent goo that pins Hapless Teen #47 to the floor of a life-sized roach motel in *A Nightmare on Elm Street 4: The Dream Master*.

From then on, Wolfe and I hung out pretty often, though we rarely made firm plans. Planning, after all, typically involves questions. For example, I might have to ask something along the lines of, "What are you doing this Saturday?" to which Wolfe would have no choice but to reply, "Are you shutting your bitch-ass mouth this Saturday?" No, Wolfe preferred to simply show up at my house on random afternoons, expecting me to be free. Sadly, the fact that I usually *was* free made it difficult to effectively discourage this presumptuousness. And anyway, I found it nearly impossible to be annoyed with Wolfe; I was always so thrilled to see him. I'd have chosen an afternoon with him over a hundred mall trips with the girls, over a thousand awkward keg parties. We'd walk down to the park so he could show me his latest skateboard stunt, or to the video store to root through their pile of used display posters, or take my camcorder around the neighborhood to stage horror flicks of our own (all agreed that *The Merry-Go-Round of Death* was an instant classic).

He never brought me home with him, though, and it went without saying that I was never to show up on *his* doorstep unannounced. Nor did anything change at school. At lunch, he still sat with boys, and I still sat with the girls, never mentioning our exploits of the previous weekend, barely even speaking on most days. Except for geometry class. There we'd speculate about the gore-factor of the upcoming Chucky movie, crack jokes (more specifically, *he* would crack jokes, for which I would serve as the butt), blatantly ignore the teacher, and, on particularly special occasions, rap. Yes, in addition to being a film buff, Wolfe was also an aspiring rap star and a devout fan of Cypress Hill. This was one interest we didn't share, my music tastes running more along the Joni Mitchell/Stephen Sondheim spectrum. For the sake of our friendship, though, I tried to develop, if not a passion, at least an appreciation of the stuff—approaching it with the same grim determination I employed when gulping down beer at parties. I never really grew to like rap (or beer, for that matter), but even if I didn't love the words themselves, I was unquestionably amazed at the way they flew so effortlessly from Wolfe's lips—no stumbling, no hesitation, no self-consciousness—just long, lacquered streams. Sometimes he'd even enlist me for call-and-response lines, and what I lacked in skill I made up for with blind enthusiasm.

Him: And when we rock the mike we rock the mike. . . .
Me: Riiiight!

Or, his all-time favorite:

Him: I want to get high.
Me: Sooooo high!

By sophomore year, though, Wolfe didn't just like the song, he *lived* the song. This turned out to be another interest we couldn't share (though, again, it wasn't for lack of trying). I didn't particularly like pot. I didn't have anything against it, exactly; I just didn't have a very pleasant reaction to it. Pot brought out my brooding side. I became the guy who sulks in the corner, doing his best to ruin everyone else's good time. I'd sit in forlorn silence for hours, breaking occasionally to toss out a fatalistic comment or two:

Me: Go ahead, dance, laugh, sing, but it's all a pathetic, meaningless, futile game.
Bystander: Who invited this kid?

That kind of thing.

People didn't like me high. *I* didn't like me high. But Wolfe liked to get high. More and more, Wolfe liked to get high all the time and, determined as I was to keep common ground firmly beneath our feet, I thought I needed to get high, too. Problem was, Wolfe didn't like stoned Jack any more than anyone else did. We'd smoke and I'd try to just relax and laugh at his even-more-nonsensical-than-usual rants, but all the while I'd feel the involuntary lecture building in my throat and, try as I might to suppress it, the whole thing would eventually come barreling out of my mouth. I'd go on and on about how useless it was to do this, how pathetic we were, how he was throwing his money and life away, all the potential he was wasting. There were other things I wanted to say but didn't, like how crushed his mother would be, how she didn't go to jail just so he could repeat her mistakes. But, even high, I knew better than to open that door. I'd never even met the woman, after all. And what I did know had come from Riley, not Wolfe.

Wolfe let the condescending rants slide for a while, hoping I'd get used to the stuff and stop being such a drag. Then one night he brought me along to see his dealer.

"We're going to have to stay and smoke with the guy, okay? He gets pissed if you just buy and run." Wolfe's instructions for me were simple: "Just keep your mouth shut. He can be mean. Real mean."

And I did keep my mouth shut, retreating to the non-committal language of smirks and throat noises I had used on Wolfe in those early days of geometry class. But sitting there shivering on the filthy carpet of this house with no furniture and no heat, passing a joint to some strange girl in a sweat-stained tank top and Day-Glo Windbreaker, terrified that if I so much as yawned I was going to incite the famed rage of this greasy-haired, acne-spotted kid in a leather American flag jacket, I realized that, however bizarre the situation, the way it made me feel was all too familiar. I was back in eighth grade, pretending to like rollerblading all over again. I thought about how long it had been since Wolfe and I had just gone to the park to walk around, how long it had been since we'd camped in my living room with a stack of videos. I watched him take a hit across the room, his whole body curling in as he inhaled, and I felt my own limbs collapse, melt. I was so tired.

In the car after we left there was the usual swirling in my chest, that familiar pressure at the base of my throat. I opened my mouth to release a sermon, but instead of words, I found sobs. I just sat there and cried. Wolfe didn't make fun of me, didn't get mad. In fact, he didn't say anything at all. We drove home in silence.

After that, his skateboard appeared in my driveway less and less often. But I didn't give up. I was determined to hold on (whether for my own sake or his, I wasn't quite sure). I'd invite him over to help him with his homework, but he'd always show up high, get the answers out of me, and leave. I'd bring him film-school brochures, tell him it wasn't too late to get out of this state. We could go together.

Me: Look, NCArts doesn't care about your grades or SAT scores. You just have to make an audition film. You're a great cameraman.

Him: Look, NCArts doesn't care about you sucking it.

Riley didn't get it. She told me he was a lost cause, that he was taking advantage of me. "He's not even nice to you, for God's sake." But I insisted that she just didn't understand, that friendship with Wolfe was different, that friendship between boys was different. As the weeks went on, what had once been mere eagerness to spend time with Wolfe quickly turned to desperation. I left too many messages at his house, talked too loudly when I ran into him in the hallway. I just couldn't bear to write him off, to write us off. And so, eventually, Wolfe did it for me. The summer after junior year, he stopped returning my phone calls.

We'd still talk occasionally at school after that—he didn't completely shun me—but his eyes were always somewhere else, his voice dull and distant. He was coming to classes high by this point, smoking in the senior parking lot before first period each day. He never rapped for me anymore. By graduation we were pretty much strangers. I was headed for college in New York, and he'd landed a job waiting tables at our neighborhood pizza place. That summer before I left, I dragged Riley in a couple times, sat in his section. He was nice, gave us free soda, entertained us with nasty jokes about the other customers. But he never mentioned getting together, never told me to give him a call.

When I first came out to Riley that August, she wasn't surprised. No one was, really, I soon learned. She did have one immediate question, though: "Were you in love with him? With Wolfe? Was that what it was?"

I was about to unleash a flip negative, but then paused. I realized I had to think about it.

Certainly, I knew I'd never really *wanted* Wolfe, not in that way. I didn't entertain frequent or intricate sexual fantasies about him. I won't lie and claim I didn't entertain *any* such fantasies, but that's really not saying very much. After all, I was a teenager and sexually inactive in the extreme. If a guy was close to my age and anything shy of revolting, I'd probably tossed the idea around at least twice.

My point, though, is that my attraction to Wolfe wasn't based on a physical urge. It wasn't lust. Yet it *was* a romance. Not in the wine-me-dine-me-by-the-light-of-the-shooting-stars-in-your-eyes-like-the-sea-on-a-summer's-day sense, or even in the sweaty-handhold-in-a-darkened-movie-theater mode so common to ninth graders, but on a much more abstract level. I romanticized Wolfe in the way that I romanticized the moors of Yorkshire after reading *The Secret Garden,* in the way that I romanticized life at Louisa May Alcott's Plumfield School for Boys. I loved the idea of him. I loved the idea of a male best friend. I'd never had that sort of powerful bond with another boy, never felt that kind of asexual affection. I was a stranger to true male comradery, to uncomplicated loyalty. And I wanted it. Desperately.

Ironically enough, the drugs and the delinquency only served to make that idealization even easier. Because I started to think I could save Wolfe. I thought I was the only one who saw him for the creative, intelligent boy he really was. I thought I could be the one to encourage him, the one responsible for getting him into college. I was convinced that I was the only one who really *understood* him. I would be the Tom Sawyer to his Huck Finn, the Ponyboy to his Dallas, the Dr. Loomis to his Michael Myers.

So no, I didn't want to date Wolfe; I wasn't really in love with him. But I did want a relationship with him—something that mattered. I had so many wonderful girls in my life, so many female ties. But I wanted a boy to be close to. Not naked with, just close to. And so I invented one. I'd spent years trying to convince myself and everyone else of a connection that didn't exist, of a Wolfe that wasn't there.

And that's—more or less—what I told Riley: I'd loved Wolfe conceptually, nothing more. And having explained it to her, I felt I finally understood it myself. Safely analyzed and dissected, Wolfe could at last be filed away with all the other now impotent denizens of my high school experience, no longer able to cause me pain or pleasure, simply available for viewing at a comfortably nostalgic distance.

And then, of course, I saw him.

It was the summer after my sophomore year of college, and Riley dragged me to a local house party. She promised a good time and, to her credit, it wasn't all that bad. I even ran into Jeff Simpson, the bug-eyed, red-haired jerk of history-class fame, without incident. I stood my ground, refusing to feel awkward or meek, and he responded by being almost obnoxiously friendly, eager to hear all about my new school and classes and life in the big city. Perhaps, I thought, I really had at last discarded all my high school baggage. Perhaps it'd never been all that heavy to begin with.

That's when Wolfe entered the house. He looked, frankly, like shit—his eyes sunken and bloodshot, his ponytail sheared, its spiky remains left greasy and matted on his head. Already drunk and high, he moved extremely slowly, seeming about to tip over with each step.

And despite all of this, just looking at him I felt instantly transported back to geometry class, and all I wanted was for him to talk to me, to show up at my house on his skateboard, to teach me the latest track from Cypress Hill.

"Hey, Wolfe," I almost whispered from my post by the kitchen door.

He turned slowly, took a minute to focus. "Hey. You."

We stood in silence for a moment, and I racked my brain for small talk. I couldn't let him just walk away so quickly. "I heard you're working at the Wal-Mart photo lab now."

"Got fired. Stole some film."

"Oh. Living at home?"

"Where the fuck else?"

And then, for old times' sake, I threw out a question I knew he'd hate, just to hear the predictably obscene response. After all, it wouldn't be geometry class without one.

Me: How's your mom?
Him: Bad. She's got hepatitis C. Real bad.

It wasn't a non sequitur. It was an answer—a real answer. And I was entirely unprepared.

I didn't know much about hepatitis C, but I knew it was the bad one. The chronic one. The incurable one. The terminal one?

The revelation seemed almost comically bizarre, as unintentionally goofy as one of *Elm Street*'s overly elaborate death sentences. The disease sounded too obscure, the lettered name too complicated. Friends' mothers didn't get hepatitis C. They got straightforward terminal illnesses: breast cancer or ovarian tumors, the diseases mothers die of in movies on the Lifetime network. I'd never heard of a mother with hepatitis C. It just didn't sound right.

Maybe it *was* just an obscene joke, one of Wolfe's inappropriate responses turned up a few notches. Maybe his sense of humor had bounced even farther off the wall in my two years away. I waited for his trademark self-congratulatory snicker. But he didn't look back my way. He didn't smile. And he didn't speak.

Neither did I. I *wanted* to say so much. I wanted to tell him I was worried, let him know how often I still thought about him up at school. I wanted to offer my help, my support. I wanted to provide simplistic solutions, outline unreasonable plans. He could move to New York, sleep on the floor of my boyfriend's apartment. We'd help him find a job, find a life, a family. He could still go to school; he could still make films. I wanted to tell him that he shouldn't be afraid to cry. I wanted to tell him that I knew how much his mom meant to him, that I knew how hard this must be.

But the truth was, I didn't know how hard it was. I didn't know how Wolfe felt about his mother. Certainly, I'd never discussed their relationship with him. I'd never even seen them together, never even been inside their home. Who was I to tell Wolfe it was okay to cry? Who was I to grant permission? Maybe he'd been crying every night; maybe that's why he looked so awful. I just didn't know. I couldn't possibly know how he felt. I only knew how I *wanted* him to feel, how the Wolfe I'd imagined and longed for would feel.

I couldn't tell this Wolfe what to do. There were too many questions that needed to come first. And you didn't ask Wolfe questions. I didn't know *how* to ask Wolfe questions—not real ones. And who was I to ask them, anyway? Some pushy stranger from New York, some kid he used to watch scary movies with?

Instead, I just swallowed and said, "I'm sorry." Then I stared, willing him to understand how much I meant it.

I wish I could say that for a brief moment Wolfe met my gaze, that he blinked back tears, that a lifetime of conversations passed between us. But that's not the kind of movie Wolfe and I liked to watch together. Ours were simple tales with clear stakes and clearer options: painful death or painful survival. There was no time for meaningful gazes on Elm Street, no room for subtext in the terse dialogue of its nightmares. *Scream* made it clear that physical love is off-limits to horror movie protagonists—"Sex equals death," one character earnestly informs his friends—but in truth, emotional intimacy is equally forbidden. Genuine connection, after all, isn't suspenseful. It's isolation that creates tension. That's why any friends our hero makes along the way are inevitably picked off by the villain: He can't be allowed to find solace. Solace doesn't make for a good story. He has to keep running.

Wolfe didn't match my stare. Instead, he cast his red eyes to the floor and muttered, "So you're in New York now. Big successful fucker in New York."

"Not so big."

He shrugged and started to walk away.

"Hey, Wolfe," I yelled. Or, at least, it felt like yelling.

He turned back.

"Did you see the new Freddy movie?"

"Yeah, really sucked, huh?"

"Yeah, I guess it did." It had. Sucked. Majorly. But it hurt me to admit it somehow, hurt me to say it to *him*.

He grunted and took a swig of his beer. "They all sucked, probably. We just were too stupid to know it."

"I don't think so." I thought of that awful Freddy board game, still gathering dust in my closet at home. I thought of my well-worn Cypress Hill CD, of rocking the mike right, of the special edition director's cut of *The Merry-Go-Round of Death*. I pictured Hapless Teen #47 writhing on the sticky floor of that roach motel. "No, they didn't all suck. The first ones were really pretty great."

He opened his mouth as if to argue, and then stopped, his lips curling into what almost looked like a smile. "Yeah, guess they had some pretty good moments."

Then he turned and ambled slowly toward the circle of smokers in the back.

Trans-ventures of an F2M
by Alexzander Colin Rasmussen

I thrived so much on small displays of affection and love. I spent so much time living in a body that wasn't mine, and hearing my mother, father, and other people in my life tell me that I was useless and nothing, that I wasn't worth being loved or cared for, that I would never amount to anything. This is what I believed and how I felt before I came out as transgender.

I guess it started when I was five. I didn't like girls' clothes, and instead of playing with dolls and playing house, I wanted to play with fighter jets and Tonka trucks. I had this notion that I would eventually grow a penis and that the mistake would be fixed. It was like I had the flu or a cold. With some medicine, rest, and a little tender loving care, this would be cured.

My mom, Katie, was a cocaine addict, and she was searching for love in all the wrong places. She would bring home men who would beat her in front of me and my sisters. I watched my mother literally waste away from the effects of the drug. It was scary. But I was so young that I was oblivious to what was going on.

Along with the addiction came the abuse toward me and my sisters. At school the nurse or my teachers were always questioning me about why I was so thin or why I had bruises. I would not answer because I had been told that no one had the right or business to know what went on at my house. The teachers always told me to go home and soak in the bathtub, put on some clean clothes, and eat more food.

My father was never there. He left when I was really young and faded in and out of my life. He only came to see me when he was drunk because that was the only time he could handle seeing how badly he had screwed me up. I was very scared of him because he beat my mother in front of me.

He was a very violent man and he taught me at a young age that the best way to let people know when you were angry was to break or throw things, or hit people you care about. That was how he got heard. When he didn't feel as though he was in control or that my mom was listening to him, that is what he'd do. I didn't like him even when I was a little kid. But I so badly wanted him in my life so he could play catch with me or show me how to shave.

People from my school found out about how I was living, and my sisters and I were torn away from my mom and everything that I thought was normal, all in a period of fifteen minutes. With nothing but a trash bag with some dirty clothes and a thought in my mind that it would only be a month before I would come back, I got into a red Department of Youth and Family Services car and was taken to live with my family on Cape Cod, Massachusetts.

For the first few weeks it was good. This lady from the Department of Social Services came to question me and my sisters about the abuse we were victims of while living with my biological parents. This is when things initially started to career out of control. I wasn't used to getting hugs and having people care so much about me. The woman asked me all these questions about things that my mom used to do and whether I was sexually abused. I answered all the questions with complete honesty. That was the only time during the next ten years that I would be completely honest about my life.

After the woman was finished asking the questions, I looked over to my aunt and she was crying. She picked me up and held me. She felt so warm and smelled so good that I didn't want to let her go. She got up and carried me into the house and held me while I cried myself to sleep. I didn't want that feeling to go away because then everything would go back to normal. She would pretty much pretend that I wasn't there and that I was just something that she had to deal with.

I longed for that warm smell again on so many occasions but was too afraid to ask. So I went to her with tears running down my cheeks and told her about what had happened to me when I lived with my mother. I got a warm, smell-good hug and felt so good.

I soon noticed that the only time that I would get that love was when I told them something that happened to me when I lived with my mother. So I told them everything, sometimes repeating stories, and over time adding exaggerations to them because the reactions weakened. I would still get hugs, but they got shorter. As a result, I began fabricating stories. They knew I was lying. I hated myself every time I told a new story but the love and affection was so important to me.

My older sister started showing a lot of her problems, and in response my life at home became World War II. I considered school my refuge. It was the only place where I could escape from the sound of my grandmother and sister physically fighting, and the sounds of their screams and cries.

Watching my grandmother pile things in front of the basement door so that my sister could not come out was hard. I could not stand it. I was cutting myself almost every day. To numb my pain, to find the boy inside, to feel pain and know that I was alive and awake rather than in a dream. I questioned the point of my life and attempted suicide for the first time at the age of twelve. I took some clonidine, my sister's medication. It didn't work but I wanted so badly just to fall asleep and never wake up again, to escape these lies I had created and this life that did not really exist.

I wanted it all to disappear. I hated myself, everyone who was around me, and everyone who believed my lies. I hated everything about myself. At the age of eleven, I'd begun throwing up after I ate because my grandmother constantly pressed into my brain that I had to be the intelligent, skinny, strong, and sensible one. She wanted me to be the example that my older sister should learn from. For me, the desire to be perfect soon became a need. It became the reason that I lived, the reason I breathed. How, though, could I be perfect if I had the wrong body? By this age I knew for certain that I was a boy inside. I just did not know how to face it or what to do. I was holding this horrible secret inside me that hurt more each time I got dressed in the morning and went to bed at night. Every time I heard someone call me Heather, I cringed and something didn't feel right inside. Deep down I knew that it wasn't.

In August of 1999 I was admitted to the hospital for the first time, and at the same time as my older sister. I stayed for almost three weeks. When I went home, I was told that my sister would not be returning to live with us. I was devastated. My sister and I had always been close, and even though our relationship crumbled when we left my mom, I loved her and had a bond with her that no one saw from the outside.

I hated everything and myself. I didn't want to live with my grandmother, because the pressure to shine to perfection was too much without my sister around. I wasn't allowed to bring home a school paper unless it had an A on it. I didn't eat anything unless it was salad. I threw up even lettuce and woke up at three in the morning to do sit-ups. I stayed up until early morning completing homework. I threw myself into my books and studies, even making up extravagant assignments to learn something new and have an excuse to be up studying. And if I wasn't studying, I was cleaning my house.

I spent the seven years after I left my mother living my life to make my grandmother and family happy with me. It was never enough, though. I always missed a spot with the vacuum. I could have gotten an A+ and not an A. I should have studied for three hours, not just two and a half. I could not do anything that would make them love me. I cut myself up to sixteen times each day, and wore long-sleeve shirts to cover the cuts.

Again I was admitted to a hospital. I wanted to go, though. It was a chance for me to be sad and have people there who cared enough to ask me what was wrong. It was a chance to get away from being perfect. I had a week or two where I did not have to clean the house or stay up late doing homework. I still threw up and eventually chose not to eat for sometimes up to four or five days. The cycle of hospitalizations continued until 2002. I entered Pembroke Hospital in July, and was there for five months before I entered a residential program on New Year's Eve.

So much happened in those months at the residential that a year and a half passed in what seemed like a day. I went through some very scary times. Just the thought of cutting seemed like a death sentence for me.

I ended up going to a partial hospitalization program after cutting two arteries in my wrist. (I went to the hospital every morning at eight o'clock, and came back to the residential at night.) I had gone into the bathroom hoping that no one would find me until I had died. But when I saw that I had lost control of the bleeding, and that my life was pouring out of my wrist and leg, I prayed that someone, anyone, would find me before I died. I made it through, and life seemed to get better. But one thing was still wrong.

For twelve years I had been eaten up by this terrible secret. I was a boy and I was a girl. I was trapped. I was something that no one else I knew was. I confronted my situation by speaking to a staff person at my program. She told me to pick out a name and just be myself. Often in my life I had thought about names. I went through Adam, Alex, Zack, Trevor, Xavier, and many others. Finally I settled on Alexzander Colin Rasmussen. I talked to my program director. "What would you say if I asked you to call me Alex and use *he* pronouns?" Her response was that it was not going to happen because she did not call people by nicknames, that I wasn't a boy, and that it would not be allowed because I lived in an all-girls program. Thinking that my attraction to girls could only identify me as a dyke, I identified as just that. I was, in that program, known as "Heather the dyke."

The need for me to find out what was wrong with me and my body, and why they did not match, grew urgent. I met some friends that I still consider very close, Billy and Kevin. They were both identifying as female-to-male (F2M) transgender. What was this word to me then? Absolutely nothing. I had never heard it before and didn't know that something like it existed. Investigating, I found the term described me virtually to a T. I am transgender. Settling this into my head before speaking to the program director again, I prepared for what I would say. I sat with her that day and explained what I needed to. Her response was the same.

I went onto the Internet and looked up transgender, finding a plethora of information from youth and adults: support forums, Web pages, clothing and passing tips, and legal information. I was overwhelmed at first but excited for myself. I had found the answer to something that had troubled me almost my entire seventeen years. Betty, my family worker, set up a meeting with the Gay, Lesbian, Bisexual, Transgender, and Questioning (GLBTQ) Group Home called Waltham House, and they came to speak with me at my program. I was set free from my cage within the first three minutes of meeting Kerry and Anne. The second I walked into the room, they asked me how I would like to be addressed, what pronoun and what name. I was stunned and quietly replied, "Alex, and, um, in the male pronouns, please."

Before the meeting, I had a lot of trouble. At school, the teachers were instructed not to accept my papers if they had Alex on them. Kids were getting suspended for calling me Alex and the girls who I lived with threw hurtful and homophobic/transphobic insults in my face. Ten minutes into the meeting, the advisors from Waltham House said that there was no reason why I could not live as Alex. And so began my adventure living as an out transgender youth.

The reaction from the people around me was mixed: some good, some confused, and some ignorant. The teachers slowly began working on switching the name and pronouns they were using when addressing me. It was extremely hard for them because they had known me for a year and a half as a female. The kids at my house were ambivalent about it and some accepted the idea while others hated me. I faced so much adversity that at some points I wondered whether it was worth it to be myself.

Now, as a resident at Waltham House, I live full-time as Alexzander Colin Rasmussen. I am eighteen years old and can't wait to legally change my name. Some days are harder than others, and it makes it so much easier knowing that I have a home where I am cared about and embraced for everything I am and everything I come with.

Recently, I was faced with a harsh reality. Since the age of nine I have wanted nothing more in life than to become an orthopedic surgeon in the United States Air Force. It was the one thing in my life that I wanted to do to make myself happy. However, a very important person to me, who is in the reserves, told me that due to the ignorance of the nation's government, I would not be able to serve my country.

First, I was told that I would not be able to serve because I am transgender. What does it say about our country if we are denying people the right to serve their country and tell them that their desire to put their lives on the line for the sake of America is not honored because of their gender identity or sexual orientation?

I am also ineligible due to the fact that I am medically diagnosed with cerebral palsy. This is a muscle disorder caused by my mother's drug use while she was pregnant with me. I went through ten operations to have the ability to walk. This is a physical disability that doesn't stop me from running two and a half miles in twenty minutes, or doing three hundred push-ups, among other things. I am fully able to live life like a normal teenager, and enjoy skateboarding, snowboarding, lacrosse, tennis, Hacky Sack, and other activities.

I am the type of person who gets a dream and stops at nothing until I get it. When people tell me "no" or "you can't do it," that makes me want it even more. Even if I don't serve my country, I will spend my life fighting for the rights of others like me to fulfill their dreams.

I am part of the up-and-coming queer generation, and standing on the front lines of the battle. Growing up and living as a transgender youth has been quite an adventure. My name is Alex and I am an eighteen-year-old female-to-male. I am strong. I am smart. I am willing to fight, not quit. I am willing to show the world and everyone in my life that ever challenged my abilities that I can do the seemingly impossible. I am courageous and brave. I am hurt and in pain. I am angry. I am a perfectionist. I am stressed, worried, and scared about my future. I need love and acceptance. I need support, and I need confidence. I am an eighteen-year-old male who is trapped and scared. But I am not alone.

I have been given the chance to write my story and my hope is that it will not only help me, but that it will help any other youth who is feeling alone, trapped and stuck. I want to let them know that there is hope and a way out, but one has to keep fighting. For those who feel trapped, alone, diseased, scared, and stuck, there is hope. There are people out there who feel the same. You are not alone. There is someone out there who cares.

Queer: Five Letters
by Kat Wilson

Dear Mr. Lindstrom,

Your last fifth-grade class gave you hell. The girls were cruel to one another, constantly hurting each other with sharp words and cutting silences. The students competed for grades like their lives depended on it. They taunted you about your earring and asked if you were gay. You said it was none of their business, but they wouldn't drop it. They were so involved with their squabbles and speculations about your personal life that they didn't absorb what you had to give them as a teacher: the proper form for a business letter, accurate spelling, good cursive, and the all-important ability to express themselves with words.

And of course there was that one student. She was in the thick of the cruel girls, and without fail she believed herself to be the wronged party. She was bright, but defiant. You'd assign a report on North America and she'd turn in ten pages on the Canadian parliament. You'd assign an essay on "My Magic Racecar" and she would turn in an essay on why she thought it was a dumb topic. She scrawled "I HATE WRITING" on the cover of her creative-writing notebook; you'd bought one for each student out of your own pocket.

Well, Mr. Lindstrom, here I am. It's been ten years, but I hope you will accept my apology. I'm sorry that I didn't speak up when my classmates taunted you. I'm sorry I defaced the writing notebook. I'm sorry I was too busy rebelling to take in what you were teaching. I've come to appreciate how right you were about business letters, proper spelling, and neat cursive. I want to thank you for the emphasis on daily writing. I didn't take to it at first, but two years after I left your classroom behind I caught the writing bug, and I've been feverish with it ever since. Thank you for laying the groundwork.

Hating writing no longer,
Kat Wilson

Dear Joanna,
You'll probably never read this letter. That's okay; even though it's to you, I'm not writing it for you. I need to explain why I'm angry, and why my respect for you ended when you came out.

As I child, I idolized you. You were a beautiful, independent college student. You were loved and respected by the people I wanted love and respect from. You were wise, you could sing, you could paint. You were radiant. You had a marriage everyone admired. I wanted to be what you were, and I wanted to have what you had.

When you moved to Indiana, I missed you. Like everyone else from our church, I was proud when your art started to bring you success. And maybe more than anyone else, I was glad when you came back. By then, I had started making friends across age differences like ours, and I thought we could be friends. I tried to build a bridge to you, but somehow it was never more than a one-way effort, an incomplete arch.

That untraveled bridge hurt, but it was the least of my problems. I was learning the hard way that the Christian church we shared wasn't ready to walk their talk about inclusion. I stood up one Sunday in worship and laid it all out, my homosexuality and my daily battle wondering if God had built me this way. There was no unified response. Some people told me I was an embodiment of God's love, and some people told me I was going to hell.

Being fifteen and the only out person at church was tough. As I battled despair and tried to name what would help me feel safe, there was one thing that kept coming back to me: I needed a role model. I needed somebody to help me lead the way, somebody who could speak from personal experience, someone who could make it clear I wasn't a representative for all queer people. As wonderful as my straight allies were, there were some things they just couldn't do. I needed somebody I could laugh with about the awkwardness. Living with the loneliness of being a single zebra in a herd of horses was sometimes so painful I didn't want to live at all. I had one close call, got near enough to see the whites of Death's eyes, but I stuck it out even though I was scared, even though people said ugly things.

A year after the worst of my ordeal at church had passed, you quietly divorced your husband. There were rumors you were gay. You packed up your house, sold your art. Almost as an afterthought you came out to me. I tried to welcome you, tried to tell you a little of what I'd learned from being first, but I didn't know what to say. You didn't stick around to see if the path I'd forged was trustworthy. You moved three thousand miles away. You said it was what God was calling you to do, but all I could see was that what I had achieved toward safety for people like us at church wasn't good enough for you. That was when you lost my respect.

Where were you when I needed someone to help me explain that being gay isn't about what two women do in bed, or that gay and pedophile aren't synonyms? How dare you stay hidden when you could have brought me the hope and company I was starving for? How dare you run away when even I could muster the strength to stay?

I understand why you didn't want to be the first, but once I came out, why didn't you join me? I was desperate for reinforcements. My life was hanging in the balance. I'm haunted by the nearness of my escape. You had the power to transform my hell into something more livable, and you didn't use it. I don't know if I can forgive you for that.

Kat Wilson

Dear Mom and Dad,
At the time, I didn't know that coming out to one's parents should be carefully planned, preferably with brochures on hand and prepared "I" statements. I didn't know that there were whole Web sites, whole books, dedicated to the subject of how to say "I'm

gay" without shutting down the lines of communication. I just knew I wanted you two to know what I knew about myself, that straight didn't fit the shape of me.

My method wasn't complicated. I checked out every book the library had on queer youth, fiction and nonfiction. They had seventy-six. I spread the books over the house, stacked on the kitchen counter, balanced on the arms of the couch, perched by your desk chairs, piled on the coffee table, and liberally scattered around my bedroom. A few days later one of you said in passing, "So, you think you might be gay?" and I said, "Yes." Just those three letters. You've been behind me ever since. As I've gone public and activist in the queer arena, I've suffered plenty of doubt, but never about your support.

When people ask me, in that careful tone used for approaching sensitive topics, "And your parents, are they okay with it?" I tell them this: If parents are assigned by lottery, I won the hundred-million-dollar jackpot.

I love you.

Your daughter,
Kat

Dear Margaret,
It must have been terrifying to see your only child, your precious daughter, turn thirteen and grow into a head-turning beauty strangers lusted over. I know it scared me to see the girl I'd been a tutor,

babysitter, and friend to become a young woman in possession of her own sexuality. I think we were both afraid that someone would try to force sex on her. Never mind that she was, and is, strong and able to defend herself. We were both worried beyond reason, you as a mother, and I because I am an only child, too, and she was the nearest I had to a little sister.

I was frank with you from the beginning. I wanted you to know from the outset that I was gay so you couldn't use my hiding it as evidence against me. I knew you were uncomfortable with homosexuality, so I was careful with physical boundaries with your daughter. When she initiated hugs, I kept them one-armed. When she, ten-year-old that she was, asked me to tickle her, I suggested we play cards instead.

We are two different people, and we coped with the gnawing fear for her in different ways. I dealt with my fear by trying to arm her with knowledge about the carnal things you kept her ignorant of. I had no right to trespass on your decision to keep words like *penis*, *vagina*, *clitoris*, *masturbate*, and *lesbian* from her, but I thought that having words for those things might help her protect herself if someone tried to use those words to have power over her. I tried to use them in a safe context, to reduce the squirm factor so no one could take advantage of her discomfort with them. I remember being thirteen, and I know there were times at that age when my knowledge about sex helped keep me safe. I knew your daughter was uncomfortable with my talk. I didn't know that she spoke of it to you.

You dealt with your fear for her by trying to control her life, trying to keep out any monsters and molesters. When she told you about my use of sex words, it got combined with your suppressed homophobia. There I was, and in your view, I was the monster in waiting, ready to become a molester at the first opportunity.

It was all very rational. You explained carefully to my answering machine, talking as fast as an oncoming train, that I would no longer be seeing your daughter without a chaperone, because otherwise I might rape her. You'd known me my whole life. You went to college with my parents. I thought there had been a mistake. I called back, tried to listen well enough to hear what you were saying underneath your accusations. All I heard was that you saw in me the embodiment of our worst fears. I hung up, numb.

The next few weeks were a haze of pain for me. Several people tried to orchestrate a reconciliation between us, but I wasn't having any of it. I felt that the only way for me to function was to avoid you altogether. Our families had many friends in common, and you called to try to arrange logistics, so that I could see my friends without worrying about seeing you. In retrospect, it was a sweet thing to do. You even sent a card, which I still have in a box somewhere, with a near-apology written on it. I remember being amazed by that, even then. We are neither of us good at admitting to being wrong.

I did not have the courage then to give you a chance to see if we could rebuild what was broken. I don't think I had the capacity for that kind of courage at the time. It's only in these past two years, as I have healed from your words (which I know you would take back if you could), that I have found the depth of compassion and forgiveness I needed then. There will always be some scar tissue that sticks out funny, but I know the shape of it better now: I was wrong, as well as wronged.

I miss having the next best thing to a little sister. I want to be part of your daughter's life again, if she will have me. Will you talk with me again about what parameters would let you feel she is safe when I am around? If that means sitting ten feet away from her at all times with you in between, I'm okay with that. I don't want to miss out on any more of her life than I already have. Please call me.

In hope,
Kat Wilson

Dear Steve,
I miss you, your warmth, the way I felt safe with you. I know, rationally, that I was too young when you were alive to remember you. I was only two those last months when my parents and I lived with you and they nursed you through pneumonia again. My dad says it wasn't the AIDS that killed you, or the pneumonia (you'd beat that before), but that you died from giving up.

It's a rare week when I don't think of you. There are places in my mom's life that haven't been refilled since she lost her best friend, and I think of you when I see them. I wonder how my life might have been different if you had been able to stay, to provide some ballast for her. There are things you did for her that I will never be able to do, no matter how hard I try, and she trusted you in ways that she has trusted no one since.

When I hear about other people's harsh, hurtful families, I think about the stories my parents tell about you in their soft moments. I know it was you who took my father in hand and took the rough edges off his homophobia, and you who taught my folks how to be parents who never left any doubt that they loved me regardless of sexual orientation.

I wish you hadn't died, that you were here to see me growing into my dreams. I wish I could ask your advice about the things I don't talk to my parents about. I wish you could give me a hug. Mostly, though, I am thankful that you lived long enough to give me a legacy of love.

I remember you in my heart always.
Kat

Falling Off My Bike and Riding into the Sunset
by Christopher Wilcox

In March 2002 I began what would become some difficult months and years in my life. For this would officially begin my coming out to friends, co-workers, and most importantly, my family. I had questioned my sexuality before but had never acted on any impulses. At the time, I was twenty—twenty-one in a few months— and came from a divorced family with a very strong Catholic background. I had attended a private Catholic grade school and had gone on to a public high school, the first in my family not to attend the local Catholic high school. Of course, as a Catholic I had been taught that being gay was bad and that gay people were sinning by not following the Bible, and thus would burn in hell. I was afraid that if I were gay, I would be sentenced to hell for eternity and wouldn't be with my family in heaven. I didn't want that and, needless to say, neither did my family.

On March 1, 2002, I attended a dinner party hosted by a gay couple, one of whom I had met at the police department where I worked. John, who would become my best friend and my rock, had always known that I was gay and would try to persuade me that it was okay and that I wouldn't burn in hell. Mike, John's partner, had invited a boy, Patrick, who was nineteen and single. The thought was for the two of us to meet and see what, if anything, would happen. So I met Patrick and was instantly attracted to him. He was tall, blond, and had the most wonderful eyes. The feeling between us was mutual, and for the weekend we were inseparable. After the weekend, Mike took Patrick up to the south suburbs of Chicago so he could visit his friends.

He was back in Bradley three days later, staying with John and Mike. I, too, began staying there, because of Patrick. I was finding myself falling in love with him. He would become my first love and first boyfriend. I couldn't stand to be separated from him and could hardly wait for my workday to end so I could see him. He was in town for a week and then had to go back home. He lived in Indiana, two and a half hours away from me. Within two weeks, we realized that we had to be near and with each other. With the permission of John and Mike, Patrick moved in with them.

Soon after Patrick returned, he pushed me to come out to my mom, something that I wasn't ready for and something I didn't want to do. One night I called my mom to let her know I was once again staying at a friend's house and used the lame excuse that I had been drinking and didn't want to drive home. She had always, just like other parents, wanted me to stay put if I was drinking or to call for a ride. I didn't want her to know where I was staying because she was already having a hard time with me spending time with my friends Mike and John. She said they were too old for me and that they would corrupt me—turn me gay. She told me that she wanted me home and didn't approve of me staying out during the middle of the week. We argued on the phone back and forth. Patrick pushed me, prompting me to tell her now, if I really cared about him. I blurted out to her that I was gay.

She yelled, screamed, cried, and eventually hung up on me. She didn't want to talk to me; she didn't want to try to understand. All she could say (and still does to this day) is that I'm going to hell because I'm sinning. I cried all night long. I was upset with myself that I'd disappointed my mom, something I didn't ever do. I was the good child, the angel, but not anymore. I cried because I knew I'd hurt my mom and hadn't intended to or wanted to. I cried because I had finally been able to tell someone what I was feeling inside. And I cried because I didn't have to hide my secret anymore. It wasn't the best time for me to come out to her, but it felt great to tell someone.

I tried to talk to her over the next couple of days but she didn't want anything to do with me. I gave her the space and time she needed to come to terms with it. I wished at the time I had waited and done it under different circumstances, but you can't change the past. Patrick and I talked about moving in together and found a nice one-bedroom apartment in Bradley. We moved to the new apartment in the middle of April and began what we both thought would be a lifetime together. My mom told the entire family about me coming out, and since they were devout Catholics, I was ridiculed each time I visited them about my ways and told that if I changed now, God could save my soul. My mom blamed John for turning me gay. She said it was his fault and if I stayed away from him I'd be normal. To this day my mom won't call me gay. She won't even watch *Will and Grace* because there are gay guys in it. She simply refers to me as being "funny." She went to a family friend's wedding and afterward told me that while she was in the church she prayed to God that I would see the light and realize what I was doing was wrong, and that I should make her happy and marry a girl, just like our friend had done. I told her thanks and changed the subject. When she and other family members get going on this issue, it makes me feel worthless and a disappointment to my family. I let it eat me up on the inside and I try to just let it pass, but it's too hard.

They quote the Bible to me and remind me almost daily what the Good Book says. And for the longest time I thought I was going to hell and had a hard time dealing with what the Catholic Church teaches. It's hard for me to believe that a God who is all-loving and forgiving would send me straight to hell. I've listened to opinions, read books, and come to my own conclusion, which is that God loves everyone, straight, gay, black, and white. We were made in His image. And since God made man, I don't think He would purposely create a certain group of people to send to hell. I find it hard to believe that He would do this to me. I even once sent my mom an e-mail about how the Bible is misinterpreted. She didn't care for that and said she didn't believe me and criticized me for not following my faith. Only time will tell who is right and who is wrong.

After Patrick and I moved in together, one of the girls whom I worked with at the police department finally asked about this guy I was always talking about. She asked if I was seeing him, to which I replied yes. She was shocked and didn't understand, as most people don't. She thought it was nasty and that if I just tried sleeping with a girl I'd see what I was missing and would be straight. She was the first co-worker I'd come out to, and really she was the only one I needed to tell, since the rumor about me being gay spread faster than a wildfire in California. Most of the guys at the police department are basically homophobes and I wasn't sure if I wanted to deal with telling them. I still wanted to remain in the closet, afraid of people not liking me or thinking of me differently. The rumor, which was now confirmed, also spread to the fire department where I'm currently working.

In a way it was a good thing—less people I would have to tell and confront. It was a hot topic, especially in the fire department. People just couldn't get over it and some of them still can't. One payday, Patrick and I stopped to pick up my check at work and I parked in the front lot. The Village of Bradley complex, as I call it, houses the main office, police department, and fire department. The dispatch center and fire department face the parking lot for the main office and police department. As I got out, you should have seen the faces of the fire guys in the window trying to catch a glimpse. As I looked their way, they all turned around and acted like they weren't watching. It was quite humorous and still to this day they all deny it.

I was soon working midnights at the police department and started working with Rennetta, who would become a great friend and someone I could fully trust. She allowed me to talk freely about what was going on, which would become a necessity later on. Working midnights began to take its toll on my relationship with Patrick. Things didn't feel right and I started to suspect that he was cheating. He was also becoming verbally abusive toward me and later would become physical and more violent. In June he confirmed my worst nightmare and admitted that he indeed had cheated on me twice within the span of one weekend. It was horrible and even more devastating to find out that one occasion occurred in my bed with two other guys while I was working. Patrick couldn't hold a job down and still can't to this day; I was the one making the money and paying all the bills. I felt so betrayed by him. I wanted him to stay because I was in love. He wanted to move out and live with the couple that he was messing around with. We fought nonstop about him leaving. Eventually I gave up and told him if he wanted to go he could, but that he could always come back. He moved out while I was at choir practice. I came home and his stuff was gone—I couldn't stand to be there. I felt so alone and empty without him. I decided I would use this as a new starting point for my life, a chance to rebuild myself.

I began to visit more with my mom and her family. I hadn't seen them much while I'd been with Patrick. I needed my family during this hurtful time but I couldn't talk to anyone. I had a very hard time dealing with all of us alone and became so overwhelmed. The only way out that I could see was suicide. To me it seemed like there was no other option and this was the only way I'd be happy. I tried suicide multiple times—everything from overdosing to hanging and cutting myself. I began to self-mutilate. And there were times that I was very close to doing it but I just couldn't. I know this sounds silly, but I thought of my cat, Lilly. I thought that if I killed myself, who would take care of her? I couldn't do that to her; I had to know she'd be safe and okay. She is like a lot of my friends who played a very important role in my life. I realized there was more to life and that I needed to stop feeling sorry for myself.

During the summer of 2002 I brought Patrick, who was still living elsewhere, out to my dad and stepmom's house for dinner. They had said he was more than welcome. I introduced him as my roommate, but parents are smart and I was sure they knew he was more. (I would later find this out to be true.) I was excited that they had invited us out together. Was it possible for my dad and stepmom to accept me being gay?

I was getting ready for a pilgrimage to Toronto for World Youth Day 2002 in August. This would be my first trip to see the Pope, one of my lifelong wishes. No one at church knew at the time I was gay, and I wanted it like that. I didn't want to lose my job there playing the organ and piano at Mass. I prayed before I left that while on this pilgrimage, God would show me how to be a better person. I had a lot of anger inside, and wanted Him to show me what He wanted me to do with my life. A few days before I left, I agreed to let Patrick move back in. He was seeing someone else and I told him it would be okay as long as they stayed out of the apartment—to respect me. I left for the trip on bad terms with him. I cried most of the way to the bus in Downers Grove, about a two-hour trip from Bradley. The overall trip was amazing, the most powerful experience in my life yet. And I had accomplished at least one of my tasks—to become more peaceful, a better person. On the trip I met two people in our group who were gay. When we arrived back at Downers Grove, one told me he was and that he knew I was, too. I came home and realized that I needed to keep my peaceful life and stop building up hate again.

The relationship between Patrick and me became physical and he became violent. He would beat me for no apparent reason and got great satisfaction out of the fact that I wouldn't fight back. As the months went by, it got worse. The comments from the fire department got worse and they occasionally slammed me. I had enough and went to the assistant chief and complained about the harassment. The people named in my complaint were brought in and told to knock it off. I got apologies from most of the people involved. The biggest one said something that I won't ever forget: "No matter what you do or who you are, you're still our friend and we love you no matter what." Little does George know that this has helped me get through some tough times. I knew that I had more friends than I had thought or realized.

The year was coming to an end and I got tired of Patrick's crap and began to stand up for myself. He would beat me for whatever reason—only now I fought back, something that I regret I had to do. I didn't want to hurt anyone that I loved. It hurt me more than it probably hurt him. One night we fought long and hard and he came after me with two knives and blocked the door so I couldn't leave. At this point I knew that he really didn't love me as he claimed he did. Someone who loves you wouldn't or shouldn't do this to you, nor make you feel like crap. He went on a rampage, stabbing the couch as he passed me. He ended up leaving that night and not coming back until the morning. I fought back smarter than he ever could—I began locking the door after he left so I could sleep in peace for the night. I kept it a secret from everyone, even my closest friends. I didn't want it to be known because of where I work. I've sent officers to gay domestic disputes and fights and have had to listen to the comments come out of their mouths. I was too afraid to say anything or complain, so I let it go on more than one occasion.

Christmas came and Patrick went home for the holidays and I went to be with my family. Honestly, I can say that I did miss seeing him, but didn't miss his crap. He came home late Christmas night while I was at work, a twelve-hour shift. He didn't call or stop in to visit, but called his sex buddy to come to the apartment. I was at wits' end and ready for something to happen.

My friends were telling me to kick him out, but I said he had no place to go. They said he could move back home with his mom. They asked what day my trash was picked up. I told them early Tuesday morning was trash day. They told me trash day was the day I needed to put him on the curb with the rest of my garbage. They told me to pack his stuff and leave it outside, and if I had a problem, then they would do it for me. They also told me that they still loved me but were tired of my complaining about the situation since I didn't want to fix the problem. Finally I had had it. I came home from the store one day and did what I feared. I sat Patrick down and began crying. I told him that I didn't love him anymore and that I needed for him to move out so I could move on. He thought I was joking with him and then it was his turn to beg and plead with me. I stuck firm and said no and began to pack his belongings for him. And in a week he was gone and I was so afraid and alone. This would be the official end of Christopher and Patrick.

Mike and John decided I needed to make my first trip to Boystown in Chicago to forget about Patrick. It was a cold night downtown but it still was fun. I was exposed to just a little bit of the gay life in Chicago. They dubbed it my coming-out party and thus I got free drinks from bartenders. There was so much to take in, in such a short period of time.

I met another friend in June 2003 who would become another support for me—Jacki. Jacki knew right away that I was gay and absolutely loved it! She didn't think any less of me, which was awesome. She had a gay cousin, so she was familiar and okay with it. Jacki and I would become best friends and would hang out whenever we could. She was someone who I could comfortably talk about my problems and life with. Life became normal for the most part, nothing new happening. I began to become less embarrassed about being gay and came out to my high school friends and friends in general. Overall, the support was amazing and they, too, echoed what George had told me: they loved me no matter what. Still, I had another group of people that I needed to come out to— my dad, my stepmom, and her family.

The entire family got together the weekend after Christmas 2003 to celebrate and open presents. My stepsister, Julie, was there. She's someone I've always admired and could always talk to. Julie, her brother Josh, and I were standing in the kitchen downstairs just talking, mainly catching up. Julie asked if Patrick was living with me. I told her no, that it hadn't worked out and he'd moved out. Josh asked me if I cared if he asked me a question, and if he could be blunt. I love being blunt so I said to go ahead. Josh asked if Patrick was just my roommate or if he was more. Julie looked at him as if she couldn't believe he'd asked that. She commented of course we were more. I confirmed that he was more and thus I came out to them. Being curious and not sure how my stepfamily would react, I asked both Julie and Josh for their opinion, if my dad or stepmom, Beth, had any idea. Julie told me that Beth knew a while back that I was gay, and that neither she nor my dad cared. The even better news was that my stepfamily wouldn't care or didn't care that I was gay.

I was honestly surprised. But from that point forward, the acceptance my stepfamily has given me, for the most part, has been extremely wonderful. It's truly hard to find a good family who supports their GLBT child. I used to be jealous of others who had families who supported them, but now I am blessed to have part of my family support and stand by me.

In early 2004, I heard from a co-worker that one of my good friends from high school had moved back into town from Tampa. Eric had taken a job working at Steak and Shake, so I stopped in to see him. There were two reasons I wanted to see Eric: to catch up on lost time, and more importantly, to come out to him. I had not seen him since the night of graduation back in June of 1999. We met for lunch and he was talking about his ex and I commented on how he sounded similar to my ex, Patrick. He looked at me, asked what I said, and I repeated myself. He got a big grin on his face and said, "See, I knew you were. I knew you were back in high school." It was great to have my friend back in town, and even better—he was gay. Eric showed me that it's okay to be gay and show it, for it's who I am. To be perfectly blunt, Eric is a little flamboyant, plain and simple. He doesn't hide it from anyone, not even at work. Just by hanging out with him I've become used to this and it's helped me. Not only have I become more comfortable with myself, but also I've stopped hiding the fact that I'm gay. There's no reason to be ashamed.

On one shopping trip we went to the local mall and stopped by a "little girls" accessory store. The store had a big supply of rainbow rings, stickers, and purses. You name it, they had it in rainbow. I had nothing with rainbows on it—I was too afraid. I purchased a ring and so did Eric. I wear it almost all the time—even at work at the police and fire departments. The only time I take it off is in front of my mom's family, which is purely out of respect, and of course at Mass.

Now that I am hanging out with Eric I find myself spending

more time in Chicago. Being gay in Chicago for the most part is not a problem and it's accepted. But where I come from, only fifty-five miles south of Chicago, you won't find two guys walking down the street holding hands or kissing. You won't even find a rainbow flag flying high and proud. In Chicago it's like I can be a different person—be me without having to be afraid or embarrassed about who I am. It's a shame that I and many others have to feel like we need to escape to Chicago for the right to be ourselves.

I now subscribe to *The Advocate* and *Out* and I don't read them at home in seclusion. I take them to work with me and read them during the slow times while wearing my gay pride ring. In the past three years I've learned a lot and have become happy with myself. In the beginning I wouldn't have taken *Out* to work, let alone acknowledge that I was gay. I've learned that I have nothing to be afraid or ashamed of. I've gone from someone who was depressed and thought about taking the easy way out, to wanting to work and lobby for gay rights and joining PFLAG and subscribing to gay magazines. I'm happy about who I have become and I am looking forward to what the future holds for me. All you need is a plan, and friends and family who support you. Some are lucky, while others are not. But it's important to remain faithful to who you are, not to what or who somebody wants you to be. Granted, it does hurt having to go through the coming-out process alone and not having your loved ones support you.

I had to think, should I do what would make my family happy and be miserable, or do what I want, which will make me happy? It's all about me when it comes to happiness. I'm not here to make other people happy with my decisions, but rather to make me happy. It's because of my good friends and family who love, care, and support me that I was finally able to get back on the bike that I've fallen off so many times and ride into the sunset a happy and proud person.

The Night Marc Hall Went to the Prom
by J. J. Deogracias

May 10, 2002

"I feel at ease now just knowing that we're getting free of discrimination."

Seventeen-year-old student Marc Hall said this to reporters as he and his twenty-one-year-old boyfriend, Jean-Paul Dumond, hopped into a limousine and headed to the prom at Monsignor John Pereyma Catholic High School in Oshawa, Ontario. He said this just hours after a judge ruled Hall had the right to take his boyfriend to the dance. The school principal and the school board had told Hall he could not bring his boyfriend to the dance on the basis of Roman Catholic teachings.

"We think it's so cool that he's coming," said a girl classmate who knows Hall. "Because he's the GREATEST! Ahhhhhhhhhhhh-hhhhhhhhhh!"

The school board, disappointed with the decision, will abide by the judge's ruling but plans to fight it in court.

"I'm prepared to take it to trial in order to set a precedent so that nobody else will have to go through what I had to go through," Hall told reporters.

"Wow, that's so amazing," I say. I press the AM/FM button, and the neon green display flips from AM 680 to FM 97.3 in my boyfriend Wesley's silver 1992 Toyota Camry. I lie back in the gray passenger seat in the new black tearaway pants my mom originally bought for herself and my white T-shirt depicting a teddy bear doing weights, with "I'm in no shape to exercise" in baby blue print on its shirt. The commercial for Sleep Country Canada jingles, *Why buy a mattress anywhere else? (Ding!)."*

"I don't think I could ever be so brave," I say. "It took me until my final year to come out in an all-guys school."

"Yeah, me neither," says Wesley, who wears a blue sweatshirt and blue jeans. He steers the car, driving past orange-and-white-lit lampposts and the streaking lights of other passing cars. I stroke the small hair bristles on his right cheek.

He giggles. "Bunny?"

"Puppy!" I bark back.

"BUNNY!"

"PUPPY!"

"Bark, bark," he barks back. "Too bad we didn't know each other back then."

"Bark, bark," I respond. "At least you wouldn't have been shafted by that girl and left all alone at your prom night."

I reach over and clench his right hand. He smiles. I smile.

"Well, if I had to go back to change my prom night, I don't think I would," I say. "Everyone was so shocked that I actually brought a girl. And then everyone at my table was so shocked that I didn't get drunk when I downed that screwdriver."

Wesley laughs. "That's right. This little bunny likes to drink."

"That's right! And that's why whenever there's alcohol, I'll drink for both of us," I say. "It's a sacrifice I'm willing to make."

Wesley smiles. He laughs. I laugh.

"Well, we're here," Wesley says. "I'm surprised you didn't fall asleep."

"Sometimes you just keep me going all night long," I say, smirking.

We drive into Markton Park. The place where we first kissed when we met a year and a half ago. The place where we kissed for five hours on a cold January night. The place where we learned how much fun two people can have in a sleeping bag in the nearby forest. The place where we made a lot of memories.

Backseat down. Lying in the back compartment. Kiss. "I love you," Wesley says. Selena sings "Dreaming of You." Kiss. "I love you, too," I say. Embrace. Kiss. Tickle my armpit. Kiss. Glasses off. Stare into his light blue eyes. Kiss. Stroke his dirty-blond hair. Kiss. Massage. Kiss. Car swooshes past. Duck. Breathe. Kiss. Takes his blue sweatshirt off. Kiss. Pulls down his blue Levi's. Kiss. Takes my "I'm in no shape to exercise" teddy bear T-shirt off. Kiss. Pulls down my black tearaways. Breathe. Kiss. Rubbing. Kiss. Windows fog. Kiss. Soft fingers caress. Kiss. Car lights approach. Kiss. Car lights stop. Red and blue flash. Kiss. Duck. *Shit*. Door slams. "Shit," Wesley says. He scrambles for his jeans. Pulls them up. Knock, knock.

Wesley, bare-chested and wearing Levi's jeans, opens the car door. I huddle at the far end of the car, far away from the door. Naked. A cool breeze wheezes into the car.

"Yes, Officer?" Wesley asks.

The police officer's voice shoots through the door. "Is everything okay in there?"

"Everything is fine, officer," Wesley stutters. "I assure you."

"Can I see your ID?"

"Sure," Wesley says. He reaches into one pocket, and keys clank. He picks his other pocket, and fumbles for his wallet. The wallet clinks with coins. He pulls out his driver's license, and hands it to the police officer.

"Okay, sir," the police officer says as he hands the driver's license back to Wesley. "I would also like to hear from the woman, if you don't mind."

I groan. My eyes narrow. I crawl forward, naked, toward the open door. Wesley lays his hand on my shoulder. I face the police officer. His face blurs with the flashing red and blue lights from the police car. I squint.

"I'm FINE, officer," I mutter in a deep voice.

The police officer steps back. "Well . . . I'm sorry . . . for, um . . . disturbing you."

Quick crunches of gravel. Door slams. The police car roars off.

Wesley grabs for the door and slams it. We sit there in the back compartment for a few minutes. Silence. Wesley bursts into laughter. I jerk my head to him, my eyes still narrowed. Then, my eyes widen. A smile emerges on my face. I break out in laughter.

"Oh my God," I giggle. "Could he have run any faster?"

"You should have seen his face," Wesley laughs. "When he saw you, he looked like he'd seen a ghost."

"I think we better get out of here, before things get worse."

"I think you're right," Wesley agrees.

While Marc Hall—in blue-dyed hair and a blue tie, in a white tuxedo and white patent-leather dancing shoes—dances the night away with his boyfriend, my boyfriend Wesley and I tear out of Markton Park.

"Okay," I say, "let's make sure that we do not let this happen again . . . and let's not tell anyone about this."

"Why not?" Wesley giggles. "It's so funny."

"Yeah, I guess," I say, smiling. "At the very least, we can always say, 'The night Marc Hall went to the prom with his boyfriend . . .' "

". . . we fooled around," Wesley continues. "And got caught by a cop."

"And the cop thought I was the woman. . . ," I groan. "So I came out and flashed him. . . ."

". . . and the police officer ran," Wesley concludes, laughing again.

A few months later, Wesley takes his class G driver's test. His examiner looks at his driver's record and asks, "So . . . did you and your boyfriend have a good time at the park that night?"

Don't Tell Me That I'm Overly Sensitive and Paranoid
by Alex Weissman

My camp counselor and personal hero, Hank, is babysitting me and my brothers one night. He says that if he saw two men walking down the street holding hands, he'd take a baseball bat and beat them. My brothers and I argue with him, but to no avail. My hero is lost.

At Hebrew school, with our teacher Adam, we are studying Leviticus. We get to the famous passage and I learn that I am not to lie with a man as one lies with a woman, as this is an abomination. Adam tries to put a positive spin on it, but I wonder how a religion that teaches us to love thy neighbor as thyself could breed so much hate.

Mrs. Green's Language Arts class takes a field trip to a retirement home so we can learn about what it's like to be old. When we begin to get off the bus, my best friend Paul pushes me so I fall on top of his stepsister, Melissa, and says, "Look! Lesbians!" I apologize to Melissa for falling on her and glare at Paul. He thinks it's hilarious.

My best friend Steve is sleeping over my house on the weekend. Somehow, we end up talking about sex and he says that anal sex is disgusting and so are gay people. Without the language or confidence to convince him otherwise, I feebly argue that not all gay people have anal sex. Our friendship begins to dwindle over the years and eventually we stop hanging out

I spend some of my time after school doing makeup for the high school show, *The Crucible*. My mom tells me she thinks it's "not good for *my* development." I cry because my mom is worried I'm going to grow up gay when I know it's already too late.

During Japanese class, in which we do nothing, my best friend Danielle writes things like "Alex is gay!" "Alex likes cock!" and "E-mail Alex for hot butt sex!" all over my folder. I laugh, but only because I know it's true.

Coach Waters of the varsity volleyball team makes a joke about one of the players spending too much time on his knees. Everyone laughs because sucking dick is funny. I quit the team and do theater instead.

The summer before college, I begin to come out to some of my friends from high school. One girl is very excited because now we can go shopping together! I wonder when I mentioned anything about suddenly enjoying shopping, but she seems determined.

I'm walking down the street with my first group of gay friends in Boston. A man passes us and coughs the word "faggots" as he passes by. The other faggots keep walking. I stop dead in my tracks with my jaw hanging on the sidewalk.

The guy who lives next door to me consistently says "That's so gay" to refer to stuff he doesn't like. Every time, he looks over at me and apologizes, saying he didn't mean it like that. I give up on him monitoring his speech and spend most of my time with the girls down the hall.

I'm walking across the quad before spring break and out of nowhere I hear someone scream "FAGGOT!" from one of the dorms. I look up to see a head quickly retreating back into a window. I go home for break, angry before I even get there.

I study abroad in Chile and live with a host family for five months. They make comments about a gay character on TV that make me uncomfortable. I lie to them for five months about my sexuality and go home unsatisfied with my study-abroad experience.

While abroad, my friends and I get invited to a Chilean family's house for dinner. During dinner, the mother says that she would not be happy if her son turned out gay. She elaborates by explaining that she has nothing against gay people. Hell, she'd even have one over her house for dinner! I feel awkward, afraid to speak my mind to this homophobic woman who kindly, naively, invited me into her home.

I am forced to take a biology class in order to graduate from college. One week, the discussion topic is the biology of homosexuality. One student comments that "gay men do not have lasting relationships. Maybe fleeting intimacies, but not lasting relationships." No one, not even the professor, says anything to challenge her. I raise my hand but get ignored in the large lecture hall. I disengage from the class and end up getting my worst grade ever at college.

I'm walking down the street, holding hands with my boyfriend. People stare at us, totally perplexed by the existence of an interracial, same-sex couple. I stare back, confused by their racist, homophobic existence just as much as they are by my existence.

I participate in a psychology study over the summer to make a few extra bucks. The researcher and her assistant are chatting about the human male's inability to decorate. Men apparently didn't get that gene. The researcher quips, "Unless they're gay, then that's all they got!" I'm shocked and feel like a fish in an empty bucket . . . my mouth moves but nothing comes out. Instead, I fuck with her experiment and lie about my answers.

I go to the special Shabbat service at Hillel that is designated to be the week when they especially welcome the queers in the community. I know the rabbi would never marry a same-sex couple, and gays are only indirectly referenced in his sermon. I leave, disappointed in my religious community.

I begin dating a semi-closeted guy, John, whose straight housemates I know well. One of them says that he's never heard John *admit his homosexuality.* He hopes that he can talk to John and get him to *admit his homosexuality.* I wonder if a Catholic confessional and a priest will be necessary for this admission.

Exams are over and I'm celebrating with some friends. My friend is trying to describe someone whose name she can't remember . . . he's tall . . . brown hair . . . wears peach and pink a lot. Carmen's boyfriend seems shocked that a guy would wear peach and pink a lot. It's subtle, but I still make a mental note to keep my distance.

I am home for vacation and my older brother tells a joke that has homophobic undertones. I get pissed and stay quiet the rest of the night. Finally I tell him why I'm annoyed. He explains the joke and it turns out I had heard it wrong. It wasn't homophobic at all.

People aren't as homophobic as I think.

I'm just overly sensitive and paranoid.

My poems
by Isaac Oliver

I hate my poems.

I used to love them, back when they knew their place.
Poems are like dogs you walk in the park
to attract off-duty firemen who love them and in turn love you.
Not my poems.

My poems used to be shy; they used to stand in front of the
    mirror
and complain about their bloated syntax and pimpled thematic
    structure.
But now they leave the house in couplets I don't remember
    rhyming,
and when I ask where they're going and with whom they're going
    out,
they say, "He's not your style. He writes think pieces, political
    pieces."

Oh God, not think pieces, not political pieces.

My poems see a guy across a crowded room,
start talking pretty, saying things like, "Your eyes are like moons,"
and before I know it, I'm left standing alone at the punch bowl.
I'll grab a stanza's arm and say, "Just let me have this one, please."

"You snooze; you lose," it responds, rolling its eyes.
"You think you're so hot with your semicolons," I shout after it,
"but I wrote you for a class assignment! You weren't even
    inspired by anything!"

My poems make better theatre dates than me.
They make jokes; they offer multilayered compliments;
they know someone in the chorus.
My poems spend money without thinking twice.

They hold hands with men on the subway no matter who's
    looking.
"How'd you get so fearless?" I ask a particularly savvy poem that
    insists
on all lowercase letters and refuses every title but "untitled."
"I don't know. Are you jealous?" it replies,
its thumb making circles on the palm of a modern dancer/social
    activist.
My poems are bitches.
So they've been to some festivals; that doesn't mean they know me.
"You're much less grateful than my earlier work, when I used to
    title poems," I snap.
"You mean the ones you wrote with Tori Amos playing in the
    background
and without the sense of humor?" "untitled" retorts.

My poems also come knocking in the very early morning,
and I let them sleep on my couch, and they cry about cruel men
and betrayal and Karl Rove,
and I hold them and remember why I wrote them.
I've needed to be fearless, to not capitalize words,
to laugh, to spend money, and to leave something untitled.
I've needed them to be my spies,
to have their hearts broken and their spirits tattered,
and to come back to me for punctuation.

Sacagawea
by Laura Heston

When I was 16, you offered condoms
to a virgin, and gave me a Sacagawea
coin with advice not to give it away.

Like Lewis and Clark, Kathleen and I took her
on our expedition. We traded her
for pleasurable plastic mysteries
in a truck-stop bathroom.

You listened intently to my misadventures
with boys. One faked a brain tumor,
another was a beekeeper,
and I'm allergic.

When I gave back the rubbers
and confessed I loved a woman,
you said not to give up
on men. I would awake one morning

to realize my Catholic destiny
and ask you to make my dress. No sense
disappointing my father too.

You wished for me to hide my Sacagawea
in the bank, to never touch her
in front of you.

A Fairy's Tale
by Travis Stanton

Like all things, I suppose my fairy tale started at the beginning. Pardon the cliché, but for me, it really did. People often ask when I first knew I was gay. My answer: since I was a fetus.

The fact is, I truly believe I knew I was different from day one—or at least as early as a child can have coherent thoughts. I'm not naive, or New Agey enough to believe that I was having homoerotic fantasies in the womb, but I do believe I sensed the fact I was somehow special. Looking back on my childhood, so many confusing memories now make sense—certain feelings I had for childhood playmates, bizarre emotions surrounding my heterosexual dating experiences, and specific moments that stand out in my mind like photographs.

But for me, knowing I was different and realizing I was gay came at two distinctly different moments in my life.

I remember growing up in a small town in eastern South Dakota, where everyone wore the same kinds of clothes, had the same kinds of childhood aspirations, and did the same sorts of things. Looking back, I sometimes wonder how growing up would have been different if so much of my early years hadn't already been predetermined by small-town societal norms. Would I have still played baseball with the other boys, or would I have taken up gymnastics with the neighborhood girls instead? And how would that one tiny variation in my path affect the person I am today? Similarly, I sometimes wonder what life would have been like had I grown up in a world where being gay was accepted and understood. Would I have still been taunted by school bullies? Would I have still dated girls in high school? Would I have taken a boy to the prom instead? Would I have fit in better by being myself than I did by trying to be who others expected me to be?

In the end, I always remind myself that when questioning the past it is less important to ponder what could have been different, and more important to take inventory of the lessons reality taught us along the way.

Part of the difficulty in growing up gay, for me, was having this overwhelming internal understanding that there was something unique about me, but not knowing precisely what it was. Some of this was alleviated by the elementary school message that we are all unique. But I sensed what made me different from everyone else was more significant than your everyday individuality.

I remember wishing I had some sort of visible difference to which I could attribute these feelings—to be outwardly beautiful, visibly wealthy, or to have a different skin color than the rest of my homogeneously white schoolmates. At times, I thought even being particularly unattractive, or visibly impoverished, would have made being me simpler. That way, others would accept the fact I was not entirely like them. I suppose I thought being markedly different would be a Get Out of Jail Free card when it came to the expectations people placed on me, to walk a certain walk and talk a certain talk. But to most, I was your run-of-the-mill child—and that mediocrity, coupled with the intrinsic knowledge I was anything but, was suffocating.

And yet, despite the fact I sensed I was different, I never really thought the difference had anything to do with my attraction to other boys. In fact, I assumed that in that respect I was just like everyone else. I assumed all boys had these feelings, but didn't act on them. I couldn't comprehend that something so basic could be what made me different.

In so many ways, I grew up like I imagine many young girls do. I enjoyed the company of girls, didn't particularly enjoy sports or the rough-and-tumble activities typically associated with young boys, and was noticeably more sensitive and compassionate than most male children. In hindsight, I don't think I confidently embraced the male side of myself until high school.

In elementary school, I experienced difficulty in fitting in with my classmates. I don't believe I had a hard time making friends, per se. I got along with most people, but didn't have that one group of close friends that most kids have growing up. When you think about those early friendships, they are almost always based on chance occurrences—your parents are friends, or you live in the same neighborhood. But for me those childhood friendships seemed to disintegrate when chance occurrences didn't translate into commonalities beyond geography and parental acquaintanceship.

Sunday evenings were awful times for me while attending elementary school. My family would spend them with my grandparents, eating together, playing games together, watching made-for-TV movies together. That togetherness, in stark contrast with my lack of close friends, made the idea of starting another week of school unbearable. I sank into something of a childhood depression. I was lonely, but not because others weren't there to eat lunch with and talk on the playground with. I was lonely like a foreigner who's away from home—who longs to see someone who resembles them.

I began meeting with a counselor. While I enjoyed having someone to confide in, I felt that the therapist violated my confidence by discussing our sessions with my parents. I don't know for a fact this occurred, but certain things they would say and do seemed to be the logical result of the funneling of information from my counselor. The other thing I noticed about therapy is that, while it made me feel better (if for no other reason than verbalizing internalized frustrations), it didn't alleviate the outward problems. The feelings of isolation didn't disperse that easily.

Throughout counseling, I sensed tension building between me and my parents. They were always supportive, but as with most parents unknowingly raising gay children, they couldn't begin to understand or comprehend the emotions of my young mind. I sensed their frustration in attempting to understand, and that alone made me try to hide my problems from them.

In addition, it was all too obvious to my fellow students that I was going to counseling. That indicated there was something *wrong* with me. And as anyone who has ever worked with children will tell you, they have a keen ability to sense and exploit weakness.

I was at something of a standstill. While the problems had not gone away, I could no longer discuss them with my therapist because doing so would alert my classmates there was something wrong, as well as my parents, who appeared to be as affected by what troubled me as I was. So began a process of bottling up all the crap life threw in my general direction.

It's interesting when you think about it, the idea of holding things inside. Part of me marvels at how strong I must have been—a kid holding back his pain to spare his parents the frustration of having a son who for one reason or another can't fit in. But on the other hand, I suppose I was weak, or at least too weak to deal with things as they happened. Either way, the decision to keep it all inside was an unhealthy one. I've always marveled at those individuals who are able to keep things to themselves—not in order to hide them, but just in order to live a more private life. I guess I'm just not good at keeping things private—or at least not major things. As much as I tried to restrain myself from letting the world get me down enough to let it show, it did.

In middle school, I remember wondering how I was ever going to survive the experience. I certainly never expected I would ever be sharing my story with others—who else would care to listen? Who else could possibly understand the turmoil that I tried to ignore, all the while being beaten by the reality that I couldn't escape it?

I doubt a single day went by without someone calling me a fag, or threatening to hit me, or actually doing so. Somehow I managed to make it through middle school without sustaining any visible wounds, but the ones that went unseen likely hurt more. When these kids taunted me with anti-gay epithets, I knew instinctively they were right. How they could possibly know my most intimate secret, I couldn't fathom. At this point in my life, being gay simply meant having the occasional thought about other boys. As I hadn't acted on those feelings, it baffled me how anyone could be observant enough to notice.

Growing up completely isolated from any positive gay role models, I never considered coming out. Instead, I contemplated ways to prove the bullies wrong. But how can you prove to someone you're not gay? I later read somewhere, " 'Straight' always has the possibility of being in the closet."* Had I known that at the time, I suppose it would have empowered me. Still, as much as I may fantasize that being openly gay would have disarmed the bullies—my reclamation of words like "fag" and "homo" leaving them unarmed—it is likely far from the truth. I wonder how much time and energy I spent dreaming up ways to make those insecure little boys believe I was straight. I dated girls, but that didn't stop the name-calling. Sometimes when I happen to run into ex-girlfriends of mine, I feel the need to either apologize or thank them for being there for me at an absurdly difficult time. Without knowing it, they made life a little bit easier. Even though the other boys didn't stop harassing me, these girls gave me something to throw back in their faces. And while one could make the assumption I was simply using these girls, I believe they needed me as much as I needed them. Middle school is a tragic time for us all, and as we held hands at school dances, the skeletons in our closets were able to tango without too many people noticing.

I vividly remember one individual who seemed to exist for no other reason than to make my childhood a living gay hell. On nearly a daily basis, he would stand up in class, in front of my home economics teacher, and announce to the students that I was gay. He yelled it down the hall between classes, yelled it in the

*Benjie Nycum and Michael Glatze, XY Survival Guide (San Francisco: XY Publishing, 2000).

locker room before gym class, and yelled it in my face one night while he and a friend of his took a few swings at me.

When I reported the harassment to a school official, I suddenly found myself in the office of one of the school counselors. The counselor never asked me if I was gay. He assumed I wasn't. It's funny, the majority of kids assumed I was, and the majority of adults—including my parents—assumed I wasn't. The school official gave me tips on how to walk, talk, and appear more masculine. This, he assured me, would prove to them I was not gay. What a wonderful lesson to teach a young person: If someone makes fun of you for being different, try your hardest to act just like them, so they'll see you're just the same. What happened to everyone being unique?

I will always harbor some resentment to the gentleman who thought it easier for me to change who I was than to solve the real problem of intolerance and homophobia in the halls of my school. But life is too short to hold too much of a grudge. I ultimately forgave the bully who taunted me—I later learned he was just as gay as I was. And I hereby forgive Mr. Elshere for never asking me the most obvious question, "Are you gay?"

I forgive him mostly because I'm not sure I would have answered honestly. And even though I believe I deserved the option, I can't expect people to think in a way they may never have been forced to think before. I only hope that the children of Watertown Middle School are no longer assumed to be anything but individuals who deserve to be themselves, to walk their own walk, talk their own talk, and be as masculine or feminine as God made them.

Oh, I almost forgot about God. In the midst of middle school, there was another force at work. Having grown up in the Wisconsin Synod Lutheran Church, I was making my way through two years of confirmation at the same time I was starting to realize I was gay. Growing up gay is a series of baby steps—knowing it, realizing it, acknowledging it, living it. And I was still just beginning the journey.

Spiritually, I always took the teachings I learned in Sunday school to heart. The fact was, Christianity made sense to me. You could attribute that to the fact I grew up in a Christian household, but I think the basic concepts of forgiveness, unconditional love, and striving to avoid temptation were what made sense. Now the problems with Christianity were about to unfold in front of me. See, Christians like to construct implausible expectations of how everyone around them should live their lives. Then, at least in my church, they attempt to deceive the rest of the congregation into believing they must meet those unattainable standards of heavenly perfection. Sermons in my church seemed to damn people to hell for the most ridiculous reasons—divorce, marriage outside the church, worshiping in a different and therefore wrong way. How awful it must have been for churchgoers who fell into those categories to listen to such an ungodly message. Before long, I found myself falling into the worst category of all. I wasn't just a sinner, I was an abomination.

Religion was something of a mystery to me. I think that's because the church that I grew up in tended to imbue religiosity with a sort of smoke-and-mirrors ambiguity with regard to logic and reason. Congregants were expected to believe wholeheartedly, and were discouraged from questioning. Like a parent with no answers, the pastors I grew up with expected me to be content with "Because it says so in the Bible" as the answer to some of the most important questions I was asking. The source of infinite wisdom, the Bible, was selectively utilized—some passages set in stone, while others were unimportant or dismissed when they inconveniently threw a wrench into the aforementioned illogicality.

Why, for instance, if homosexuality inevitably results in damnation, did it not make God's Top Ten list? And why, if homosexual intercourse trumps all other sins, does the Bible clearly state that no sin carries any more weight than another? And if I was wrong, and they were right, and being gay was a sin, then why didn't Christ forgive that sin—like he promised to forgive all the others?

For many years after that, and still in some ways to this day, I turned away from organized religion. I personally believe that the road to one's own spirituality should be a journey, not a roadmap handed to you by your parents that you blindly traverse. If it weren't for my frustration with my church, I may have never found my own personal relationship with the spiritual side of myself—a relationship I am still courting.

Despite the chaos of those two years of religious indoctrination, I survived—sanity intact—and began high school ready to start anew and reinvent myself. I don't know if I had a particular grasp on who I was in middle school, but I knew I didn't want to be that person anymore. I wanted to find my own voice, even if I wasn't quite ready to use it.

I began competitive speech, an activity I seemed to have a talent for. I made friends and began to build a reputation for myself—aside from simply being the kid everyone thought was gay. In fact, the anti-gay epithets seemed to decrease—or maybe I was just too busy to notice them. Either way, life improved. And for a moment, I thought just maybe I would never have to face the difference I felt.

I don't need to go into the details of my first homosexual experiences; doing so would out individuals who may or may not appreciate my openness. Suffice to say that high school opened doors for me—doors that I didn't entirely understand.

I remember the first real sexual encounter I had as a young man. For years I blamed that particular individual for making me gay, as ridiculous as I now know that to be. The relatively innocent experience made me sick by how dirty and wrong I felt afterward, and for many years, I wondered if those negative feelings meant that being gay was wrong. Hindsight seems to lend credence to the fact that the negative feelings were a combination of disappointment and fear as I began the lengthy and confusing process of shedding society's expectations and creating the me I was born to be.

In a way, my high school busyness was just a diversion. It left me little time to worry about what other classmates were saying about me, both behind my back and to my face. But as with any diversion,

I soon realized that the problems I was trying to escape from didn't go away. Luckily, instead of losing myself in drugs or alcohol, I was losing myself in activities like speech, debate, theater, and student organizations. After three long years of working to establish a name for myself other than "faggot," I began to realize that no matter what sort of reputation I earned for myself, being gay would always be a part of it—and the sooner I could accept myself, the sooner other people would be given the chance to wholly accept me as well.

The relationships I cultivated in high school were tenuous at best. I always wondered if the friends I had would still be my friends if they knew my secret. So while I was outwardly surrounded by friends and acquaintances, I couldn't help feeling lonely. Despite the progress I had made, not much had changed since elementary school.

But one thing had changed. The journey, even though not yet finished, had armed me with tools I would later use to defend myself. Having to stand up for myself in my conservative Midwestern hometown had taught me how to stand up for myself, and that lesson proved to be an invaluable one.

I will never forget the first time I actually came out to myself. My senior year in high school, I traveled to various parts of the country speaking on the issue of gender roles and individuality. In the speech, I made an untrue confession. "I'm not a homosexual, I just don't fit the standard," I said, in reference to the rigidity of gender stereotypes. Sometimes I look back and fault myself for not having the strength to come out in high school. Surely I would have opened minds and helped my sleepy little town wake up to the fact that gay people are not so different from the rest of society. But it wasn't that easy. I spent weeks in Internet chat rooms, typing away about my problems to nameless, faceless strangers who offered some degree of comfort. A pen pal provided solace as we both came to grips with our sexuality simultaneously. And one evening, alone in my room, I said it aloud—almost as a way of testing myself to see if I could really do it. I'm not sure what I expected to happen. I think part of me honestly believed that verbalizing this internalized part of me would somehow stop time in its tracks— and, in a way, I suppose it did. At first I said it quietly. Then again, and again, louder and louder, until my face was awash in tears, and the words "I'm gay" were barely audible beneath the sobbing. The world didn't stop turning. The experience was both empowering and terrifying. I had finally taken the first and most important step in accepting myself—and accepting my path unconditionally. Now that I had, in effect, admitted what I had known to be true for so long, there was no turning back. The path ahead looked dangerous and difficult—definitely the road less traveled. But I suddenly realized I was stronger than I had ever given myself credit for. And as I sat there, alone in my room, drying my tears, I was both proud and ashamed of that strength.

While saying it aloud to myself was the first step in coming out, it was only the beginning. Moving away to college, I again had the opportunity, as I did in high school, to reinvent myself. I spent a lot of time deciding whether or not to reinvent myself as loudly and proudly gay, or if I should continue to hide my secret and attempt to maintain the lie I had been living.

One evening, I had the good fortune to hear Archbishop Desmond Tutu speak to an arena full of students and faculty at my small private liberal arts college in Sioux Falls, South Dakota. Toward the end of the presentation, Tutu allowed for a brief question-and-answer period. One student stood up and addressed the archbishop. She noted the work he had done in his own country of South Africa to address the issue of gay and lesbian equality, and asked, "Isn't that contradictory to what the Bible has to say about homosexuality?"

The archbishop paused for what seemed like an eternity. I remember naively thinking that his answer would change the world—either opening up the hearts and minds of the audience members, or forever slamming the door on my neatly appointed closet. Then he started to laugh. "The Bible says a lot of things I hope you don't believe," he chuckled.

That evening, empowered by the archbishop's message, I came out to my best friend. I hope that someday I am able to thank Archbishop Desmond Tutu for the strength it must have taken to live his life in such a way that led him to that auditorium to deliver his message of acceptance, tolerance, and unconditional love.

Later that year, I came out to my sister in an airport before I boarded a plane for Germany. "I love you," I told her. "I love you, too," she said, somewhat surprised by my statement. "Well, then, there's something I should tell you." "Okay . . . ," she responded. I hugged her as I said my next few words, partly because I was shaking so hard I needed her support to stand, and partly because I wasn't sure I could look her in the eyes for fear she'd turn away. "I'm seeing someone," I said. "His name is Nolan."

She hugged me back and said, "I am so proud of you."

There are moments in life when no matter how strong you are, you feel too weak to keep yourself from falling. Some people describe those moments as feeling like the weight has been lifted from their shoulders. But I had been carrying that weight for so long, and the burden was so heavy, that I nearly collapsed when it was removed from me. My sister's support, both physically and spiritually, held me up, and continued to support me, encourage me, and love me unconditionally.

The next step out of the closet was the most difficult. Several months later, a familiar scene played out. Again at an airport, this time in Atlanta, moments before boarding a plane for Ireland, I stood, trembling as before, as I held a letter I had written to my parents. My friend Keryn, whom I came out to after the archbishop's speech, held me as I dropped it into the post office slot, addressed to my mom and dad. I cannot begin to put into words the range of emotions that flooded my body as that letter left my fingertips and became lodged in the mail slot, forcing me to once again summon the strength it took to make the impossibly difficult decision to mail my coming-out letter.

I will forever cherish these difficult moments, both for the intensity of the experiences and the unbelievable strength they demanded of me. We've all read about moments of tragedy where people are able to summon superhuman strength, lifting cars off of victims trapped below, or racing into burning buildings to rescue those inside. These moments of greatness astound others, who wonder how otherwise normal individuals were able to do such unbelievable things. And while some may disagree with the comparison, these coming-out experiences were my moments of greatness.

Luckily for me, these moments all ended happily. I never experienced the difficulty of losing friends, or having relatives turn their backs on me.

For several years after coming out to my parents, I lived life as a loud, proud, out gay man, eventually earning a job writing and editing a GLBT magazine called *Lavender*. Still not out to my grandmother and extended family, I walked a tightrope between being proud of myself and living the lie I created so many years ago. Just a few months ago, my grandmother happened upon a copy of *Lavender*. She saw my picture, and read my coming-out story. It was both awkward and interesting to find myself back in the door frame of my closet, taking the final step out.

When I was younger, struggling to come to terms with myself, to be comfortable in my own gay skin, I read a lot of books, watched a lot of television, and listened to a lot of people talk about homosexuality, and I never saw the rainbow that I see today. Maybe it was the fact that gayness was always the punch line of a joke, or the insensitive remark used to hurt, rather than the adjective it really is. Gay is not positive or negative, it just is. And being gay is not a good thing or a bad thing, it's just a part of who you are. For me, it has proven to be a big part of who I am, and in many ways contributed to aspects of myself that I am extraordinarily proud of. Knowing what it's like to be different has made me tolerant and accepting of diversity. Recognizing the benefit of diversity has shown me the value of being different. And being different has given me the chance to discover myself.

But the world is still a scary place, and we are still in the minority. We live in a day and age when being gay is not nearly as difficult as it was decades ago. We exist in a society that, while not fully accepting, is far less hostile and intolerant than in the past. The world is changing, and we are a part of that change. Someday we will win the war for equality, but not simply by virtue of being the good guys. Someday coming out will be a non-issue; but until then, we will continue to fight for the right to be different.

We have all heard the saying that hate is a learned behavior, but acceptance is also a learned behavior. I've watched firsthand as friends and family members have learned to be accepting of homosexuality. Today my relationship with my parents is wonderful. They accept me, and will welcome into our family whatever man wins my heart. But that didn't happen overnight. My father had questions, my mother had concerns, and they both had to struggle with their inability to understand. Some people will take longer than others, and some will never quite come around. That's why it's important for us to be visible and tell our stories, because that's how we win the acceptance and the understanding of the mainstream community. And the straight allies we earn in that struggle are the allies we will need as we continue to push for GLBT equality, and same-sex marriage, and employment nondiscrimination, and the host of other issues that we need to create a more accepting America.

We must continue to tell our stories in hopes that others are listening.

Unlike my fairy tale, I'm not so sure how or when that acceptance will begin, but I am confident it will. When it does, my happy ending will have just begun, and we will all live happily, or at least equally, ever after.

A Boy in the Girls' Bathroom
by Dylan Forest

I was fifteen the first time I used a men's restroom. I was fifteen
when I first saw a urinal. I was in high school when I did something
that most little boys do as soon as they don't need their mom to
help them up onto the toilet or button their pants.

I hadn't been into a public restroom in almost a year. See, I didn't
stop going into the women's room when my mom no longer had
to help me. I kept going into them because when I was born the
doctor gave me to my mom and told her she had given birth to a
healthy baby *girl*. I'm sure if I hadn't been so disoriented, I would
have given him a funny look.

So there I was, fifteen years later, squeezing my legs together
and gritting my teeth and trying not to pee my pants, all because
of that doctor's mistake. I guess any doctor would have said it, or
any person at all, really. Anatomically, that's what I was: female.
And every report card or ID or legal document reminded me of it
with a big fat F. It felt like my grade in life.

But I tried. I wore frilly dresses on holidays and smiled for the
camera on picture day and grew my hair so long that if I wasn't
careful I'd sit on it. I was my mother's little girl. I got good grades
and never got in trouble. In fact, I barely ever talked at all. Everyone
told my mom what a good little girl I was. I was perfect. I was
miserable.

The first time I got my hair cut short I stared at myself in the
mirror for so long I started to get dizzy. Looking back, it was a terrible

haircut and the woman at Supercuts hadn't understood what I wanted at all. But I loved it. All of a sudden I could see myself. I could see glimpses of the boy I had felt like all along. I could see him in the angle of my jaw and the broadness of my shoulders, and he looked back at me from the mirror with fearlessness in his eyes. That just made it more real and more frightening. I bought a lot of girly underwear after I got that haircut, like I thought a floral print or a little bow in the front or the color pink would turn me into a girl. But a boy in frilly undies does not miraculously transform into a woman. Believe me. I know from experience.

How do I possibly explain what it's like to just *know* something about yourself despite everything and everyone telling you otherwise? The best way I can describe it is that when I see myself, I see a boy. It's not about the little things like how I dress or what my hobbies are. I can't say I always knew I was male because I didn't like dresses or Barbies when I was little. The truth is, a ton of girls fit that description. I don't base my gender identity on stereotypes. It wouldn't work if I tried, really. I'm not a stereotypical guy. I'm terrible at sports. I cry regularly at movies. I'm a feminist. I'm not straight. I'm not gay, either, although that stereotype would fit better. I'm just me. And part of who I am is the fact that I am a guy. I'm not a man; after all, I'm still a teenager. But someday I will be a man.

Right after I got my haircut I started getting "mistaken" for male. I didn't like it because it was pushing out in the open something I had been trying to hide my whole life. I was ashamed, but what I hated most was the fact that I lived for the few times a day a cashier or waiter or bus driver would call me "son" or "young man." My cheeks would burn with shame, but my stomach would rise up into my throat in pride. I was battling myself. There was a full-on war going on between who everyone thought I was and who I really was. Who I really am.

So, to put it simply, I let go. I let go of my mother's daughter and my grandmother's granddaughter and I stopped trying to be who everyone expected me to be. But it didn't happen all at once.

I didn't wake up one day and decide to embrace something that was such a source of pain and humiliation for me. It took a long time, but gradually I learned that the only way it was going to stop hurting was if I stopped running. So for a while I was very anti-social and introverted. I read a lot, I spent a lot of time alone, and I got more and more comfortable with who I was.

I started looking more and more like a boy. Strangers called me "he" more often than "she," and I stopped feeling uncomfortable when I was seen as male. People would stop me when I tried to use a women's restroom; they'd tell me I was in the wrong one. And most of the time I felt like agreeing with them. I *was* in the wrong bathroom. So I stopped using public restrooms unless they were unisex. I learned how to not use a bathroom from the time I left in the morning to the time I got home, and sometimes that was more than ten hours.

It's very hard for me to verbalize how it feels to finally feel right. The way I felt the first time a guy my age acknowledged me with that brotherly nod and the first time a girl flirted openly with me in public or little things like getting called "man" or "bro." It was re-lief, like eating something delicious when you haven't eaten in days, like coming home. Things were finally starting to fit.

I started to feel more and more comfortable socially, but physi-cally I was still far from home. It's very easy to blame all of this on my body. It would be easy to hate my physical self because that's where most of my problems come from. Many transsexual people have terrible body image and absolutely despise their bodies, which is entirely understandable. I've been like that most of my life. Puberty made me want to die; I felt like I was being betrayed by my own body. I've lived with hatred for myself for much too long.

It is much more difficult to accept than it is to resent when something makes your life much harder. But when it is something you will have forever, no matter what, acceptance is something you need to work for. I am not perfect by any means and I still have is-sues with my body. Sometimes I still look at myself and wish with every thought in my head that I had a flat chest and bigger, tougher hands. I wish my cheeks were like sandpaper, I wish my body had less curves and more angles. But I will never be exactly what I want to be. I will never be able to take a shower in a men's locker room. I will never have a Y chromosome.

This body will carry me through my life. Every memory I have is from within this body and everything I will ever do will be experienced from here. It will change in the course of my life, but it will still be this body. Someday I will have a flat chest but I will have scars to remind me that it was not always that way. Someday male hormones will fill my body and my voice will drop and I will grow facial hair, but I will never have the one thing that most people see as the defining characteristic of a man. I will never have a penis.

It would be easy to dwell on that. I could cry for hours in my bed because I won't ever be able to have sex like they do in the movies. I've lived like that before, and I still have nights when I do. But I am learning acceptance. I am teaching myself to love the one person that will always be in my life, without fail.

This life is hard. It has been almost unbearably difficult at times, and I'm only sixteen years old. But I'm getting to a point where I am happy with the person I am, both inside and out, and a majority of people *never* get there. I don't regret anything. I love who I am, and I wouldn't change it even if I could.

Our Space
by Jovencio de la Paz

We are the sum total of our places. Our lives accumulate the cities we visit, the rooms we occupy, the doors and windows we touch in passing. Like magpies we gather our surroundings and hide them in the nests of our subconscious.

My first memories are of open spaces. I recall the wide green valleys of Oregon. I remember limitless passages of water, rivers that went as they pleased. There was no place to stop, no ditch or barrier to deny my passing from point to point. I remember vastness. The names of the places are forgotten, but the vastness remains. I knew that there was truth in the openness. The namelessness meant freedom. When I entered high school, the fences came up. Suddenly open fields grew streaks of boundaries, white posts grew from the ground, and beams of wood shut away acres of free-flowing grass. Walls were built. Down rivers, dams burst through the surface, altering the direction of the water after millions of years. I desired parameters, safety, definition. To know where one area stopped and another began. And to know where I belonged.

I took him to such a place. Somewhere I belonged. We sat together and watched the sky, noting various heavenly bodies. We sat together in empty fields in the middle of the night, surrounded by idyllic space. Sometimes he would smoke and I would watch the glowing end of the cigarette move like a living thing in the dark. I watched how he sat, his posture, the length of his arms, his hands moving from ground to lips.

We sat together in empty fields and talked. For hours we discussed the intricacies of youth, the promise of the future, the strangeness of love. The 2 a.m. sky filled with the sounds of our chatter. I don't remember what brought him to me. His girlfriend had broken up with him. He was having a hard time with relationships. Something had happened in his life and he needed someone's sympathy. At any rate, he arrived. He came to me like a boy from my past, the boy I never was. At the time I was preoccupied with the arrival of college and the departure of my childhood. When he came into my life, he gifted my childhood back to me. He recalled the Saturday-morning cartoons that, for fear of embarrassment, I chose to forget. He resurrected the silly superstitions that belonged to schoolchildren, the rhymes I had put away for the coming of adulthood. Once again, boys with bedsheets as capes were still superheroes and summer days slowed to the speed of molasses. Time did not move but bent to allow us to see it and what it was doing to us. He smiled as he avoided the cracks in the sidewalk.

He sat up and I saw his impression left on the grass in that huge, empty place.

He told me about his past, his family, the beauty he found in everyone. He had an ability to see the world innocently and describe it without the fear of honesty. Our intimacy came from this honesty. Because whatever he saw, whatever he feared or whatever joy or love he felt, he experienced without pretension. So when he reached out to me, it was easy to reach back.

We were not afraid of being alone in the middle of nowhere so early in the morning, so early that the faraway lights of houses turned from yellow to orange and finally disappeared completely. In fact, there was safety in the open, empty space. We trusted that openness and that openness was reflected in us.

Being in an open place pushes you close to who you are near. So he told me about the girls he had loved, girls with long hair and incredible eyes and fingers that made sounds in the dark. Girls who moved their hands to tie ribbons, pulling hair back into buns.

Girls of all colors, round like fruit or thin as blades of grass. He would shut his eyes and tell me about their lips, the architecture of their kisses, the structure of an embrace in sudden passion or in quiet grace, and I dreamed of a time when I would understand that closeness.

And though I did not know the name of our closeness, I could not avoid its presence. Though I did not know what our relationship was, I held it close to me the way I held my memories of open fields. I thought back to my boyfriends, the boys who came and went so casually, the ones who smiled and said nothing and were nothing to me. And I realized that I had never been so close to anyone.

We only appreciate the largeness of a place when we are standing in it. So we stood and he put the cigarette out on his shoe and we walked toward a better view of the field. I followed him. We came to a place where there was a fence, and he climbed over it. I did not. We both looked down its length. It stretched out, turning slightly to the right and then up a rise in the earth, dipping behind to where we could not see it anymore. The fence went on in the other direction, breaking the openness of the place, cutting it into two distinct parts, signifying that there was a limit to the field. I could not join him. So we sat and watched each other from opposite sides.

We sit at the edges of many fences. We find things around us filled with barriers. I see the walls crisscross and stitch the landscape and segment what was vast and new and open. I remember when the valleys and fields of grass flowed into each other, the way one melted into the other so it was impossible to separate one from its neighbor. Now I see the formations of the limits. I see where I could not be close to him, the reasons why he could not be close to me despite how close we were. We learn to recognize those borders. And we know where we stand.

We are the summation of our places: the total worth of the borders we define for ourselves.

Four Photos
by Justin Levesque

I.

"the sun is down, the blue glow of the tv is on his skin and my body shakes, with a stranger's glance, the first touch, imprinted, permanent, rushing running blood, everything so fast and everything spinning, here you are, with the world's gravity pushing down, whispering 'forever . . .' "

II.

"with his hand, falling fast, and my eyes going to the sky,
finding meteors, moving so quickly, from this spot seeing all,
seeing so many eyes around, seeing me, rooted by the ground,
shake no tumbling, because in the silence, in humility, he got
what he wanted, and i, blushed and torn, with indigo brands,
and i, not making a peep, and i, without a name . . ."

III.

"him, so far away, distances, the reaching, sending waves, spinning around, the lines, the lines they are stretching far and wide, across and through doorways. snapping shut at the closure of knobs and clasps. and they are snapped and propelled back, falling, losing footing, last second reaching for anything, and standing. a little unsteady, a little unsure, but standing.

the aching heart, pushing on our ribs, filling through our ears. . . ."

IV.

"this early morning, having left him, the thoughts rampage
through my head, i am never resting always going, thought after
thought, swelling, coughing thick syrups of doubt and guilt, and
happiness, and guilt . . .

. . . my patience is not infinite . . ."

Break-up in Slow Motion
by Joshua Dalton

So my first boyfriend and I, I guess we kinda bypassed the whole "dating" thing and stumbled right into deadly serious commitment. It was a matter of availability, mostly; I only knew one other gay guy at my school, an overweight *Queer as Folk* wannabe, and was still hardly comfortable enough with the whole homosexual thing to waste the emotions on him. Of course, it probably didn't help that Ryan and I were both lonely, introspective teenagers, still naive and overly romantic, overflowing with testosterone.

The first time we met was straightforward enough. My friend Courtney brought him along as an afterthought to see *The Ring* with us; he'd been at her house when I called to invite her, and it would have been rude to just send him home. In my dad's pickup, Ryan and I shared the backseat, a big pit with two little chairs that faced each other. His knees kept brushing mine, and both of us kept turning our heads to avoid the awkward business of being two strangers staring directly at each other. The only word to describe him, really, was goofy, with his overly large head, laughter that burst out like a sputtering engine, random clothes, and wild eyes. He bubbled with this endless manic energy, fidgeting and tapping his fingers. When we ate, he spun the coasters around and shared lame jokes, looking around and laughing whenever an awkward pause crept up, anything to break the silence. There was something so relaxed, so self-assured and *cool* about him.

At the movie I was in the middle, Ryan to my left and Courtney to my right. Between jumping at the scary parts and whispering predicted endings with Courtney, I kept looking at Ryan's hand. It was just perched on the armrest, long fingers delicately planted like a bird on a telephone wire. I felt funny around him—that's the only way to say it. I'd never had a real guy crush before, or hadn't let myself—at least not with a real, live person who wasn't miles away because we'd met only on the Internet. I liked being around him, after just that short time. I liked his aura of coolness, felt I could bask in it and maybe soak it up, get a nice tan of confidence to block out my usual worried self.

Wandering around at Barnes & Noble, waiting for our ride, Courtney said that Ryan had something to tell me. They were both laughing a lot and exchanging odd glances. My brain did that thing it always seems to do at crucial moments, completely checking out and leaving my body to stupidly perform on its own. I never had the conscious thought that Ryan was gay, but of course I wasn't surprised when he handed me the note, written with a pen borrowed from a bewildered cashier. Having someone else be gay made it suddenly acceptable. "Me, too," I said, and we all kept laughing.

That night I talked to Courtney online. My brain was doing that thing again. "So," I IM'd her, "what's Ryan's screen name?" She asked if I liked him. I said of course not—he was just funny and stuff, another fun person to chat with.

Naturally, I became completely infatuated. Ryan and I started e-mailing each other, gooey notes with awkward lines about how he wished I was there on the couch with him, or me pointing out that I'd never been kissed, just to get him to say "You could practice on me." Checking my e-mail during second period, while I was supposed to be working on the school Web page, I was happy for the first time in ages, genuinely happy.

That lasted about a week.

God popped up. He has a habit of doing that, just when things are getting good. I heard the voice of Jesus himself, telling me how wrong this was. I shouldn't be having e-mails like this. I shouldn't be with a guy at all. If I didn't get right with God, I knew the horrible feeling in my stomach would never go away. I asked Ryan if he believed in God and he said, "Fuck God. Who would believe in someone so angry, someone who wants to send people to hell?" Words like that scared me even more than my burgeoning homosexuality. He dared to vocalize the doubts I squashed, and that made him dangerous. I had to break it off.

One year later, all religion abandoned, outed to most of my friends and frustrated that the only gay guy in my grade was still so obnoxious, I looked up Ryan again. We'd talked some, in the intervening months, but only for a few brief phases, a couple of weeks here and there. This time I asked Ryan if he wanted to go see a movie.

My parents didn't really understand. "Ryan who?" they asked when I begged them to drop me off at the theater. I tried to jog their memories: "You gave him a ride once, remember?" They gave the parental equivalent of a "whatever" and dropped me off, happy that I was at least getting out of the house. I waited awkwardly, leaning against a column, hands burrowed deep in my pockets. Then I looked over, and there he was—my Ryan, mostly the same after a year. I had picked out my clothes carefully, choosing streaked jeans and one of the tighter preppy shirts in my closet; Ryan never cared what he wore and stood in a bland jacket and wind pants. His gray T-shirt didn't even have a logo on it, much less some mildly subversive phrase thought up by the marketing wunderkinds at Abercrombie & Fitch.

We said hey.

The rest of it is all very disjointed. We ended up in the theater—we were supposed to be seeing some lame comedy. It started with hand-holding. Then him showing me the silver charm bracelet his friend Natalie had given him, which I grabbed and challenged him to get back. All innocent and flirty, until I slid the bracelet across my crotch, daring him with my eyes to grab for it now.

Next thing I know we're on the floor in the unisex bathroom, door locked and lights out, fumbling all over each other. At one point on top of me, he began ramming his tongue in my mouth and swirling it around. When I started laughing, he admitted, in the same casual tone with which he'd later dump me, that he didn't know what the hell he was doing either. I didn't need the lights on to see his characteristic shoulder shrug.

Afterward we slid against the wall of the theater's small arcade, looking at each other and vaguely smiling, miles apart, still processing. We ended the night simply saying goodbye. No one said we were going out; he didn't give me his letter jacket and ask to go steady. But all of a sudden we talked on the phone every day and he was at my house every weekend. Suddenly we were both Committed and Very Serious, always having chats about the state of our Relationship. Before this, my problem had been just allowing myself to *have* a boyfriend—I never realized how difficult it would be to maintain.

Every few nights some new conflict arose. For a while he decided that he was bi and maybe liked girls. Another night he worried that he was in love with an online friend instead of me. Often he returned to the whole "I-can't-care-about-someone-because-I'll-just-end-up-moving-like-I-always-do" argument. I didn't help matters much, worrying each day that while he was at school, all the girls who constantly had crushes on him would finally win him over. Our online chats were tainted with my knowledge that while he talked to me, he could also be chatting with Zach, the classy New Yorker who shared Ryan's love affair with music like I never could. Just as one conflict subsided another one would pop up, rearing its ugly head like a nightmarish game of relationship whack-a-mole.

Not to say there weren't sweet times: finding his violin performances on my voice mail, or rare blissful moments when we would both forget that we could fall apart at any second and actually enjoy each other, lounging around watching movies or playing on the computer. And we had our share of adventures. Once we skinny-dipped in the neighborhood pool, ignoring the fact that it was the middle of the day and the windows of the surrounding houses were open. Another time we nearly gave an old security guard a heart attack when we emerged from a golf course bathroom together late one night as the guard was trying to lock everything up. We ran away, hearts pounding, checking over our shoulders for his golf cart. And, of course, there was the time my parents came home from work unexpectedly for lunch and Ryan had to hide under the bed. I smuggled him some food and a 7UP, then forgot it was lying there. When my mother asked about the errant can lying on the floor, I had to make up some ridiculous story explaining why I wanted to sit in the corner and drink a soda, squeezed between the bookcase and the bed. When she bent over out of habit to pick up a dirty sock lying dangerously near the gap below the bed, I leapt to the floor, shouting that I would get it, so she wouldn't see his silhouette among the old boxes and stray books.

But the arguments never stopped. We were like a really boring soap opera—constant melodrama without any exciting twists; we had no evil twins or baby abductions to keep our relationship from cancellation. We were a bitter married couple with impending divorce overshadowing our every moment, and we didn't even have the legal process or custody battles to slow things down. So I guess it was easy for him, calling me that day, to break up.

At first I couldn't believe him—we'd "broken up" several times before, so how was this different? And my brain did that thing again, deciding that it would be a good idea for us to do something as friends, right that second, instead of staying home and giving myself time to process.

When I got to his house to pick him up, there he was, fresh out of the shower and wearing a towel, running late as usual. Empty house, semi-naked boyfriend—usually the towel would have gone flying. But this time he shut the door while he changed, and my defense mechanism began to crack. Once he emerged from his room, I kept hugging him, my words saying that I just wanted hugs to say goodbye, but I wasn't thinking or feeling a thing, just wrapping my arms around him with no plan to let go.

On the car ride to the theater, we didn't hold hands. I didn't buy his ticket. And while standing in line in the wait to get seated, our casual conversation lacked any emotion. But it still wouldn't hit me. Letting myself even have this relationship, then all the stress of keeping it, had been a long process, and this sudden ending just would not compute.

He sat to my left again, only this time I didn't have Courtney to turn to on my right. Staring firmly at the screen, I resolved that this wasn't over. I put my hand on Ryan's leg, testing. Held it there and waited. He didn't budge. We both just watched the movie. Earlier was just a misunderstanding, I told myself, and slowly I slid my hand into his.

He pulled back and said, "Josh . . ."

It was our first movie alone together, all over again, only in reverse: my hand reaching out, not his, followed not by happy images but shards of painful memory. I know at one point that I took his keys, the only sharp thing I could find, and tried to cut myself— driven by instinct, a trapped animal trying to bite off its own leg in a struggle to escape. He didn't even stay, not wanting to deal with me any longer. He went to the bathroom. I found myself alone in this crowded theater, halfheartedly attempting suicide, when I suddenly decided I would not let Ryan's slinking away be the end of the only first love I would ever get.

So I followed him to the bathroom, finding him at a urinal, and closed myself in a stall. We peed awkwardly among the unaware men around us, so much unsaid. At the sink, trying to ignore others' curious glances, I convinced him that we just needed to go back to the movie, that I'd be fine.

Naturally, I ended up on the floor, just inside the screening room in the little hallway leading up to the seats, crying and kicking like I was auditioning for *The Exorcist*. "Get hold of yourself," Ryan said, sounding angrier than I had ever heard him. I rattled off a list of apologies but none of it made any difference. Ryan asked me then, as he would again and again, what had he done? How did *he* do anything to cause this break-up? I tried to explain that I cared about him more than he ever cared about me, but he didn't understand.

He just sat there, aloof as always, as much a stranger to me as when we first met, sitting in the pickup more than a year earlier.

I asked him if there was someone else, and he admitted that he did like another guy. Later, I found out that my replacement was Stuart, a kid I'd gone to elementary school with. Stuart had thick glasses and a nasal voice, and his mom wouldn't let him go to camp with the rest of the fifth graders. "He's gentle and sweet," Ryan answered each time I would ask what Stuart had that I lacked. I tried to tell myself that what Ryan really wanted was just someone passive who wouldn't expect anything from him, but this was too hard to believe. Ryan had chosen someone else over me, so of course I had to have done something wrong.

Crying is hardly ever the beautiful single-tear-falling as movies would lead you to believe—it's messy and noisy. Still at the theater, coughing and wiping snot from my nose, I called Ryan's mom, Maggie, who I'd actually been pretty close to. She answered and from the voices in the background I could tell she was at a party somewhere. "Hi," I forced out, in between chokes and gasps. "Just wanted to say bye, and thanks for being so supportive of us, and . . . say bye to Billy for me, because he was always so nice to me." Ryan's younger brother had always made me fit in, and the thought of losing him along with Ryan sent more shock waves of grief through my body. Maggie said that she was sorry and asked if I was going to be okay, and told me to not do anything drastic, knowing how dramatic I could get. I understood what she was saying: Don't kill yourself over my son. Don't kill yourself over him, even though he meant more to you than any other human ever has, even though you fought past a rocky beginning and all sorts of fights and you tried so hard to make it work, so sure that you'd be together for-ever, soul mates who met as teenagers like your parents did. Don't kill yourself, because I don't want that on my conscience, and nei-ther does he.

Ryan didn't say anything throughout my brief conversation with her. I called my mom next, just asking if she could come, unable to explain why. Confused and sounding slightly irritated, she said that she was on her way. I told Ryan that I would never see him again, and walked off. Of course, we saw each other seconds later, outside the theater, standing on opposite ends as we waited, people streaming in and out, oblivious.

Both my parents were in the car to get me, which only happened when they were worried. I climbed into the back, still crying, barely able to explain. "I don't understand," my mother said. "If he was going to break up with you, why did he make us drive you to the movies first?"

I couldn't explain my stupidity, my insane thought that somehow, if we were together, Ryan would change his mind. That my brain had done that thing again.

Ryan was my first boyfriend. Although I managed, for better or for worse, to fast-forward through the early stages, nothing could make the ending unfold in anything other than wrenching slow motion. While he went on to date Stuart, I staggered through a series of unsuccessful flirtations and months of misery, often regretting Ryan as much as longing for him. Maybe Jesus had been right all along.

A Story Called "Her"
by Alison Young

It is warm. Her hands are everywhere on me, on my thighs, breasts, shoulders. She laughs softly, and it echoes through the room. I'm not sure where we are, but it's a bed, and the sheets smell like lavender. She leans closer and kisses me, fingers and palm slipping between my legs.

I push her on her back, and now I can see that the sheets are pale blue, reflecting the lightest shade in her eyes. She's laughing again, and her eyes twinkle when she does that. I smile sheepishly, and my heart flips when she smiles back.

"I love you, Kitty," I whisper and kiss her again.

I wake up sweaty, my thighs sticky. The room is too warm—my fan had cut off sometime during the night, but I hadn't kicked off my blankets.

I dreamed again.

I dreamed about *her* again.

Frustrated with myself, I slide out of bed before the alarm goes off. The floor is relievingly cool against my feet, tendrils of cold air and sanity creeping up my legs like vines, finally reaching my brain. Clothes are more of a bother than they are worth, but I have to be dressed to go to class, so I pull on jeans and a T-shirt. As I brush my hair—tangled from tossing and turning—I hope that class will help drown out her face smiling up at me and the sounds of her groaning my name. I know, though, that it won't.

When the professor lets us out early, I am not sure if I'm angry or pleased. Being let out early means permission for my mind to wander, permission to daydream about her.

Lunch is quiet, with Dylan and Lysi.

"You know Kitty? My best friend in Australia? I'm in love with her."

They look at me, more surprised that I've suddenly started spilling out my innermost secrets over cheeseburgers from the dining hall than the actual contents. Dylan hugs me—his solution to many situations is a hug—and Lysi watches me for a moment, silent.

Then she smiles gently. "We know." Left unspoken is that they've been waiting for me to figure it out. I smile helplessly back. "You should tell her." The smile falters.

It's late that evening, and I am furiously typing at the computer. I don't realize until halfway through writing the piece I'm so fervently working on that I'm crying harsh, angry tears. Why did I have to fall in love with her? Why does it have to be so hopeless? Why does she have to live on *the other side of the damn globe*?

More importantly, why can't I work up the courage to tell her in person?

I think it's the last part that's making me cry, but I'm writing anyway, typing without planning or outlining or anything good writers do, just an outpouring of feelings in little black and white pixels on the screen. Even if I finish the piece, I don't know if I have the courage to put it online where she could see it, read it, and know. I am far too paranoid to open myself up like this, but the pressure of holding in these feelings every time we speak is driving me insane. For once, I'm glad we are separated by a computer screen, or I would have pushed her against a wall and kissed her a long time ago. I'm sure it would have been disastrous.

I see Sarah get online, and rush to instant-message her. I need confidence. We talk for a while, and then . . .

me (9:10:18 PM): Him: "Marry me, Sarah. Make me the happiest man on earth!" You: "Llama."

me (9:10:31 PM): You: "Erm . . . I mean, yes. Sorry."

Sarah (9:11:49 PM): *giggles!*

Sarah (9:11:54 PM): Should I send out the invitations already?

Sarah (9:11:55 PM): hehe

me (9:12:02 PM): Sure

me (9:12:10 PM): And you should name your kids Llama and Monkey

me (9:13:22 PM): *swallows* Asenath Caitlìn Ryan-Young, Celia Alison Ryan-Young, and Mathin [still debating a middle name but I want Kavanagh] Ryan-Young.

Sarah (9:13:49 PM): Aw, how adorable

me (9:13:52 PM): I'm not sure how we will afford 3 rounds of invitro, but we'll make do.

Sarah (9:14:05 PM): *grin*

me (9:16:56 PM): I don't think you realize that I'm dead serious.

Sarah (9:17:26 PM): and what does Kitty say?

me (9:18:17 PM): For now? Yes. But that could be us just joking. I don't know. *sigh* We don't talk about it, or who it involves. It's just acknowledged.

Sarah (9:19:58 PM): *hug* I still think you should just give it time, since those dreams could mean any a number of things.

me (9:20:48 PM): I love her. I know it and it's really brought a new level of serenity and peacefulness to my over-fraught brain.

Sarah (9:25:32 PM): any idea what Kit would say?

me (9:25:38 PM): Not a clue

me (9:25:54 PM): It could be anything from "Oh, thank god, I love you too" to "You're joking"

me (9:27:38 PM): Or, worse, "No you don't"

Sarah (9:27:46 PM): eeep . . . *HUG*

me (9:29:23 PM): *sigh, hug* If it's not me, she'd let me down gently, I know, but why the hell would I tell her when she's a day's flight away? It has to wait until we're closer together physically, because I have no desire to have an online relationship of that variety.

Sarah (9:30:49 PM): maybe you should ask who it is

me (9:31:10 PM): Why?

me (9:31:17 PM): What purpose would that serve?

Sarah (9:32:04 PM): to find out how she feels.. if it is you

me (9:32:17 PM): It'll either not be me—leaving me disappointed, and very likely having to tell her that I'm in love with her (no way would she tell without a "I'll tell if you do" sort of clause)—or it would be me and then we're still 27 hours by plane and $2000 apart

Sarah (9:34:17 PM): but wouldn't you rather know than spend your time wondering and having to keep your side hidden?

me (9:34:59 PM): It's not worth the embarrassment. Better in person, when I won't go into paranoid fits that she's not online because she's angry at me.

Sarah (9:35:21 PM): heh.. that is very true

me (9:35:37 PM): god knows I'm paranoid like that, too

Sarah (9:36:15 PM): oh trust me, I am too.. if I said something to somebody that could possibly make them angry, and then they're not online or I don't talk to them at all, I feel absolutely horrible

me (9:36:25 PM): exactly

me (9:38:58 PM): and if it is me, what can I do on it? Nothing! Nothing more than we already do—talk online. Long-distance phone time would be more than I can afford, and I don't just want a computer with her on the other end. I need to be able to hold her hand, to hug her, to touch her. Spending a week with you was so totally different than online—though, sorry to disappoint, I'm not in love with you—and it's changed our online conversations for the better. But without that face-to-face? I don't know it could work.

Sarah (9:42:17 PM): aye, meeting in person does change the entire perspective. so that makes very much sense, and I suppose it would be much better to wait.

me (9:42:38 PM): So stop pushing me, mooooom

Sarah (9:42:44 PM): *giggles*

Sarah (9:42:45 PM): Sorry.
Sarah (9:42:46 PM): I'll stop.
me (9:42:53 PM): heehee
me (9:43:08 PM): can we be done with this serious crap now?
Sarah (9:43:19 PM): absolutely

Being a masochist, though, I can't stop writing, can't stop hoping and dreaming and needing. In a moment of complete and utter foolishness, I decide to post the drivel I've been working on at FictionPress.

me (10:56:36 PM): *swallows* New story
me (10:56:42 PM): http://www.fictionpress.com/read.php?storyid=1599445
Sarah (10:57:48 PM): uh oh, a swallow
Sarah (10:57:49 PM): ?
me (10:58:00 PM): just read it, dork
Sarah (10:59:49 PM): oh, Ali *hugs!* It's beautiful
me (11:00:24 PM): That will be the only hint she gets from me. If she figures it out, then I'll admit it. If not, I'll suffer quietly
Sarah (11:00:44 PM): She'd have to be pretty dense not to figure it out, and Kitty is not in the least bit dense
me (11:01:07 PM): *winces* Is it that obvious? I'll change it, I don't want it obvious.
Sarah (11:01:16 PM): Yes, it is rather obvious . . .

I don't know where I got that courage from, but I wish it hadn't deserted me the moment I clicked *add story*, leaving me vaguely nauseous with nervousness. My head hurts. I lay down after a little longer talking to Sarah, and curl around my pillow.

I wish my pillow was her, and cry myself to sleep.

Dylan can consistently be counted on to know when there is something wrong with me, and today is no exception. I sit down at lunch and he looks at me for a moment contemplatively. I'm busy pushing salad greens around my plate, trying to eat, but the nerves are keeping my stomach upset, still. I didn't check my e-mail when I got up, for fear that she would have left a review, and now I'm torn between wanting to know and wanting to be Hermione Granger so I can have a time turner and reverse it all so it never happened. Foolish overconfidence, even if it was just for a moment, will be my downfall, I'm sure.

"What happened?"

I sigh. When did I become this overdramatic soap opera character? When did my life become eerily fictional—just a normal girl, in love with her best friend, and agonizing over it—and why doesn't the fact that it is so cliché bother me? "I wrote a story last night," I start. Another sigh. "About how I feel about Kitty. And I posted it online where she'll see it. Except now she'll see it and hate me."

There is a serious advantage to having a tranny boy as a close friend: he thinks like a guy. "I seriously doubt Kitty will hate you. You've said it yourself—you're best friends. She loves you." His logic is calm and rational and linear. "Besides," he drawls, "you're just so sexy."

I hit him in the arm, hard, giggling, but the knot in my stomach does not loosen.

Oh god. Oh god oh god oh god oh god, she's online. And she doesn't *seem* upset. Either she is so angry and upset she has repressed it, or she's trying to figure out how to let me down. Or she hasn't read it. I'm desperately praying for the last. Maybe I'll have time to take it down before she gets to it.

Sarah (9:07:23 PM): gotten any more reviews, Ali?
me (9:07:43 PM): Nope, just you. *glares all around*
Sarah (9:07:49 PM): hehe
Heather (9:07:54 PM): Oh..!
Heather (9:08:01 PM): *dutifully goes back and reviews*

• • •

Damn you, Sarah, for ruining *that* plan. We are in a conference, Sarah, Kitty, myself, and another friend, Heather. Heather knows, too. I feel like burying myself in a hole and dying now.

Kitty (9:08:17 PM): What's this?
me (9:08:52 PM): I have a few new stories on fictionpress. No big deal. But Hez and Sar were on last night when I posted them, so they should have reviewed, those bums

She's going to go look. She'll look at my FictionPress account—there's no secret there, for her—and see the new piece and read it and know. I'm cold and shaking now, all the blood in my body working to keep my heart at a steady, normal pace instead of rushing. I am frozen, unable to type or think or move, waiting for her to do something. Say something. Please yell at me, hate me, but this silence is deafening and deadly.

Kitty (9:18:05 PM): *is not dead, silly. Is simply . . . er . . . blushing* *a lot* *is not dense, indeed. Though I wouldn't be scared to tell you I loved you in person*
me (9:19:07 PM): *dies. Tragically* It's not exactly something I wanted you to know—god, you're my best friend of five years. But I had to at least write it down.
Kitty (9:20:11 PM): You wrote it beautifully. I don't deserve it.
me (9:20:18 PM): Yes you do.
me (9:21:03 PM): I won't bring it up or anything. I don't want you to be mad at me.

Her Internet connection fails, and I scream in frustration. I need to know, because that wasn't enough to reassure the compulsive worrier in me. I need to hear her voice, but it's not possible at the moment.

me (10:00:30 PM): *is doing her best not to cry*
me (10:02:17 PM): *best is obviously a relative term, because I'm crying*

me (10:05:12 PM): I love you. I love you. I can't say it enough.

Kitty (10:05:28 PM): Good *hug*

me (10:06:04 PM): *curls up in lap* I assume this means you're not angry with me.

Kitty (10:07:35 PM): I'm amazed you think I would be

me (10:08:38 PM): I'm paranoid, you know that. I can come up with the worst possible result to any given situation and firmly believe that is what will happen. I've been on pins and needles, worrying you would tell me never to speak to you again.

Kitty (10:11:47 PM): The only thing I'm worried about is us eventually meeting and you deciding that I really am a horrible, awkward, nervy less than amazingly gorgeous person.

me (10:13:17 PM): No. Never. You are amazingly gorgeous. *hiccup-y laugh* I had printed one of the pictures to show Stina and Dylan as explanation—"Can't you see why I love her?"—and the consensus is that you're far too pretty for me.

me (10:13:55 PM): And the rest . . . I know already (though I don't believe you're horrible). And they're just parts of you, and I love them too.

Kitty (10:16:03 PM): *sheepish look* You know, for about three seconds after reading "Her" I thought "this can't be me she's talking about!" and got incredibly jealous of the non-existent other person that you must have been referring to. I hope that sums up how very "not angry" I am

me (10:16:49 PM): I think that might be the best reaction I could have gotten. Ever.

me (10:17:37 PM): You know, I've been crabby and jealous all week, thinking your dreams probably had nothing to do with me?

Kitty (10:20:00 PM): Who else could they have been about? I thought I made myself entirely clear on that score

me (10:20:54 PM): No . . . because I was looking for the worst, not best, case scenario. And I didn't want to ask, because then I'd have to admit it, and then you'd be angry . . . I'm sorry I was scared.

Kitty (10:22:05 PM): Don't be

Kitty (10:28:29 PM): Now, I'm sorry, but I really have to go lie down for a bit. I'll try and be online later

    me (10:28:42 PM): Okay. Feel better.

    Kitty (10:29:54 PM): *grin* I do, in every way that isn't physical. I love you, and tell Things one and Two that all is well

    me (10:30:11 PM): I will. I love you.

I swallow, and lay down, too. I scream again, this time with joy. I have the presence of mind and courtesy for my neighbors to muffle it with a pillow.

Her smile is radiant, and I am crying. My head is pressed against the hollow of her throat, my ear to her shoulder. Our hair is tangling together, red from me, brown and blonde from her, mixing in a cascade of color down our backs.

She is whispering to me, soft, her voice mellow and calm. Song lyrics, beautiful and sad. She's singing now. "For you my sweet babe . . . I wish . . ."

I pull back to look at her, and swallow harshly. "I love you, Kitty."

Her smile makes my heart skip. "I know. I love you, too."

As I haul myself out of my warm bed the next morning and onto the cool tile, I am relatively confident that this is all just a wonderful dream. I am relatively confident that I don't care what it is, as long as it never ends.

Shirt, pants, sandals, book bag. As an afterthought, I grab my sketchbook. This is the sort of day I can feel the inspiration bubbling up before I've even had my coffee. No, wait, that's not inspiration, it's a giggle.

"I love you, Kitty Ryan!" I yell to the empty room. I can feel the answering laughter, like a sound I know is there but too far off to hear. I smile widely, and set off to class.

It's evening again. We have been honest for twenty-four hours, and I have never felt better in my life. My hands are shaking, not from cold or fear this time, but from anticipation as I dial her phone number. Cost be damned, I have to call.

Her voice is soft, our connection crappy. "Hello?"

I sigh and laugh and mumble "hi," all at once. She laughs, too.

There is a pause, neither of us sure what to say. We have never spoken on the phone before. Would she like a few minutes of pleasantries, or does she prefer to get straight to the point? How does she stand, or sit, when she's on the phone? I'm curled up under my covers in my bed, wishing I were wrapped around her. The silence drags on, edging into uncomfortable.

I smile, though she cannot see it, and murmur into the mouthpiece, "I love you, Kitty."

She does not say anything for a long moment, and then, "I know. I love you, too."

Moment: This Could've Been Me
by Evin Hunter

The name Matthew Shepard is now very familiar to me, but it used to evoke barely any emotion from me. Just a name, just a symbol, just another story from another time. After all, at the time of his murder, I was a third grader in a different part of the country—1,748 miles away, to be exact. I don't even remember hearing about it on the news. Certainly it didn't affect my family in any way. I grew up with two conservative parents in the suburbs of Philadelphia, and I didn't learn what the word "gay" meant until a fellow fifth grader clued me in on the playground. It was not an issue I ever had to deal with in my childhood. To me, Matthew Shepard means the hate-crime agenda, the fight over the "lifestyle" of gay people, a reminder of the constant threat that I'd better watch my back if I'm going to live as an openly gay person. He never really struck me as just another human being.

Once in a while I get the chance to step back and reread *The Laramie Project,* and on a couple occasions I have seen it performed on-screen and onstage. The first time I read through the story my throat clenched up and my hands started to shake. I may have been a straight female ten-year-old when this happened, but now I am a gay transgender male. This could happen to me. I remember hanging out with my friends one night, and a drunk teenager shoved me and said, "What the hell are you faggots doing around here?" I turned and walked back inside the nearby coffee shop and sat in the bathroom, on the verge of tears. Another time, someone once told me I was "fucked" when they found out I was a guy without a dick. I was on the phone with my best friend the night she was stabbed with a knife by a group of gay bashers. She lives in Akron, Ohio, and has been in five or six gay beatings, ending up in the hospital more than once. You know what that fear and hate does to you? It makes you suicidal. She didn't want to live because everywhere people were telling her she didn't deserve to live. It is incredible to see the power with which some people can hate. For example, a Web site titled "God Hates Fags"—a campaign by Fred Phelps, the Baptist minister, to show every faggot that they are condemned to hell. Phelps's group even showed up at Matthew Shephard's funeral and shouted to whoever would listen that he wished Matthew had a chance to repent his homosexual sins as he lay dying, tied to the fence. Both the Web site and Fred Phelps are part of a Baptist church, located in Topeka, Kansas, right in the center of our country. "Welcome to the Westboro Baptist Church homepage. This page is dedicated to preaching the Gospel truth about the soul-damning, nation-destroying notion that 'It is OK to be gay.'" Politicians are going out of their way to create things like the Federal Marriage Amendment proposal, so that millions of gays and lesbians may never walk down the aisle in holy matrimony or even get any of the 1,100 rights given to any normal heterosexual couple and their children. I mean, even just the passing glare of disgust, or the shifting in a seat when I grab a boy's hand in a romantic way, or somebody saying for the millionth time "That's so gay"—it's the same kind of hate as the hate that killed Matthew Shepard. It hurts to see my identity being used as a clichéd insult to mean something along the lines of "stupid." I mean, this murder victim could've been me. This could've been one of my gay or trans friends.

After experiencing this story, this account, to hear him called "Matt" lovingly by his close friends, and to see his dad break down in tears . . . it just puts this damper on my spirit, and the pain of the murder really sinks in. If I had lived in Laramie, Wyoming, no doubt Matthew Shepard would have been one of my close friends.

He was a short guy like me, 5'2", 110 pounds, and he had this head of beautiful blond hair. I wish I had the chance to know him before he was killed—as the person he was, not the controversy he stood for. I give his family and friends so much credit for having their child and friend turned into this national symbol, and still staying strong for the purpose of preventing other hate crimes, through the spirit and memory of Matt. I mean, he was just like you or me—a kid with a big heart and a big future.

A Quietly Queer Revolution
by Laci Lee Adams

I do not know how to be Christian apart from being queer, nor do I know how to be queer apart from being Christian. For me, these two realities are fused together. Two images from my childhood are similarly fused together. First, I had a girlfriend in kindergarten. She had porcelain-white skin and these absolutely gorgeous jet-black Shirley Temple curls. During nap time, we would lay our mats next to each other. I can remember falling asleep with my little finger twisted in her curls. Just as striking as her hair was the light blue–tinted paste she brought to school. My mission was to eat as much of that light blue paste as I could. In retrospect, however, I remember the look and feel of her hair far more vividly than the taste of the paste.

Second, I have wanted to give my life to God ever since I was a little girl. At six or seven, my class went on a field trip to Avery Island. One of the stops on the trip was a Buddhist shrine, which housed a very large statue of the Buddha overlooking a mossy pond. My classmates and I would play church near the statue. (I realize now the inappropriateness of this action.) I always wanted to be the head priest. By nine, I was ready to enter the convent. And by fifteen, I had forgotten how much that little girl wanted to give to God.

Sweet sixteen, however, brought major changes that seemed anything but sweet. I made the transition from being a young Catholic to being a young Methodist. During that time, I reveled in the prominence of the Bible. I thirsted for the ability to seek God on my own terms. Participation in worship left me wanting more. I became involved in worship planning and liturgical reading. My call started to form.

This time also brought with it drastic physical and sexual changes. I was a late bloomer, but once I bloomed I made up for the delay. My hips grew wider and wider and wider. The only thing that grew faster than my hips were my breasts. It seemed like one night I was a little girl and the next morning I was a fertility goddess. The external changes were accompanied by profound internal changes. I started to realize that I was not straight. I started to admit to myself that I dreamed about women. Not innocuous dreams, but dreams that were charged with sexual yearning. I imagined sexual acts that I had no intention of acting out! Looking back, the whole experience seems hazy. I remember experiencing a tremendous amount of self-loathing. But mostly I was afraid of who I was becoming, and what all these desires meant. I felt like a stranger in my own life and in my own body. Mostly, I think I was afraid that God could not love a young woman who loved other women just as much as she loved men.

On April 27, 1998, during my junior year in high school, I joined the First United Methodist Church in New Iberia. Having hailed from half a family of Roman Catholics and half a family of Baptists, I was the first person in my family to become a United Methodist. That same day, I realized how powerfully God could use me. As I preached for Youth Sunday, I felt this fire growing inside of me. When I spoke, I felt like that fire was spewing forth from my mouth. My words and my voice were more powerful because God abided in them. I knew then that God had something in store for me, but I just couldn't believe that I was worthy enough to do the will of God.

Many respected church members questioned me about my future and encouraged me to look into ministry. I was so resistant to their guidance. How could I possibly have anything to give to God? I was an abomination in the eyes of God. Over the next few months, I cried a lot. I prayed more than I cried, though, and by the summer, I was at a crossroads. Two things seemed clear: My head told me that I could not be queer and Christian; my heart told me that God had made me beautiful, queer, and with a purpose. I could not figure out if I should trust my head or my heart. With the exception of my best friend, no one knew how painfully I was struggling. And, in reality, the struggle was killing my soul. I went on our summer mission trip with a heavy heart. During a worship service, we were invited to pray. The leader of the service said she would pray and if God placed anything in her heart she would share it with us. The prayer time seemed interminable, but I dropped to my knees and I bargained with God. I told God that I needed to know if my heart was right or if my head was right. I just kept saying, "My heart or my head?" I must have prayed those same five words a hundred times. I basically demanded that God tell me what to do. And there was no answer!

As the prayer time came to an end, I was desolate. Then the leader came and stood right next to me. She placed her hand on my back and with the most confused expression she said, "I have no idea what this means and I normally would not have even told you, but I feel like God is commanding me to say this: Heart!"

I experienced an awakening. I awoke to the reality that I was a child of God, loved by God, sought by God, but most importantly called by God. Accepting myself allowed me to face God as a whole person. I could seek God now, because I knew who was seeking! After coming out to my friends in high school, I found myself happy, at peace, well-adjusted. My life finally made sense. I began to understand my call as tied to the United Methodist Church. I finally accepted that my life made the most sense if I would be an ordained elder. This was not an easy decision. At the time it felt like simply a concession. God wanted it and I accepted it. Even then, at sixteen, I knew that the church's position on homosexuality was not positive, to put it lightly. I knew that my ordination was not an option, but I was also very idealistic and naive. I truly believed that God would swoop in and fix the problem, fix the church, fix the world. Out of this conviction came a covenant. I promised God that I would not cut my hair until I was ordained. Still in high school, I realized that I had a good eight years before I would finish all the education and requirements for ordination. Surely, the church would have changed by then!

College proved an amazing time of expansion for me. I felt capable of expressing myself sexually and relationally. I finally came out to my mother in a Mexican restaurant. She said she knew and wanted to get back to dinner. My mother had to tell my father because I could not muster the courage. My father still saw me as the five-year-old girl who thought that doves were actually angels. I was innocent to him. I had always been a daddy's girl and I did not want that to change. The next time I was home I was reading a book called *Bi Any Other Name*, about the bisexual movement. I had left the book on the coffee table while I was online. My father came into the living room and stopped. He looked at the book and then at me and then at the book again. Finally, he said, "I take it that's yours." My only response was "yes." He said "okay" and we have been better than okay since. Once I was out to them as queer, I began to come out to them as called. In many ways, I think my parents understand my sexuality better than they understand my call. They are endlessly supportive, but not always knowledgeable.

My college years brought clarity about my call, my purpose, my place. To that extent, clear areas of my call started to form in my mind and soul. First, I am called to be a preacher. I felt the closest to God when I was preaching. The Gospel message of liberation from enslavement spoke to my queer experience, and I found that preaching allowed me to give voice to my own feelings of enslavement and oppression. More importantly, I was able to reach people and to influence them. Second, I am called to relational ministry. Small groups came to be an integral part of my spiritual journey. My junior year I started a small group Bible study for gay, lesbian, bisexual, and transgendered Christians. In that circle of six, I realized that God also calls me into relationship with all God's children, especially those whom the church and world have marginalized. I understood that my own journey and experience could serve as food for others' journeys. In those college years, I became the great gay index. I was the one that young men came to when they needed to come out. My own struggle with my sexuality equipped me; I understood their pain and fear and excitement. Finally, I am called to be a church reformer. I feel very strongly that part of God's will in my life is to bring about justice. Micah 6:8 (to do justice, and to love kindness, and to walk humbly with your God) has been a focal scripture in my realization of my call. With clarity came deeper conviction, which then led to action.

During my college years, I organized the queer community. For three and a half years, I led a queer student group. I became an active and vocal queer member in many mainline religious student groups. I preached about liberation to my peers. Such publicity does not come without consequence. In my first four quarters of college, I received twenty-seven pieces of hate mail. Some of the letters were almost kind. They only suggested that I was leading Christians away from Christ. Other letters scared me. One such letter plainly explained that if I did not justify myself by God, they would be forced to do it! I started to have horrible nightmares while I was receiving the hate mail. I would dream of being at a large family gathering with my kids and my extended family. In the dream, I would be breast-feeding my youngest, and some fanatic would come into the restaurant and murder me at point-blank range in front of my whole family, and then pray over my body. I always remembered him calling me the Antichrist. Between the dreams and the hate mail, I was paralyzed with fear. So I moved off-campus and established a safe home for myself. The move really invigorated my organizing. Consequently I started the GLBT Bible study. In response to the Bible study, I got a very kind and curious e-mail that said, "I don't mean to be mean, but can you be gay and Christian?" I politely replied yes and included some explanation. I found the interaction absolutely delightful. I was no longer afraid and felt like I could live my life again. This change of outlook prompted me to start my ordination process.

I am convinced that any ordination process is as much bureaucracy as it is sound spiritual discernment. In the United Methodist Church, the ordination process reminds me of really steep steps. If you try to skip steps, you will fall on your butt. During my junior year of college, I made my first attempt to jump through my first local church hoop. The first big step in the ordination process is to get the approval of your home church. My first attempt at the process unfortunately led to me falling on my butt. My mentor and I thought that I was ready to meet with a representative body of the church called the Charge Conference, but alas, we were wrong. So I took about a year and a half to regroup. In the interim, I received a new mentor.

Then I moved from Louisiana to Denver to begin my graduate education. There I was granted the genuine pleasure of attending the 2004 General Conference of the United Methodist Church. This conference meets every four years and has the gigantic undertaking of stating what the United Methodist Church officially believes. Issues surrounding homosexuality were addressed at the General Conference.

When I first realized my call to ministry more than seven years ago, I believed that the church would have changed its position on the ordination of homosexuals. In many ways I was right. This last General Conference did change the church's position on homosexuality. Now the United Methodist Church has a harsher stance than it did seven years ago. For this reason and many others, the General Conference weighed on my heart. Where is my place in a church that does not seem to want me? How can I be of maximum benefit to God and to inclusivity? What can I do? In response to this last question, I decided that I must force the issue by allowing my struggle to be made known. Church members and people in the pews must begin to understand that the issue of ordination of GLBT people is not some distant reality, but that our struggle for full inclusion fundamentally speaks to how we will be the church. I felt that the best way to effect change was to bring my story, my struggle, my experience, to the people that need to be transformed. During fall break of my second year of seminary, I decided to begin climbing the steps again in order to begin a dialogue in my southern United Methodist Church. Before I went home to tackle the epic struggle, I had the privilege of preaching on behalf of FLAME, which is the queer community at the seminary that I attend. In many ways, the sermon I gave synthesized the reason I struggle for ordination. I think it also reflects the mind-set that I brought to these most recent ordination proceedings.

FLAME Sermon

I will not be silent anymore. I stand before you today as a lover of God, a lover of men, and a lover of women. I stand before you today as a bisexual woman, and I am coming out. For me, coming out is deeply tied to being a Christian and to being a United Methodist. The scripture from Romans is such an amazing piece of scripture because it articulates three important themes in the Christian journey and in the coming-out process: choice, death, and resurrection.

The scripture begins with remembering our baptism. Our baptism is the event that ties us to Christ and remembrance is an act of choice. When we remember our baptism we choose God again and again. For Christians, that choice should empower us. Choices also empower queer people. When I came out, I chose to see myself through God's eyes because God doesn't make junk. Let me say that again: God doesn't make junk. I chose the queer community and that was a powerful choice. In that community, I have found friends and family. I have found colleagues and comrades. But most importantly, I have found a deep embodiment of God in the world. The queer community has taught me to be a better Christian. It has taught me about the transformative power of suffering. Suffering that empowers people, deepens community, and transforms the world. When we make choices about who we are and how we will live, those choices will empower us. But beware: Those choices have consequences, and some of those consequences are not always good.

From baptism the scripture immediately turns to death. I read the scripture and these powerful images of funerals surface in me. Death is a key part of the Christian journey. There is no resurrection without death. There is no Easter without the Crucifixion. There can be no new life without a death of an old life. Coming out is a death. It is a death of an old way of living! It is a death of a life of lies! It is a death of unhealthy expectations! It is a death of fabricated personhood! And let me tell you, death is difficult! And we need to be able to sit with death because when we can really embrace death, we can more fully appreciate resurrection.

And that is the Good News: When we die with Christ, we are also resurrected with Christ. Resurrection also has a lot to teach us. It teaches us about a new way of living in the world. The Resurrection teaches us about being a new creation. The image of Easter taught me how to come out and be out. The Resurrection taught me how to shed my old life and put on the life God intended for me. The Resurrection taught me how to shed a life of victimization and lead a life of empowerment.

The Resurrection also requires us to dream. It demands that we dream about the sort of world we want to live in. It demands us to dream about the churches we are a part of. It forces us to dream about the Kingdom of God. The Resurrection forces us to dream big dreams, unthinkable dreams, outrageous dreams, even undignified dreams.

I dream about a world where every child has the ability to come out. Where our children and youth can honestly figure out how they will be in the world, how they will love, and whom they will love, and then be able to publicly declare that. I dream that when our children come out, all of their parents will love and support them. This is what I dream, but mostly I dream about a church much closer to the Kingdom of God. I dream of a church where candidates for ministry are judged on their gifts and graces for ministry, not on who or what they do in their bedrooms. I dream about the United Methodist Church.

I am a United Methodist, and I love my church. I joined the United Methodist Church when I was sixteen. I chose the United Methodist Church. It was a beautiful choice, but before I could do that I made another choice. I chose to live as a bisexual woman, and those choices together have brought me to this path. This path has not always been pleasant. My ordination is not currently possible. My full participation is unwelcome. But this scripture from Romans gives me hope and forces me to dream. I am reminded of this praise song that goes "I will dance and I will sing to be mad for my king. Nothing, Lord, is hindering this passion in my soul. And I will be even more undignified than this." See, the Resurrection gave me the power to live a truly undignified life for God, because I have already died with Christ!

Now I mean to live with God. I can see the church's old self, but I can also see the church's new self. Because of this, I can say with all the confidence in heaven, I love my church, and I will love it until it loves me!

I began the ordination process knowing that my ordination was not a possibility. I refuse to closet myself to do the work of God. And I only know one way to be me: Queerly! The meeting was set. I was supposed to be with a church committee called the Staff-Parish Relations Committee on December 14, 2004. I was certainly afraid. At times, I was devastated at the possibility of them not seeing my gifts and graces. I cannot think back on the days before that meeting without seeing the face of a woman who has been my support, my confidante, and even for a short moment, my lover. For days she was the rock of salvation, the balm of Gilead, the ancient of days. She was the incarnation of God for me! My hope every day is that I can be the same for her. In the midst of my angst, though, was great expectation. I was so ready to speak to them about who God had made me. I wanted to tell them how they had helped to form this beautiful, faithful, queer woman. The day before I was to meet with the committee, my pastor called me and requested a meeting. In the meeting, I was told that I could not yet meet with the committee. They were confused about their responsibilities and the church's position on homosexuality. I felt angry and pissed off and frustrated. All of my preparation was met with more waiting. My pastor explained that the committee would meet with me after their initial clarification meeting. Then, I was asked to explain in writing parts of my call narrative in light of the homosexual issue gripping the church.

They have not responded to the letter I sent them, nor have I had the opportunity to meet with them. The waiting is painful, because it feels like I am waiting for bad news. What light is there in this dark and dingy tunnel? My district superintendent (DS) is certainly a bright light of God. In him I have found a colleague and a source of support and encouragement. He constantly tells me that God will complete the good work that has been started in me. My DS and I do not agree about gay ordination, but we do agree that God is greater than we can know. We are both open to God's transformative power. Essentially, this should be the nature of the church. My experience of being queer is fundamentally the same. If I let go of my expectations and my judgements, I find tremendous beauty and diversity in our queer community. I find people yearning for justice and loving whatever way they see fit. I want to choose to be queer every day! I want to choose to follow God every day! And for me, when I choose one, I also choose the other! When I am Christian, I am queer! And when I am queer, I am Christian! And that truth is a blessing that sets me free!

Hatchback
by Kaitlyn Tierney Duggan

I.

It's not until the weekend is over that I realize I haven't really thought about transit matters for days and days. I wonder what that means, if this state of mind is what people mean when they talk about a normal life. I realize I find myself wondering entirely too often, except for this weekend. I wonder what that means, as well. I feel the boy I was slowly ebbing away, more quickly than you would think. I find myself a little sad for his loss. He is dying, after all, so I may live. If he was ever alive in any real sense is something that will be left for me to think about for what I suppose will be the rest of my life.

Toward the end of the weekend, I realize I am at, or possibly well past, a certain point in my life where I was asking which was the greater cost: to lose friends, family, even those you thought were very close to you, to put yourself into debt and risk the loss of your material possessions, or to sacrifice your own identity for the comfort and peace of mind of those around you. I see now that suffering in silence is not, as I had thought, the path of least resistance.

Unhappy people don't lead happy lives. They don't have healthy relationships—they can't. Transition is shocking to anyone who knows you, and some will never get over it, true, but I realize, over my Cheerios, that it comes down to a finality, an impasse: You can either suffer the loss of others or suffer the loss of your own self.

I used to go to all sorts of meetings. GLBT meetings, youth meetings, therapy meetings, transgender support meetings. I went to the meetings; I listened to what everyone had to say. I tried to find my identity, find my self in other people's stories. I listened, and I thought, is this me? Does this describe me? Or am I something else? Sitting in a room just dingy enough to be depressing, just dingy enough for me to notice that it's dingy, I wondered if I wanted to be there, if there was a real need to be there that I just hadn't discovered, or if I was honestly capable of doing things on my own. I went through the steps, because they were expected of me. I found myself wondering how strong of a person I was, and wondered if the act of wondering made me any less strong. A lot of transitioners talk about baby steps forward. Therapists, too. They're crazy for the baby steps, those therapists.

It's true that there are baby steps. But what no one tells you is that every once in a while those steps will lead you to a huge chasm, a massive change. It's crazy and scary and fun and I recommend everyone try it at least once. The baby steps have built up such a momentum that they carry you, fast and wild, to the other side. And once you're there you realize that, without even being aware of it, you've crossed a divide that can never be uncrossed. Your momentum pushes you forward, and as you're carried off by your maniac baby steps, still trying to take your last looks at where you've just come from, you feel yourself building steam, and you're glad.

So this past weekend I was in Boston to meet my very first transsexual friends, which I keep saying because I think it's funny, because really, when you look at us as a group—the young transitioners, that is—there really isn't a whole lot of the typical transsexual thing going on.

I don't even know what that means, really. Typical transsexual. Cate calls it the young, hip, and passable TS, which I guess is what I'm trying to articulate. (Though a caveat of mine would be that I am not 100 percent passable at the moment, damn facial hair still casts ever so much of a shadow. But it's nice to be included, because in the end I know that I definitely will be passable, even pretty.)

It was a great milestone and no big deal. I'd never actually met a transsexual person (or, I should say, another transsexual person) in my life, and so I kept thinking how this must be a big deal for me. And in some ways it was, but really I just wanted to finally get to hang with my friends.

We possess a vibrancy in our identity because we have had to earn it, and that essence was, I think, a tangible thing when we were all to-gether. We have had to fight parents and right-wing relatives and stodgy school officials and dumbfuck therapists who have thrown everything they've had into convincing us to walk a "straighter" path, that there was a normality, and that we weren't it. We are at odds with our identity, or at least we have been at some point in our lives.

We have had to transform ourselves through force of will into who we should have been. We are at once ashamed of what we were, where we have come from, and proud of who and what we are. This makes us, I think, quite beautiful, and it's a rare beauty that I really was able to witness this weekend. It's in the small things—the way Cate's a little punk, Jess's quiet wisdom, Reise's confidence. Good people to be friends with, for sure.

We all have this same uniformity to our backgrounds, and it makes connection an easy thing. Our antagonism of self, our shame, our pride, the consistency of our stories of self-discovery, our sense of an earned self, make us older than we are, and this, too, is beautiful.

• • •

It's a strange thing, and something I've never been able to articulate well through self-examination, but I think observing others like me from the outside has given me some perspective. There exists a quiet center, a gravity of age underneath the surface of everyone I met this weekend. We are twenty-two years old and ten thousand years old. We have discovered our center of self in our youth when many have never even bothered to locate it, and this makes us sort of powerful. Powerful enough to claim our own lives, powerful enough to risk loss and suffering. It's not an easy thing. I have cried more in the past two days than I have in the past two years.

The weekend was magnificent in its simplicity. Going to Quincy Market to watch (and talk to) street performers. Getting lunch in some hipster vegetarian place. Having some quesadillas in a bar for dinner. Having some drinks. Our buoyancy is our armor. It protects us from those highs and lows that come so quickly. Keep that sense of humor, 'cause really, come on, you're having a sexchange, how can you not laugh?

II.

After Boston, Cate and Jess came back to New York with me to visit the big city. Their city is big, but mine is bigger, mine's the biggest. Of course, I no longer had a place of my own in the big city, so we stayed with Nick, who Cate and Jess adored. A bit about Nick: When I told him—when I came out to him, loath as I am to use the term—he was awesome. I had figured he would be. Although he had the most indescribable funny little expression on his face when I first told him. Nick is the type of guy who strives for politeness and decorum above all things. So I can only imagine that as his synapses were misfiring and his mind was totally blown, his main concern was, I'm sure, to not let me see how shocked he was. I had imparted this fact about Nick to Cate and Jess, and they could see it immediately, could see what I meant about Nick and his politeness in all things. They thought it was sweet. It is sweet.

So we're there, three girls in New York. I take them to Union Square, Washington Square Park, Chelsea Piers, The Strand, Forbidden Planet, Terra Blues, the cool places that no one ever goes to when they visit New York. Thrift-shopping in the East Village and SoHo and on Bleecker. I am, to my surprise, a size six, or smaller. I have become one of those skinny girls for whom all of those skinny-girl stores are designed. Does this mean I can no longer be grumbly and envious of skinny girls, since I can now also wear the clothes that look cool and are cut right? I shall find other reasons to be grumbly and jealous, I am sure.

We blend in by standing out, in the proud New York tradition of blending in by standing out. I get clocked a few times, and even Cate gets called "him" once by a Middle Eastern salesclerk (the look on her face is—I guess priceless really is the word. Shocked and pissed and amused all at the same time). Cate wants to visit the Trapeze School in Midtown West, so I take her there, where she promptly runs into a guy who knew her back when she was a guy in college. I guess acrobatics is a small world.

But the city is nice, and reminds me of what I miss most about it. We get some pizza for lunch, the big gigantic thin-crust slices that can only be done well in the city (it's the water in the dough). I come to the decision that it would be far worse to lose whatever spark or uniqueness I may have by burying it under some lifelong lie. I also come to the decision that many of my profound moments coincide with meals.

We get to be part of the tapestry that is sold as "young hip America." Not to sound anti-cynical, because I know cynics are cooler (see what I just did there? Being cynical about being cynical), it really *does* exist in some places. And New York is nothing if not young and hip. So, sitting in the park at the end of the day, we are just filling in the needed sexual/gender minority slot (the position is also offered to waxed DKNY Chelsea boys, fantastic drag queens from Christopher Street, and punked-out, tattooed butch dykes from the Village). At the fountain sit some hip-hopping young black kids; next to us are these preppy-looking student communists carrying a banner and handing out fliers. A businessman stands in the grass with his shoes off. We are helping to paint that picture, we are that youth culture you've been hearing about. I think how nice it is, at times, to be able to embrace anonymity, or stereotypicality, and how it's a useful ally in transition that isn't available to me in the suburbs. I wonder how Jess does it in Maine.

I am slowly but surely beginning to grasp the concept of emergence. Is that the defining statement, the transcendent arcing theme of this process I have been so in search of? If it is, should I really be drawing attention to it? By doing so, do I lessen its impact? Emergence—a new state of being forming from what already exists. The process of taking shape. As important, if not more so, than the end result. The person I am going to be is only now becoming visible from the mold.

It occurs to me that it is entirely possible that adversity, rather than success, is the true defining element of a life worth living. It is possible that the act of struggle, rather than any sort of outcome, is that which we are measured by. Growth through force of will. An earned life. It's an idea that appeals to me for obvious reasons.

The fact that I'm aware of my own growth as it is happening is uncommon, I think. Does the fact that mine is a conscious transformation make it any less organic? Does the fact that I blend so easily into the crowd make me any less unique?

But it's nice. We sit, three normal, transsexual girls, acting casual about acting casual, because we can now. To even be a girl is a victory, even having this small moment is a victory. By being here, we help complete that portrait of the city. By being visible, we push things forward, in our own small way.

●●●

It's funny. I feel sometimes as though I've been caught up in some clockwork whirlwind of my own design. I built it, I set it into motion, and I thought I knew what would happen when I set it loose. But, like with all inventors, inventors in the Frankensteinian sense of the word, when the gears started shifting and turning, I realized I didn't truly understand how wild or whimsical the consequences of my creation would be once loosed upon the world.

I hope this doesn't sound like regret. It's not. Every day for me is happier than the next. Every step forward brings a calm and contentedness to my heart I have never known. I feel . . . at ease with myself. I am finding my place in the world, and it is very much a birth. There is a great deal of pain involved, it is hard, it is an endeavor, but the end result is a joyous one. You hope.

III.

I should mention my homelessness.

It sounds dramatic, and really, I would like it to be, in a way. Later on in life it will lend my youth the mythology and theater that everyone so hopes for. I will drop the subject casually at dinner parties with fancy people: "Yeah, for a while in my, oh, my early twenties or so, I lived out of my car for a bit. Oh yeah, it was a heap, a real junker." I will shrug it off as no big deal in a way that will connote to everyone how much more vividly and intensely I have lived. They will feel foolish about their concern when they see how nonchalant I am about the ordeal. "Sure, kinda rough, but I made do."

These people at these dinner parties will marvel at what a strong and interesting person they have met, and their lives will feel momentarily cooler, in the way that comes from brushing up against those with unorthodox pasts and lifestyles.

But. In the meantime, now, I am homeless.

I am not dirty or panhandling. I do not fight junkies for a doss out on the street or do anything I would normally equate with being homeless. I have a car in which I keep all of my stuff. My stuff has taken on a much greater importance now, seeing as how I've had to whittle it down to the most essential and most precious in order to fit into a 1984 Volkswagen Golf hatchback station wagon. (The car is so old, it's not even a Gulf. It's a freaking Golf, like the goddamn sport.) I still have a job, I go out, I even have medical benefits. What I do not have is a place to stay, or the means to acquire one.

Last week, my mother saw me as a girl. She freaked and kicked me out of the house. The irony is that I wouldn't have even needed to stay at her house except that I had just lost my own apartment. I know it's not popular to say that transition is a choice, but I think it is a choice the same way breathing is a choice. You choose to go on, you choose to live. It's harder than it sounds sometimes.

Other than a place to sleep, my life is very much the same. I am a twenty-two-year-old homeless transsexual. And that is not nearly as exciting as it sounds.

I am lucky, in a sense, that these circumstances have found me at a point in my life when I am able to deal with them fairly ably. I have worked out most of my past issues of self-loathing, depression, suicidal tendencies (not the band). I have had my moments, but I am over them.

The inherent flaw of suicide is that it is not a true ending in any sense. Least of all to your problems. Consider pain to be a form of emotional energy that, like any other form of energy, can neither be created nor destroyed. The act of suicide, rather than acting as an end to that pain, instead acts as a conductor. The pain follows the path of least resistance to those who were closest to you at the time, like a bolt of lightning striking a tree during a storm.

•••

On the surface, a day in the life of the newly homeless is not a terrible departure from that of a normal life. The main difference is the intense and pervading boredom that drives you to occupy your now very long, very empty day.

Still, even the mundanities of an urban existence are available to me, and today could have been no different from a day off from work to the casual observer.

Normally I would have a bit of cash on me, and could at least stay in a Motel 6 or something if I so chose, but I spent most of my wad up in Boston, and was inexplicably taken off the schedule at work this week. Hence no money until Sunday, which seems many, many days away.

I spend the first several hours (the one thing I now have in excess) at the library. Despite my lack of a library card, I manage to talk my way into some computer time there. I check e-mail, post to some friends that I may not be able to be around for a while, do some random layabout Web surfing, and am always eventually informed that I have exceeded my gratis lab time.

Being in a library, I naturally go in search of some good reading. Read for several hours. Am inspired to write a bit, the way good reading will do, and do so.

Bored with expanding my mind in a structured environment, I go in search of some slightly more hedonistic instruction, and am off to the beach. I lay out on the hood of my car at the seawall, listening to a classic rock station, the only station that comes in clearly in the '84 Golf. I watch families and young couples go by, thinking how almost like them I could be.

I have a memory, sudden and vivid, of being in the car with my mother and my aunt. Driving along in relative quiet, my mother blurted out, "Everyone I know right now is in transition," and I started choking, I was so surprised. My aunt was not in the know yet, no family yet, not at that point.

This was before I started getting letters in the mail to let me know that I was on a list in the Vatican of special souls to be prayed for, and cards of the Sts. Michael and Gabriel to guide me through what my family considers to be a "bit of a rough patch." I take some comfort in the knowledge that I am so shocking to my family, my existence so extreme in their eyes, that they felt compelled to notify the Pope and a couple of archangels. To be so removed from them, so far from the same mind-set, only reinforces my belief that I am on the right track.

So, my mother's blurt. I occasionally forget that for most people not plugged into the transsexual lexicon (my mother included, I would assume), "transition" is, in and of itself, a relatively harmless word. Little "t," not capital "T," is how most people see the word.

So. She went on listing the various transitions of people we know. My aunt with her recent business closing and starting a new career. My mom's friend moving to Florida, another who was taking a big promotion. My brother, newly married and off to start his military career in Kentucky. And I kept waiting, knowing she was going to get to me, and wondering what in the world she was going to say when she did.

She talked about how I'm in the middle of another move (it looked like I was losing my apartment at the end of that month), and how I'd stepped up the search for a newer, better job.

I sat in the car, biting my tongue for my aunt's sake, and I couldn't help but think, how interesting. The big transition my life was going through right now, in my mother's eyes. My apartment. My job.

I remember wondering how my mother could drive with those big blinders on. If she could even see me sitting next to her.

There is a slight breeze off of the water now, enough to distract from the early-afternoon sun, enough to bring me back to the present moment. The salt air reminds me of home, and I try to remember the first time I realized this, on my first trip home from college. It's always been homecoming, never being away from home, that reminds me of what I miss.

I lay out until I felt the sun on my face—in the way that happens when you sit out on the hood of a car in the afternoon sun for too long. I sit in the car for a bit, reclining, listening to music, with both doors open to let the breeze pass through. I sit like this for a while, until Myke calls. He asks if I want to help him move some stuff from Lynn's old office to her new one, and maybe grab a bite, around five. Myke is the one friend I was most scared to tell, the one friend for whom I still had to pretend to be a boy. I had never been able to work up whatever it is I work up in me to come out to someone when around him. Courage, perhaps, though the act itself never feels courageous. I agree to meet him.

I leave the beach, still with some time to kill, and drive to a commuter parking lot, though a different one than the one I spent last night in. I call Jess and Cate, and tell them I miss them, and lie and tell them I'm doing fine. I cry, first at the circumstances, and then at my own self-serving self-pity. They console me, which is what I wanted, and the conversation ends shortly after, with me still missing them and still pitying my sad self, but feeling a little bit better and a little bit annoyed at myself for having cried.

I call Brooklynn back. Brooklynn the wild child, the party girl. (With no real way to occupy my time, a great deal of my homelessness is occupied by calling friends.) I tell her about my weekend and about my new living arrangements. She is angry with me for not asking someone around here for a place to stay, but she understands a little when I explain how I don't want my asking for help, my circumstances, coloring anyone's reaction to my coming out.

My feeling is that were I to ask for a place to stay, it would be disingenuous of me to not tell why I was without a home in the first place. Since I am neither willing to lie to my friends nor to sabotage my own chances of acceptance from them, my dilemma exists, for the time being, unresolved.

Aaron, my old roommate, fared better after the liquidation of our apartment. But then, Aaron is not transsexual. He found some co-worker friends to rent him a room for ridiculously cheap, and though I was happy for him, I was upset at my perceived abandonment. There are friends I could stay with, but it took me four months to find my last place, and I have no desire to wear out my welcome.

We talk for a bit, Brooklynn and I, about the idea of chosen family, the theme echoing my Sunday-night conversations with Cate. Brooklynn is a rarity; having been disowned by her own family years ago for turning her back on an oppressive Mormon culture, she is one of the few who can truly empathize with the life of transition without having to live it.

My cell battery dying, we say goodbye with the tenderness of two friends who do not want to retreat from a good conversation before its natural end. I tell her, as I told Cate and Jess, that I will call her soon. The absurdity that I am homeless yet own a cell phone is one I try not to acknowledge.

Almost five, I drive to Lynn's office to meet Myke and move office furniture. I arrive to find Lynn sobbing and the rest of the helpful therapy-staff-turned-moving-crew embroiled in overcoming some logistical or bureaucratic obstacle I am not able to fully untangle.

Eventually we load a few office tables, large and round like the ones you find in a school cafeteria, onto a pickup truck and then to some garage. I am considerably weaker than I used to be, thanks to hormones and poverty, and the work, though relatively simple, is difficult.

Our moving tasks apparently done, Myke and I return to his house to grill some Boca Burgers. Lynn calls from her office, still upset, and I am saved from the temptation of bending my own ethical rule about asking for a place to crash when Myke tells me that tonight might not be the best night to hang. I finish my burger-esque dinner and leave, more relieved than disappointed, and grateful for the meal.

It is early still, though. The few hours before midnight that can legitimately pass as night before becoming late are often the longest for me, and leave me keenly aware of my own boredom.

The library will already be closed, I know, and my last two dollars and thirty-five cents went around one o'clock for a can of beans and a large bag of chips that I hoped would last until Sunday, when I was scheduled at least to return to work. I haven't yet begun to plot the feasibility of working while living out of my car, but am remaining cautiously confident in it as a reality, despite the fact that I am basing that belief, really, on nothing.

Still, I am in search of diversion yet again. Movies, bars, and even coffee shops would require a down payment of some sort, my good-faith purchase that would barter me the extended visit I was sure to wallow in. I settle for browsing at Borders. A book-store is, essentially, as good as any library. I listen to new and interesting CDs, skim some old and not terribly interesting poetry, and take a look at some new fiction until the store closes.

Not yet tired of the day, and knowing that tonight will be harder to sleep through in the commuter lot than last, I go to a small suburban park, complete with gazebo and benches, to sit somewhere that isn't behind a steering wheel, and to think.

I feel suddenly like I am running in place. I try to remind myself that it's just a black mood, one of many that accompany transition and homelessness and desperation. Still, the feeling persists. I'm on a treadmill, and that cardboard panorama of life in the "Shiny Happy People" video is scrolling past me over and over again. Will I ever manage to get back on my feet and begin moving forward again? Both at the same time, preferably. Even my writing feels lazy. Cramped. Without momentum.

Michael Stipe has completely abandoned me, and I am left alone here on the soundstage with that old guy on the bicycle to keep me company.

I think about gender outlaws, who say not to be pigeonholed by societal gender norms. Buck the system. Fight it. Deconstruct it. I think of the feminist who says to break free from the shackles of gendered oppression. I think about walking down the street with my friends, and I don't want to have to be a status warrior.

I'm busily telling the maitre d' "I'm not with them" in a hushed, embarrassed tone. I feel like a traitor, but it shouldn't be an effort to be normal. I don't want it to be. I don't want fanfare. Is it laziness not to care? Selfishness, perhaps?

I'm still in my head, in my memory of just a few short days ago. My friends are with me. We're having fun. I want this to be my life—this moment here, in this instant that's already passed. I won't worry about the dismantling of some great oppressive societal force. We'll live our lives, happy and free, oblivious to the system as it crumbles around us.

• • •

I sit there, the final bit of traffic grazing slowly by. I sit and write amidst a few small clusters of teenagers, some with tambourines or bongos or long gothy skirts, as they try to delay the end of summer. I sit and write, waiting for the night to be over.

It occurs to me that transit now has more than one meaning.

Perhaps in time it will become the all-encompassing definition it was intended to be. A girl in transit. A life in transit. When are we not in motion? Up or down, left to right, fast, slow, backward and forward, we move.

We can be neither created nor destroyed, or maybe those are the only two things we can ever be. It is constant, and we call it change.

Walking the Tracks
by Eric Knudsen

I never told him, but when I got dressed in the morning before school, I always tried to look like him. Well, maybe I didn't want to look *exactly* like him, but even if I could, I still couldn't buy the confidence in his walk or his free-spirited smile. When he went out at night or was off working on the weekends, sometimes I would go in his room and look around at his stuff. I wasn't sneakily probing into his personal life to uncover any dirty secrets; I just wanted to feel closer to him. Sure, he tormented me just like siblings often do, but he also assumed the job of my protector. Even at a young age my brother had patience with me.

If I didn't tell people that we were related, they would never have guessed Bryan and me were brothers. Our personalities and lifestyles were complete opposites. With red hair, blue eyes, and a football-player build on a tall frame, Bryan didn't look anything like me. So when he approached my family and told us that he was going to join the United States Marine Corps, I was feeling contradictory emotions. I was shocked that he had such aspirations, but at the same time it didn't surprise me that he would do something I never had thought about.

Whereas younger siblings often feel left out because they can't hang out with the "big kids," more often than not Bryan would ask me to come fishing with him or join him on a bike ride to the baseball field. Although I tried, athletics never came naturally to me, but that didn't matter to Bryan. Even if he was going to do something

I had no interest in, he would ask me to come along despite the expectation of me turning down his offer. I now realize that was his way of saying I love you. I try not to have regrets in life, but I wish I had taken him up on his offers more.

Young boys like to make fun of each other to build a sense of camaraderie, but even Bryan knew the limits. He was often the leader of the pack, but that didn't mean he ignored his sensitivity to define his masculinity. If someone teasing me went too far, Bryan would let them have it. If someone didn't accept me into the group, then Bryan thought twice about his being there.

Late in July, Bryan's last week home with the family, he asked to go for a walk with me. The sun had just set fire to the horizon and the low chorus of crickets started up in the tall grasses. There was a different, earnest sound in his voice, and although spending time with my brother was nothing new to me, he'd never asked me to walk with him before. Sometimes in life an unexplained premonition takes over your body and you know there is only one choice to make. My uncertainty showed in the airiness of my voice as I obliged nonchalantly, as if I didn't sense the uneasiness in the room. It was a cool night, so I ran to get a light jacket and pushed at the screen door, hearing it slam behind me.

This night was unique for a number of reasons. Aside from being one of the marked times in my life when I was actually nervous around my brother, he was about to go off to boot camp, and the family anticipated his newfound responsibilities and duty would separate him from the life he once knew. Although our house would always be his home, becoming a man would exempt him from parental rule and render their commands as mere suggestions. I wondered if he would change as a person—I always heard the military could do that to some people. Bryan wasn't known for having the best structure in his life, nor was he known as being the most responsible person at times, so maybe these new demands would change him drastically.

We came upon a set of train tracks, one that still brings back fond memories from my childhood. I can still hear the sounds from my window of the old steam train that appeals to the tourists. I began balancing on the rails with my hands outstretched at either side of my body like an eagle in flight. Bryan and I used to place pennies there on the tracks, and whatever other objects we were curious to see flattened under the weight of a steam engine.

We talked about the summer and we talked about school, and we talked about the new part of his life he was about to embark on. I knew he had something to tell me but I didn't know what exactly, and I watched his words carefully for the anticipated moment.

"I want you to take care of the family. It's not going to be easy for Mom, but I want you to be there for her. Try not to fight with your sister. I know it's tough, but try to be nice to her." It was one of those moments when you are supposed to keep quiet and just listen, and aside from nodding occasionally, that's exactly what I did.

There was a slight pause before his voice changed tone. "But I want to make sure that everything is going to be all right with you." He turned to meet my eyes with the most compassionate and pensive look on his face. "I *know*, Eric." My heart started beating faster and my legs forgot how to work correctly. All at once I felt naked, revealed, like someone just ripped a blanket off my sleeping body. I wanted to run, I wanted to say "No, you *don't* know," but that was before he added, "And I want you to know that I don't care. I love you and I'm here for you." My vision got cloudy and the corners of my mouth began to twitch. I moved away from my brother's face as he put his arm around my shoulder and pulled me closer. I turned toward him and fell into an embrace while tears slowly soaked into his shoulder. It was a moment when I cast away all embarrassment and shame, because my brother, the man who I looked up to for so many years, was telling me he loved me just the way I was.

The rest of the night went by so quickly. I shared memories and feelings that I never thought I would reveal to my brother, but it felt so right knowing he held on to my every word. My brother and I always had a sense of humor between us, and being able to laugh about being gay and making light of the situation allowed him to understand me in a new way while giving me a newfound sense of confidence. It's amazing what good can come of such seemingly bad circumstances. My brother joined the military and is serving for his second time in a war, yet because of the initial impending situation we grew closer than ever before.

They say that siblings are a link to the past, and I truly believe this. By sharing an important part of my identity with someone I have known so long, it was as though we relived our youth in that one night without having to use words. Through the simple fact of knowing the last piece of the puzzle, everything finally made sense. In the place of a past of secrecy and misunderstanding I was finally known.

Although I don't have the same desire to join the armed forces, Bryan inspires me to reach for what I want in life even though it may be dangerous and I may face adversity in my journey. He has taught me what it means to devote myself to other people, an entire nation, and I highly honor his selflessness. I never feel in comparison with my brother, nor do I feel in competition with him. My mother feels blessed that she has such dynamic children: one son is the all-American boy, taking part in Boy Scouts and the football team before joining the Marines, while the other son excels in the arts and academics while possessing an identity that is often subject to ridicule and misunderstanding by society.

All kids have a role model in their life, whether it is a comic-book character with superpowers, a famous actor, or a prominent political figure. I always had Bryan. I will never know definitively what it takes to become a man, but I guess it's one of those things you just become, and in retrospect you know yourself in a new light with enough experience and knowledge. When I find out I'll be sure to send a postcard. But until then, I won't have to walk the tracks alone.

The Most Important Letter of Our Life
by JoSelle Vanderhooft

Junior Year of High School
Salt Lake City, Utah 1996

Dear Joey:

I hope you'll forgive me if I sound a little awkward here. I mean, what do you say to your past self now that the past is gone? "Hi. Hello. It's me—I mean, it's you—seven years from now. At 23. See, it's late where I live, and I'm lonely, so I just thought I'd write and tell you—"

Tell me what? you'd probably ask, because you were so suspicious and scared back then. Getting a B+ on a test meant that you'd never make it into college, and having a guy wink at you meant, of course, he was going to drag you into the nearest deserted classroom and rape you. But this time, Joey, no one could laugh at your paranoia. You're right to be suspicious of me, of this stranger from the future with your hair and your eyes and your voice, only not really. Because they say your cells grow and die and replace themselves, so you basically have a new body every five years or so. As for my eyes, they've seen things I couldn't even imagine at your age: New York City as an honest-to-God New Yorker, the streets of London up close and personal. September 11, 2001. And as for my hair . . . see, that's just the thing. Last night, someone touched it for the first time. And I don't mean touched it in the sense that Steve touches it when he's asking, "Want me to just cut off the split ends today?" or how Mom touches it when it's three a.m. and you're standing over the toilet bowl puking your guts out with the stomach flu. I mean touched it like *that*, touched it like it mattered, and for the first time in your life you felt like you were home.

Joey, I know this is strange but you've got to take this letter very seriously. I'm writing to tell you about something important. You don't know it now, but you've got entire rivers of fire in your veins. And in your center, where you should have a heart, there's an inferno that's slowly climbing the walls and eating you piece by piece. It's almost sad that it's you and not your house that's on fire. With your house, you could recognize what was happening. You could grab a fire extinguisher and hold off the flames while frantically dialing 911. But when it's your eyes, hair, and cells and not the carpet, lamps, and sofas, it's so easy to shut the door and say, "I'm not here and this isn't really happening." Especially when every fiber of your being is, well, just sitting there fiddling.

You always knew you were different, you just didn't know how or why. Maybe because you were adamant about dresses and long hair when everyone else wore pants and bob cuts. Maybe because at seven years old you were five feet tall and an A cup while the rest of the girls weren't ready to start titty training. Or maybe it was because you never believed boys had cooties, and actually preferred playing with them . . . when they weren't trying to cop a feel, of course. Which wasn't all that often, this being Utah in the 1980s (we'll talk about your men issues later). You didn't know for sure. You only knew that dances and dating were an insult to your intelligence, and kept you from getting to know Oscar Wilde and William Shakespeare better. Now you'd rather be studying for Academic Decathlon while your girlfriends ogle the shirtless men's soccer team practicing on the field outside Ms. Barton's window. Oh, and sometimes, even though you're happy with your boyfriend, you secretly dream about having a threesome with the cute-but-geeky girl who sat next to you in AP Art History.

Thing is, Joey, you're queer. You're a lesbian, or at the very least bisexual. Truth be told, I'm still waiting for that letter from the forty-year-old me to sort it out for sure. But you're not straight and you've known it since you were four or five years old, when you went through the mall sticking your tongue out at the men and smiling at all the pretty ladies. You're gay and you are not being honest with yourself.

I'm sorry. I'm not trying to judge. I remember being you and I remember what you were up against. You grew up down the street from a Wal-Mart and about seventeen Mormon ward houses in a suburb of Salt Lake City that still hasn't figured out what the 1970s meant. Oh, it definitely wasn't the Bible Belt, but then again they don't call it the Zion Curtain for nothing. Gay just . . . wasn't talked about, unless we're talking about playground taunts ("Oh my God, Jo-Selle!! That book bag is sooo gay!" ". . . . no it's not, it's pink!"). You had to visit your dad and stepmom in Massachusetts to hear the word used correctly, and even then you thought it must mean something dirty.

"And then they put a sign on Mr. Gonzales' back that said 'I'm gay!' and he walked around the class with it on all day and didn't notice!" said Benny, your eldest stepbrother's best friend, on the way to the annual folk festival in Lowell. The entire carload of kids laughed, including you. You weren't sure why you were laughing, except that whenever anyone back home said "gay," *they* always laughed. So it must be really funny. But after your stepmom gave you all a ten-minute lecture on what the word actually meant, and why jokes like that were wrong, you knew you'd never laugh at another one. And you also knew something else: no matter what you and your stepmom believed, the world at large still thought gay people were pretty damned hilarious. At least, funny enough to deserve public humiliation. And after having your schoolmates poke and prod at your burgeoning breasts for two years, you decided you'd had enough humiliating to last a lifetime.

The point is, while you're not being honest, you've had a lot of help hiding in that closet of yours. And the fact that one of your best friends since middle school just told you that only lesbians went into the University of Utah theater department really didn't help things, either. That and the holy hell Senator Orrin Hatch raised sophomore year about the kids who wanted a gay-straight alliance over at East High. It's no wonder you'd locked your closet door and tried with all your might to turn yourself into a prom dress. But none of that ultimately matters. I can go on and on for ten pages pointing fingers and laying the blame on school, society, church and state, and God and country, and it won't make any difference. Because no matter what "they've" done to you, you're the one who has to deal with it. You're the one who has to pick yourself out of the dirt and move on.

You've got to. Time is running out for us. In less than a year you're going to get a telephone call from your uncle. He's going to be crying so hard Mom can't make out what he's saying. When he finally manages to force the news out between sobs, she's going to say "I have to tell her" in a voice that's so small and scared and hurt you barely recognize it. And then she'll lower the phone and say the words that will hang around your neck for the rest of your life: "Your father committed suicide."

Let me tell you, when that happens all hell is going to break loose. You're going to run to the arms of your best male friend seeking a father, and think that you're in love. You'll believe that he's going to marry you and suddenly everything will be okay—you'll have children, you'll be happy, and most of all he'll protect you. That, and you'll never, ever have to think about girls again. He'll say he loves you and then leave you two weeks later with an "I'm not ready for this" speech. You'll hold it together just long enough to pass your AP tests and give your valedictorian address, and then you're going to fall apart. You're going to have a breakdown and spend most of the summer of 1998 watching Eve 6 videos on VH1. I still can't listen to "Rendezvous" without feeling sick.

What would coming out to yourself do to solve all this? Maybe not a whole lot, sure, because we all have to go through our share of high school bull. Still, it might make your first year of college easier if you did. That way you won't have to feel so degraded after throwing yourself at one man after another, even though you realize by now that it's a joke that you've long since forgotten the punch line to. It'll save you from having a fight with a good friend when you find out she's dating your ex. Who knows? It might even spare you loneliness at nineteen, twenty, twenty-one, twenty-two.

Even if it doesn't, you'll be one step closer to feeling some of that peace they talk about in church all the time. That's what cracks me up inside, you know? Knowing that at twenty-two, you're going to be sitting in a bathroom thinking maybe you should kill yourself because your gayness offends God. At twenty-two, when most of your Mormon friends are married with children, you're still fighting this adolescent war because even then, even now, you still sometimes think *Maybe it was the sexual abuse. Maybe it was the fact I had a cold and distant father. Maybe if I just called Exodus or Courage and got some therapy everything would be all right, and I could be safe and happy and know I'm going to heaven.*

I feel so old now, Joey. I'm not even twenty-five and I feel like I've been carrying the world on my shoulders. Only the world is shaped like you, and I'm not as strong as Atlas. I look back through the years at you, your innocence and your damned naïveté, and I just feel like my heart has been shattered beneath a window. I want to protect you. I want to wrap you up in cotton at each stage—at sixteen, seventeen, eighteen, nineteen, twenty—wrap you up in a little cocoon that's soft and warm and keep you safe so you can fully develop. So you won't end up like me, feeling spent before you can even run for political office, before you can even rent a car without paying a penalty. I want to hug you at twenty, when your first girlfriend leaves you, and tell you that in four years you'll meet the love of your life. I want to crouch next to you in the bathroom at twenty-two and tell you that you should read what Catholic tradition really has to say about marriage and sexuality instead of feeling like God is going to punish you just because your partner happens to be a woman. I want to tell you every day of your life that sexual abuse, your father, the fact you broke your toe on a chair once, whatever, has nothing to do with your sexual orientation.

And someday I want you to breathe and realize, in the middle of a street in whatever city you call home, that you don't have to feel ashamed anymore.

But most of all, I want to be able to forgive you for making the mistakes you had to make, for doing the stupid things you had to do in order to survive in the best way you knew how. I guess, ultimately, that's why I've written you a drawer of these things. Because someday I want to be able to really say "we're okay" and mean it.

For now, please accept that I'm still learning. You've vanished into the past and you'll never see this. But I will. I'll read it over and over until I know that my heart understands as well as my head. And on that day, though you and every other JoSelle is dead except for the one flickering in the present tense, on that day maybe I'll be able to say

I love you,

_____.

Without a Trace
by Anthony Rella

Someone's dog is chasing a trio of mountain goats across a talus slope on Mount Princeton, leaving small avalanches in his wake. His owner's screaming causes the other hikers to stop and watch this high-altitude drama unfold, as the goats leap across a precipice and pause. The dog paces at the edge, posturing and threatening. It looks like a precarious situation; a mistake might send the dog sliding down the slope, which could make it a difficult hike home. Another hiker starts yelling with the owner. We know that the dog does not belong on the mountain, just as the goats have more right to the altitude than us; certainly their hooves are more adept at traversing the terrain than our Gore-Tex boots.

I am hiking with my friends Jack and Neal as part of a two-week road trip commemorating our mutual retirement as Boy Scout backpacking instructors in New Mexico the previous year. We pause and rest our packs against the rocks. "I bet the mountain goats win," Neal says.

"The dog could probably take down one or two of them," Jack says.

"No way, those goats know what they're doing. Dogs don't have any depth perception; he has no idea how long that jump is. I bet that guy is pissed he didn't bring a leash."

"Why the hell did he bring a dog on the mountain anyway?" I say. I am not used to hiking in Colorado, so I have little experience with the backpacking culture and think that hiking with dogs is dangerous. It offends my sense of order, which is the second time this has happened today. An hour ago, we came across a man resting on one of the false peaks while his five-year-old daughter played on the perforated, spongelike gray rocks. She wore the tiniest backpack I have ever seen, possibly large enough to hold a quart of water and a baby jacket, and jumped around as though she were on the school's plastic playground equipment.

"You brought your daughter backpacking?" I asked, trying not to sound accusatory.

"Sure," he said.

"I would have been panicking when I was her age. It's so steep."

"Fear is a learned response," he said with pride. "I want her to respect the mountain, not fear it." Her ease made me a little jealous, even as I had a sympathetic twinge at the thought of her slipping. I wondered if her fearless upbringing would lead to boldness or boredom.

This dog is not bold, he's poorly trained. It takes five minutes of his owner commanding before he saunters back, unscathed. A little disappointed, the three of us continue our hike until we summit Mount Princeton and pause for lunch and the requisite nude picture that male hikers find so endearing. Then we stare at *Colorado's Fourteeners,* arguing over how we should descend and wondering why the marked trail on the map does not exist. Jack notices a ridge trail almost a thousand feet below us, and a path leading to it—which is actually a wash of loose rock nestled between the curves of the mountain, but we don't know this.

The year before, I was taking a crew of fourteen-to-eighteen-year-old Scouts through base camp to get their prepackaged meals from the commissary. It was my job to make sure the boys and their adult advisors had all the appropriate gear and supplies to survive a two-week trek through the Sangre de Cristo mountains, and then to hike out with them for two days and teach them no-trace camping skills, how to inhabit a spot of wilderness and leave it exactly as you found it, as though you had never been there at all. There were various lessons: raising bear ropes to keep food out of the animals' reach, digging a hole for excretory duties, restoring the plants crushed by tents or boots. The purpose was to minimize environmental impact, sustain the campsites so that others could enjoy them for years to come.

I was enjoying my summer until I noticed that someone in the commissary had made a handmade placard announcing *BOY SCOUTS WIN 5–4*, the Supreme Court's decision to allow the Scouts to discriminate against homosexuals. I had known when I signed my contract that it would be a summer in the closet, but permitted myself some hope that it would change thanks to the nine people in charge of deciding the fate of an entire nation's laws. I stared at the poster while the Scouts loaded up on food, willing one of the votes to move in the other direction, until an advisor came up beside me.

"Thank God," he said. "The First Amendment still means something in this country."

"Yeah," I said, "but it never should have gone to the Supreme Court at all."

"Exactly." He walked away before I realized we had not agreed on the same thing. I wondered, should I run after him and tell him what I meant? Would that get me into trouble? Should I get into trouble? My summer of ambivalence had begun.

I hate descents more than any part of the trek, especially down such slopes; my stomach always sinks with dread. Like Scotty in Alfred Hitchcock's *Vertigo*, I picture myself falling from any height, although my condition is less debilitating. I do not expect to find solitude and reflection when I go to the mountains—I go for the drama. Every success lessens the terror, broadens my limitations. I want to be like that dog, recklessly indifferent to the dangers of living. I do not know the origin of my phobias. Perhaps the flat forests of my native Indiana made me suspicious of the treacherously shifting land of scree and boulder, the curling scrub oak that reaches like a snare across trails. The arid silence of the Western wilderness unsettles me in the night, unlike home, where the summer's evening air is humid with cicada noise. On my first nights here, the fall of a stick from a tree is loud enough to send me into paroxysms of fright, sure that something thick and hairy approaches to devour me whole.

But Jack and I are from the same town, we grew up in the same Scout troop, and he seems completely unaffected by this geographical displacement. It is my life that is dominated by fear. I am afraid of spiked iron fences, electrified subway tracks, freak incapacitating household accidents, the Department of Homeland Security, nocturnal intruders human or supernatural, the end of the world, mountain lions, darkness. I took an Enneagram personality test and discovered my type, 5, the Observer, has fear as its dominating emotion. There have been many times in my life when I allowed this to intimidate me from doing anything, but cowardice is not an option now, unless I think I can build a good life at 14,000 feet. So I tighten my belt strap and start baby-stepping down the wash.

I tried to police my behavior while working at the camp, weighing the queerness of every action or statement. My somewhat butch demeanor allowed reprieve from fear of discovery, but my friends were the most visible pursuers of our female co-workers. I wondered if my disinterest, more glaring than their interest, would draw some remarks. I was lucky to be sharing tents with Neal, a vocal atheist, anarchist, and sometime bisexual to whom I outed myself within the first few days. He often went to the local bar with our co-workers and discussed his sexual proclivities loudly to our friends, telling drunken stories. "There was one time I got so drunk and made out with this baby-faced guy, and he wanted to fuck me but I can't handle that. He was so hot!" This frustrated one of our closeted friends so much that he yelled, "Neal, why the hell can you run around screaming about being bi and making out with guys when I can't say one goddamn thing about—" before he realized they were surrounded by the camp administrators. Neal may have escaped suspicion due to his visible encounters with women—well-known stories that I witnessed firsthand one night when he and Jack, who had become friends through their mutual interest in women and punk music, brought girls to our tent and made out with them on his cot. I was trying to get enough sleep to go out on the trail with my crew the next morning. After a few minutes, Jack's girl pushed herself up and asked if maybe they should leave, to which her friend responded, "You can leave if you want."

"My bed is the demilitarized zone," I said. "You can sit here and not have sex." She sat at the end of my cot and watched as her friend kissed Jack and Neal. Finally, the sandwiched girl said, "Do you really want to go?"

"Yes." The girl on my bed stood up and pulled the other girl out from their clutches, leaving them to bemoan wussy chicks who can't handle their orgies. Neal slid over to my cot, his beard smelling of Pabst Blue Ribbon.

"What?" I said. "Your girls left, so you want to taunt the gay-boy?" He laughed, and then kissed me. After a minute, during which my hormones began to shed their summer despair, he stood up and said, "Okay, time for bed." Neal's bisexuality was a few kisses with a boy if there was no girl around, with no risk to him because he would sober up to his more pressing need for women. I went back to sleep, and nothing more came of the incident.

The problem with summiting mountains, I think, is that you look from the peak and realize you have to do the whole thing again. I see my descent not as a series of exact and gentle steps but as a jagged and bloody roll down. Kierkegaard says dread is "an alien power which lays hold of an individual, and yet one cannot tear oneself away, nor has a will to do so; for one fears what one desires." I am not sure of the last clause; is my fear of falling an equally strong desire to fall? Do I have a yearning for pain and death too subtle and disturbing to acknowledge? I do throw myself into terrifying situations, promiscuously seeking fear the way some fall in love over and over again, discarding their lovers when the intensity of emotion has passed, looking for a fresh source. This is the feeling of dread, a tenuous marriage of fear and desire, an emotion of the time between the foregone and its conclusion, the desire for the stresses of fear to alleviate with finality—to either get off the mountain or die, no more of this uncertainty.

I mention the end of this thought to Neal, who has been trying to lighten the mood. He likes to develop personae, adopting the voice and attitudes of characters that he creates, and today he's "Pastor Dave," a Christian youth counselor of dubious integrity.

"God made all this shit for *you*!" he yells. "You should love it with all your heart, not fear it like some Satan-worshiper!"

"He sure is great," I yell back. I pretend to be indifferent, moving quickly, planting my heel firmly into the loose rock to form a brief foothold, and there is nothing to worry about, it's only fear that causes accidents—then my heel slips and I land on my ass, sliding. Marble-to-baseball-sized rocks line my fall, marking me with thin red cuts. The rocks counter every attempt to stand and my legs are beginning to shake from wear and near-panic.

Jack is watching all of this and seems unsympathetic. "Doesn't God hate gay people?" he asks. "Maybe he made all this to kill you." Whenever I'm around the guys, I seem to take my rightful place as the group's weakest, the slowest one, the most damaged by falling, the gay one—despite Neal's borderline bisexuality and Jack's warm appreciation of any form of deviance. I think it's a dynamic with any group of guys; it's a metaphorical position that I happen to literally inhabit.

"No way!" Neal yells. "Jesus died on the cross for sickos like him, too! Isn't that fucking *awesome*?"

The fourteen-to-eighteen-year-old boys who comprised the Scouting crews provided numerous distractions to my political angst. I had a group from Big Clifty, Kentucky, who liked to climb all over the Ponderosa pines, getting butterscotch-scented sap all over their clothes. They also supplemented their weak vocabularies with heavy doses of "fag" and "gay," which began to sound like George Orwell's

Newspeak: "You are a faghiker. This is a gaybackpack. This is a doubleplusgaymountain." Their crew leader was an eighteen-year-old bulk of fat and muscle whose face suggested a fairy tale in which the frog prince didn't quite complete the transition either way. He and his buddies would become defensive when I asked them to stop climbing the pines.

"Trees are strong," he said. He never made eye contact when he spoke; his pupils rotated with no object permanence. "Who cares if we break a few—this is a forest."

I explained that it was our policy. *"That is a plusfagpolicy."* I gave the no-trace pep talk; our campsite was so beautiful and surprisingly well preserved, considering how many Scouts we got every summer, wouldn't it be nice if the next group to camp here had the same unspoiled experience? *"That is gaythink."* I explained that it was a very long hike for medical help, so if any of them should fall and twist or break something, they would be in pain for many long, long hours. He shrugged.

The frog leader's parents were the adult advisors for the crew, and I found that I preferred them to any of the boys. I especially liked his mother, a no-bullshit rural woman who informed the boys that if the trees and rocks didn't cause them injury, she would. She told me that she and her husband went on a hiking or canoeing trip almost every other month, usually without their children.

"That's great," I said. "I hope that I can find someone like that someday."

"You've got to find the right girl who'll try it out with you," she said. "Most guys try to convince girls that they're too slow or weak to pull their weight, but if you give them a chance and try to be patient, they'll pick it up."

"Do guys still give you crap when they find out you hike?"

"Yep. The other leaders in our troop didn't want me to come. Said the boys wouldn't have a good time if they had to stop and wait for me all the time. But during the practice hikes it was a different story."

I always liked having women advisors in my crews; all of their stories about the Scouts involved some patronizing man who told them they couldn't make it. Most of the women took extra time for endurance training and arrived in better shape than the men, and never complained about the tasks, unlike some of their macho, whiny offspring. Our conversation took an inevitable turn to the discussion of James Dale and the Supreme Court case. The father said, "I think they picked the wrong person to fire; it seemed like he was a great Scout leader. I wish he was in our troop."

During that evening's debriefing, the father gave an impassioned speech about how much he enjoyed hunting, but the morons at his hunting grounds always left their trash and garbage lying about, and years of such abuse had ruined the forest. I followed with another speech about no-trace camping ethics, trying to impart some respect for the wilderness, help them to understand that it all has a reason to exist and should not be needlessly squandered. The next day the boys used the spectral whiteness of the Aspen pines as a canvas for their creative mutilations with rocks and sticks, as though I wasn't there.

We did manage to form an unexpected bond. The boys hated going to the programming provided by camp counselors at various sub-camps, especially the song-and-dance campfire programs: "I hate this gayfagcampfire. What a plusgaysong." Normally such descriptive statements are mild linguistic irritations, but I was no longer in the mood to tolerate them and had spent many hours contemplating how to criticize them without giving anything away. After one "queer" campfire program, I remarked, "You're right, if that campfire had a sexual preference, it would definitely be attracted to other campfires of the same gender." The boys thought this was hilarious, and for the rest of my time with them they tried to goad me into more similar comments with the adolescent belief that a joke only gets funnier with repetition: "Look at that gaydeer! What do you say about gaydeer?"

I hate Mount Princeton. Whenever I look down, the ridge trail seems to be as far away as it did on the peak, with an interminable decline of rock whose color varies from gray to dark brown. It's nearly noon, or past—I can't tell because I don't have a watch, but it's close to the time when experienced backpackers know they should be beneath the tree line in case a storm comes. If there were trees, perhaps the sun wouldn't feel like it was stealing the last drops of water from my body, making it easier for the rocks to jar me out of my senses. I want to move faster, recklessly, but it is not working at all. "Pastor Dave, didn't God make me gay?"

"That's devil talk!" Neal says. "You are gay because society told you it was cool and you wanted to be different. When Pastor Dave doubts his sexuality, he always finds a parishioner whom God has endowed with the greatest gifts, and invites her to his room for a prayer session, which is *awesome*. You should do the same!"

My dread of being outed was largely irrational; there were two men in upper leadership who had been "roommates" for nearly twenty years, and one of the staff sashayed through base camp in his high-riding uniform shorts and leather choker. I never heard of a wide-scale expulsion of gay leaders, and the head of Scouting himself noted in a letter that the Scouts would make no effort to discover sexual orientation. However, some of my co-workers began wearing snippets of rainbow ribbon as a silent protest.

Jack was wearing his ribbon when he met one of his crews of Mormons upon their return to base camp, which prompted the advisor to write a tirade in Jack's evaluation to the effect that gay issues were better left to parental instruction and guidance, and we should not attempt to promote our own political views on the job. Someone in upper leadership took this evaluation and posted it anonymously, stating that the ribbons were not part of our uniforms and should be removed, although others had similar adornments praising morally superior institutions, such as Texas. Several people quit, gay and straight; one guy had a gay friend who had taken care of him while he was recovering from cancer surgery, and felt that his continued employment was a betrayal.

Another left with some controversy. I had suspected that he was gay for a few weeks and cultivated a crush on him. After the ribbon policy was made public, I overheard a few instructors remarking that he had written a huge letter to the leadership and resigned. I thought that he had come out in his letter. That evening, he was sitting with Jack and a few of his other friends, so I walked over to sit with them, unsure what to say. He was hot, dork-glasses and backpacker legs, and I had never approached a guy before to vocalize my desires, being fresh from my high school closet. He stood up to leave, and I knew I had to do something, or else I'd spend the rest of the summer feeling that I had let every chance to be courageous pass me by. I walked after him and stopped him.

"Hey." The feeling of dread hardened in my stomach, I was now forced to go through with it. "I know we've never really met or talked but I have a lot of respect for you because I'm in the same boat but I don't know if I want to leave and it's too bad I didn't meet you earlier becauseIthinkyou'rereallyhot. So, uhh." I wasn't sure if I could stop speaking. There were no clouds, which meant a freezing night but a clear view of the array of constellations. I could see Ursa Major, otherwise known as the Big Dipper or the Big Bear. That did not help.

It was hard to see his face; the only light was coming from one of the offices several feet away, which glinted off his glasses as he squinted at me. I started rubbing my face in embarrassment, feeling stupid; I couldn't handle his eyes. There's the Scorpio constellation, nemesis of Sagittarius the Archer, who is hiding on the other side of the hemisphere.

He put his hands in his pockets and leaned back, looking confused. Finally he said, "Okay, thanks." I smiled and said no problem and quickly backed away, to tell Jack what happened.

"That was pretty ballsy of you," Jack said.

"Why?"

"What if he wasn't gay?"

"I thought he came out in that letter."

"No, he didn't. His letter criticized the Scouts and said he couldn't work for them because of the policy, but he never told anyone he's gay." Oh, shit.

I saw him again a few minutes later. "Sorry about before," he said. "You kind of surprised me."

"Yeah, sorry about that." I kept shifting around on my legs.

"It's okay. Thanks. It's too bad we didn't talk earlier, because you're pretty cute, too."

"Oh." I smiled. We looked at each other, crossing our arms, and I wondered if this was the moment when we would have our forbidden kiss, the moment of courageous subversion. "Well, have a good summer," he said, and turned to leave. Then he stopped. "Don't give it up. Keep fighting." But I did not care enough to fight. I wanted to have a good time and believe I was winning because my "oppressors" were paying me to hike. He walked away, and I wanted to follow, but I didn't. There was Cassiopeia, the stars in the shape of M or W—*moron* or *wimp*.

A man and his wife are approaching, so we give them space to pass, but he stops, huffing and puffing. "How old are you guys?" Early twenties. "Well, I'm sixty, and I've never done this before." He seems to want us to affirm his inexperience, compliment him on his halfhearted bravado, but I am too exhausted to be impressed. His wife is also having a tough time breathing, but she keeps hiking while he leans into the rock, complaining. I imagine him dying from the exertion; this is the kind of thing that would concern me if I had been at camp and he had been one of the adults in my crew.

Now it only makes me think about people who speak of conquering the mountain, as though it cared if you live or die. The conflict is usually internal. I think about the times I had believed myself near death on hikes, whether it was valid or paranoid, and it seems that any death not related to hiking would seem rather mundane and unfair. The only noble death for me might be to break against the rocks and be devoured by scavengers until there is no trace of me left. The fantasies flit through my head, and I understand the meaning of dread, fear, and desire as one.

By the end of my summer at the camp, I began plotting various ways to come out. I had a romanticized notion that if I told everyone I was gay, someone might change something, somewhere, even though I knew such a self-inspired catharsis was impossible.

It had become inconsequential; a week before, I had hiked in from the trail and saw Jack, who said, "Dude, last night Neal got so drunk, and he grabbed a guitar and started singing songs about the people we were hanging out with. Then he made up a song about you, and how you were a lonely fagscout in the wilderness. I hope you weren't planning on keeping this job."

I threw my backpack in the tent. "Well, coming out is easier if other people do it for you, I guess." I saw Neal a minute later and asked him to sing the song for me, but he had forgotten the words. "That was really cool of you," I said, "after this whole summer, to go ahead and tell everyone for me." I was burning from the hike; I wasn't sure if I was angry or not.

"It wasn't anyone important," he said. "It was all our friends, who don't care."

"Whatever," I said, grabbing my shower supplies. "I was going to quit anyway."

Still, I wanted to do something drastic and spectacular for my own amusement and closure. The Church of Jesus Christ of Latter-day Saints comprises a large portion of the adult leadership in the Scouts, and they have clearly stated that they will withdraw if the policy was reversed, so I took the Mormons to be an easy scapegoat. On the last day of my contract, someone from a neighboring tent came to mine with the Book of Mormon that one of his crews had provided, and asked if I wanted to help him burn it, so he, Neal, and I doused it with a bottle of white gas and set it aflame. I turned the pages with a stick to ensure that the whole book was well combusted. Some of the other staff passed by and stopped, including one of the few African-American employees of the camp, an attendee of Neal's sing-along.

"What are you guys doing?" he asked.

"Burning the Book of Mormon," Neal said. "Does that bother you?"

"Hell no. In that book it says the people knew they were at paradise because everyone was white. They didn't even believe black people had souls until the NAACP sued them."

"That's a good idea," I said. "Maybe the Lambda Legal Defense could sue them."

"Hey, at least you guys have souls." He had a point. Most of the observers shrugged and kept walking. The fire was smaller than I had wanted, leaving wisps of ash all over the ground and a small burned spot. The rain came an hour later, and washed it all away. The world remained as I had found it.

I know several men have mailed their Eagle Scout badges back to the Scouts in a gesture of protest, but I held on to mine for one of the reasons that I used to justify continuing my employment—as a reminder that I am a product of the Scouts regardless of how they feel. Unfortunately, such gestures are meaningless when they remain unspoken, unacknowledged by anyone except myself. Perhaps if I had stayed with Scouting, moving up the ranks with discretion until I was in a position to effect real change—but what a sacrifice that would be. To be good, evasive, for the rest of my life, to alter some antiquated policy of a group that is quickly losing relevance? To fight, to be courageous, you need passion for your cause. I loved my time with the Boy Scouts, but I was no longer a boy.

I used to joke that I was not scared of heights, merely falling from them. The thought occurs to me when I finally half-slide my way to the ridge trail, almost two hours after leaving the peak. Jack and Neal sit waiting for me, only able to manage an acknowledging "Dude." We're all out of water, due to poor planning, and have an hour and a half left to hike before we can make it back to the car. We hike quietly but faster, with more certainty, passing poor travelers who are only preparing to climb the summit.

After we put enough distance between ourselves and the descent, we pause to look back.

"Is that the trail we took?" Jack asks. The wash, discernible by its lighter white appearance and thin rock covering, stretches well into the valley.

"That would have sucked to fall down," Neal says.

"What a plusgaymountain," I say. I'm bitter. I never want to hike or feel that scared again. Then I notice the pine trees stretching beneath us, all the way down the slope, to the highway, which leads to the next peak, and I can see more peaks in the distance that I haven't summited. I'm tired but feeling good from the endorphins, the pleasure of success. The hatred has fled. I am a hapless lover of mountains, and I will continue on, until I find that eternal source of courage that makes every challenge a bore.

body isn't this
by Zara Iris

he checks to see if anyone's looking
before he hikes his pants up
and adjusts his breasts underneath the button-down shirt
and skirts around the topic of his first
cub-scout experience
in casual conversation
with strangers who
want to know.

he's immature and loud
louder
louder than he's ever been before, because
he feels he has a secret that he doesn't want to hide
but can't reveal for fear of
rejection and
male pride and
he's walking so quietly on the eggshells he refuses to move
because gender
is not something to change
or rename.
and it's true.
he knows this, but still he sways
and laughs effeminate, giggling, wondering
why he can't stop crying.

he was born a dick named jane,
and since birth he's been clawing his way out
toward the sun and
a son he can't believe himself to be.
he pulls seasons past with fingernails
scraping skin on the way to changing.
he's laying down his weapons
in order to become one and the same
and *son*, and *boy*, and *you, sir,* fall on deaf ears
because he's only hearing silence while
the unknowing weight of compacted words
bears down on his slim shoulders
and he's older than he remembers
when he looks in mirrors
and pictures a life less sordid
than what the photographs suggest.
the best years of his life are covered in cobwebs,
archived as evidence
of what he refuses to admit;
his past is buried as deep as his name,
(ashamed of the self-murder brought on by
[the dichotomy of gender)
which rendered him lifeless and cold.]
he's told he'll be fine if he just lets it go
but they don't know it like
he knows it and
he knows it's fluid and final,
still the reminder comes every time someone looks away
and he adjusts his breasts underneath the binding.

he's lying, but
he doesn't know which way is up and
can't figure out which truth to tell
and how he'll ever
pull himself

out
of the hole he's been digging
since his parents taught him how to continue living
as the girl they thought they created,
the girl he rejected
bound
and hated
and cut and bruised and beat
and burned to learn her to leave him alone.

that will teach you, girl.
that will teach you to meddle in business that
isn't yours
and never will be.
that will
teach
you,
girl who walked tall and broad down city streets
broken by the sight of her
tall flat frame that felt so right,
learning quickly that she wasn't hiding.
she is standing out,
out of place,
nonexistent
nevermind, she's gone . . .
he's a being all on his own
but she's towering over him
and his hands can't cover his breasts,
even when people aren't looking.
but he adjusts them anyway,
hoping that no one will see the girl beneath him,
hoping that no one will see her pretending
but not wanting to end the charade.
he's lost and afraid of
falling in between the binary,

but scared, knowing which side he's on.
and years of abuse from a father
he never wants to emulate
sends him straight back to the girl who
layed in bed
cold, alone and
raped, lonely
no example for the girl he
couldn't be if he tried,
shouldn't be if he wanted to.
he's not,
and he's not okay.

he overcompensates and laughs,
effeminate hands holding everything he holds dear,
learning how to embrace
what no one else knows he is:
he is
he
she
takes a hint when he takes a hit
from someone doubting his status
as a radical girly boy.
and her ears catching *ma'am,* and *sweetheart* and
she's gonna be a dancer when she grows up,
eating away at her.
she doesn't exist enough to care;
she is the he she never wanted to fuck,
unlucky girl to fall so far from the lines.

girl, you . . .
girl, you need to find
your body isn't this one
this time

and he clenches his fist,
grabbing belt loops in tightened fingers,
holding grief and
pain and
shame and
strife, a
life in
chains, and
still at
night he
settles into
dreaming of himself
free, unbound, flat.
his chest heaves with relief and breathing,
filled with the hope
that someday
he will
believe.

Nice Ass
by Jesse Cameron Alick

I have a nice ass
For reals.
I shit you not.
When I walk down the street,
I cause car accidents.
My buttocks are round and firm as mangos
and twice as sweet.
I could sell jeans with my ass
I could have it plastered
on billboards all over the country.
People in every corner of the United States
would be saying
"Now that's a very nice ass."
Whoa,
isn't that a weird concept?
I could make a living off my ass.
God Bless America.

"Girl + Faggots"
by Caspian Gray

So I was pretty apathetic about coming to college—all my friends were nervous or thrilled or sad, and I was blank, with only the vaguest feeling of *bring it on,* because I'm defensive by nature. I've been out for four years, and am no longer afraid all the time because I'm a dyke—I expect people to accept me, and when they don't, I don't even hate them for it anymore. Xuan Ho, who says he loves me, left weeks ago for the Marines, and Lara has already twisted my heart around enough that for now I am comfortably numb. Whitman, who is my only other friend, spends time with me eating at the Waffle House and having deep philosophical conversations helped along by liberal amounts of Tsingtao beer. I paint his nails in stripes of black and amber, but when night rolls around, he always sleeps on the couch.

I miss touching people.

Then I make it into the Read dorm, where I am a "scholar" and therefore deserving of the very best that Ohio University has to offer. This means that my room is clean and relatively large, and that the bathroom isn't supporting any unrecognized new forms of life. My roommate is fluffy and pleasant, and her inner arms have the scars that say *cutter,* but the rest of her smiles and says *well-adjusted teen.* I am jealous, because despite medication and therapy, I am far from well-adjusted, and I always had the sense to put my scars in places that wouldn't be revealed by short sleeves. So I smile back and prepare myself for a long quarter of spending a lot of time on my own, which is pretty much what I've always done. My mom asks if she can call me every day, and I say yes once I realize that she is serious.

I have the odd, uncomfortable idea that I can smell myself all the time, this warm, margarine scent emanating from my crotch. I shower obsessively, just in case other people can smell it, too.

When I go to the Coming Out discussion group, I take a little flier and tape it to my dorm door, writing *Closets Suck* on the dry-erase board above it. My roommate says she doesn't mind; this is my way of searching for any other queers in the Read/Johnson Scholars Complex.

It turns out that there are only three of us. They are both boys, both thin and flaming, but fun. Jason is short and constantly writing messages for people on their doors, and Ray is tall with a solemn side that sits oddly on him. I meet them both the same day, and it is Ray's birthday. He is nineteen.

To celebrate, they hold the Dorm Slut Olympics, and I am the torchbearer. The torch is four bananas held together with a hair band, and the first event is the Banana Deep Throat. A girl named Caitlinn goes for the gold, taking the whole banana down. Everyone is awed. Jason is silver, and my roommate gets an honorable mention. I decline, since dick is not my thing, and I have no desire to practice on produce filched from Shively Hall. Then there is the Best Fake Orgasm competition, and again Caitlinn wins hands down. This time Ray gets silver, and while he's performing, one of the ROTC boys from downstairs keeps touching himself through his pants. I laugh to myself, because it's so cliché for the faux-soldiers to lust after one of my epicene new friends.

When it's over, and most people have paired off and disappeared, Ray and Jason and I crawl under the blankets in Ray's bed, which is a top bunk. I relish the feeling of other people's legs tangled with mine, my small breasts pillowing Ray's head. It is all perfectly innocent, but I am glad to be in the middle as we half-watch *The Daily Show*. I've missed having people to be close to, to the point that this simple human connection is bliss. I only met them this afternoon, but after watching them both fellate bananas, it would be hard not to be friends. We pull Ray's comforter over our heads and say silly things and practice for tomorrow's Olympic event, which will be Heterosexual Dirty Talk with a Partner. I ask Jason if I can lick every wrinkle in his ball sack, and he laughs and pretends to feel around in my pants, telling me to just let him know when he finds my labia. We decide that we'll be funny rather than sexy, because it's already obvious that Caitlinn dominates as the official Dorm Slut.

Then Ray complains that he can't see the TV because he's in the back, and I ask him if he wants to be in the middle, because he is the Birthday Boy. It's not long before he and Jason are no longer spooning, but obviously curled up in each other. Jason keeps taking the comforter away from me so that I am outside the circle, and then Ray keeps fixing it so that I'm back in with them. I don't know if he's nervous or just trying to be polite, but I can take a hint. I climb down from the top bunk and collect the few other people still in the room, not so subtly letting them know that Ray *will* be receiving head whether they stick around or not, but that they might not want to witness it. Since no one's left but me and straight boys, they all clear out. I shut the door gently behind me and wander back to my own room.

I'm not surprised to feel lonely, only disappointed in myself. I'd rather be used to it by now, but I'm not. I don't know what I miss more: Whitman's shifty reluctance when I pull him into a hug, or Lara laughing while I kiss her chin, or Xuan Ho giving me a hickey and then freaking out in case his girlfriend sees it. They are home, or were home, and I feel like a drifter without them. My classes haven't been in session long enough to be challenging, and it feels like they might never be. With nothing to distract me, I wish that I was a frat boy chasing pussy, or at least a queer getting free oral sex because it is my birthday. Instead, I'm just me, laughing along with the ghosts in my head.

Something for the Ladies
by Danny Thanh

Whenever someone asks how it is that I have so many girl friends, I am quick to respond, "It's a gift I acquired before even popping out my mother's hoo-hoo."

I remember Mother telling me about how I was my parents' third, and final, attempt at having a son. "*Meh'* and *Ba'* already have two daughters, we wanted a boy. Every week Mommy went to St. Martin church, and I prayed we will get a son. But doctor said Mommy going to have girl again, so there is nothing I can do about it. It was like Mommy have cursed womb. *Ba'* said it okay—we love third daughter just as much as any child. But every day, I still pray. On the day I delivered, you come out and nurse wrapped you in cloth to go and clean off a little . . . and she come back screaming, *'You have boy! You have boy!'* and she shoved your pee-pee in Mommy's face.

"And Mommy *soooo* happy I forgot I hate Daddy for making Mommy pregnant," she coldly concluded, with squinted eyes and a white-knuckled fist.

All my life I was told I was a girl. My mom and dad had their "Third Daughter" story to recite at their friends' parties. The adults found it cutely amusing. I cannot begin to count the number of times they pinched my cheeks in adoration, or the number of times their children pointed and laughed, saying my name should be Danielle and not Danny.

Because I wielded athletic abilities below that of a severe

anorexic, I was always the last picked for the kickball team and relay-racing group during physical education. The disappointing final choice was between Tonya Stevens and me, and the team captain let out a reluctant sigh before pointing to my pig-tailed counterpart, who hobbled on her crutches to join the ranks. Once during a race around the school's track field, the baton was slapped into my palm and I sprinted twenty yards before lying on the ground, hyperventilating, like a spastic jellyfish. I sat up after my breath regulated and looked around to find the other kids quaking in seizures of uncontrollable laughter.

The other boys decided I was incredibly inept at sports due to the fact that I was really a girl. While they were throwing orange balls into hoops under the baking sun and jostling one another, I sat on the side staring at the frying pavement. Occasionally the players would dare a bold individual to venture up to me, alone on the bench. "Dude, like—check it out, like—why do you run like a girl?" Timothy Woods once questioned, reenacting his version of my running—which resembled a swishing model's runway trot in fast motion. I wanted to point out that though it may seem that I walked like a fashion model, it sure beat his running posture: a bull-legged gallop, suggesting a number of jagged objects were crowding his rectum. But instead I simply smiled and nodded as he returned to his cackling clan.

My relationship to sports could be summarized by the jazz shoes beneath my bed, and the stack of tapes I used to record any Summer Olympic event that required the male athletes to wear Lycra. Luckily, my parents, having immigrated to the United States from Vietnam, had a very out-of-touch sense of homoerotica. It would take a masculine-looking drag queen, singing and dancing with a chorus of animated dildos and a backdrop of men dry-humping each other, before Mom and Dad would even begin to scratch their heads thinking, "*Oi cha!* That woman with sequins and feather boa singing '*Voulez vous couchez avec moi*'—she must really be wearing a wig."

My mother would nudge my father to bring his attention to me, sitting before the television set, licking my lips to the sight of men doing tumbles in leotards and diving in Speedos. "I think Danny wants become Olympian when he grow up!" she exclaimed with hope.

High school lacked any sexual tension between the girls I was around and me. Our genuine friendship was complemented with their comfort, knowing I would never force myself near their cooters. While my father expected me to invite guys over from the judo club he signed me up for, the only friends that came through our front door were adorned with glittery eye shadow and puberty-riddled 36C Victoria's Secrets. Witnessing the sea of different girls coming in and out of our home, my mom began to worry that I had turned into a teenage gigolo.

"You make friends with too many white girls, Danny. Why don't you make friends with Vietnamese girl for Mommy? If you're around so many girls like that, Mommy's future Vietnamese daughter-in-law get scared off. She think Mommy's baby only like the white."

"Oh, Mom, we're just friends," I tried to reassure her, before returning to the phone to arrange another night of miniature golf with my harem.

With influences from my girl friends and my English teachers—their suggested literary readings of Kate Chopin and Audre Lorde—I also became a feminist. I was the only man in a crowd of topless, breast-feeding women at a public park, chanting, "Women have the right! Women have the right!" I denounced my own genitalia, and every man's, as a symbol of sexism during our American Politics discussion of *Roe v. Wade*. I was the shoulder my friend Denay cried on when she caught her boyfriend wearing a gorilla suit, having sex with a girl caked with clown makeup. "Men are pigs!" I comforted her. "Well . . . straight men, anyways. You deserve better."

I would find my friend Meling rolling around on her bed, clutching her lower stomach, moaning like a tortured cat, "God damn this period. I knew it was gonna hit like *a—ack!* It's been six months since I got the last one, and *BAM!* So irregular. I wish I were dead." Kneeling on the side of her bed, I asked Meling if there was anything I could do, and she commanded, "Go and fetch me a box of pads with a carton of cookie-dough ice cream, you bitch!"

Cradling the package of feminine hygiene products in one arm and the ice cream in my free hand, I walked to the cash register at the grocery store. As I walked by, women with babies, women arm-in-arm with their partners, and women pushing lonely carts turned and smiled at me. I looked down to make sure people weren't looking at some mysterious stain on my crotch I had overlooked.

"Fucking men. I wish guys would bleed out their asses once a month, goddammit," my godsister wailed during her heavy flow, looking at me with spite.

Though I couldn't help that my anatomy was different, I felt remorse for not having an intrusive monthly visitor. It was like surviving a plane crash and living with the guilt that it was someone else, and not you, who had to die. I did the only thing I could to make my girl friends' lives better: I began carrying feminine hygiene products in my backpack to school. This act alone gained me the importance of a drug dealer, and my lady friends became a horde of dope fiends.

Instead of fishing to find a quarter at the bottom of their purses, girls would come up to me during classes, attempting to discreetly ask for assistance with a hearty, "I'm on the rag—help me!" I would then rapidly pull out everything I had available and showcase them with my hands, like a stage girl on *The Price Is Right*.

"Do you want a tampon or a pad? I have the pad with or without wings. These overnighters with wings are *really* absorbent, so if you're surfing a big crimson wave, this is the one. But if you want a tampon, I have to suggest these superabsorbent ultrathins, because you can barely feel them *and* they're made from unbleached cotton, not rayon. If you want to be environmentally friendly, however, I just got the Instead: Alternative Feminine Protection Cup from an infomercial. You just squeeze it, like so, and gently glide it within yourself, firmly positioning it right behind the pubic bone. . . ."

I'd continue to advertise, sounding like a desperate door-to-door salesman, before the girl of the moment just snatched the closest item and waddled in a rush toward the restroom.

To my girl friends' disappointment, I eventually had to stop providing. I came home one night to find my mom standing at the door, holding out an open palm with a still-packaged tampon she had found while searching my backpack with motherly curiosity. Having seen an anti-drug commercial on TV, she was convinced that as a good parent it was her duty to invade my privacy.

"What is this? Mommy found it in baby's backpack!"

"Huh? That's not mine."

"This belong to girl you sleep with?"

"No . . ."

"You sleep with those white girls?"

"No, Mom! Ummmm . . . that . . . that belongs to Tam—"

"Who?"

"Tam . . .Tran?"

"Vietnamee friend-a huh?"

"Yeah, Mom. She's a—"

"Tam *la'* girl?"

"Yeah, Mom, Tam's a girl—"

"Oh, you make Mommy *soooo* happy. My baby find good girlfriend for Mommy."

My mother consumed the story not because she whole-heartedly believed it, but because it was easier to digest than previous suspicions. After slapping the tampon into my hands, she ran toward the back of the house and into my parents' room, calling out for my dad with a smile spanning her face.

"*Ba'! Ba'!* Danny . . . those tampon not for white hoo-chee. Our baby found Vietnamee girl!"

They cheered in the same magnificent shrilled roar I had learned to associate with a football touchdown. Quietly, I walked into the kitchen with the tampon in my hand, and reached into a drawer to pull out a small brown paper bag. I dropped the slender environmentally-safe-unbleached-cotton-plug inside. After listening to the crinkling sound of the paper bag being wrapped, I walked outside and discreetly disposed of it in the neighbor's trash can and quit my job as a feminine-hygiene-product dealer—cold turkey.

Click and Drag
by Joel de Vera Moncada

fed up
surrendering to the
Monday through Sunday search
for a meaningful
IM chat
with an unknown male
screen-named
xxsexydownepnoixxx

fed up
with fraudulent pictures
of half-naked
underdeveloped
homo-bodied impostors
of a thug's life

fed up
with countless face pics
poses of
smiles / dimples / squints in the eyes
puckers of chapped lips
as if tweaked to perfection
by adobe photoshop

fed up
with homework break searches
midnight profile snacks
hoping to stumble upon
a man of depth
soul jazz enthusiast
to hum ditties with
ambitious artist
to find inspiration with
after reading
scanning
countless
exaggerated descriptions
posted on profiles under
about me headings

fed up
with the mission
the dreary click and drag
through drop-down search toolbars
as I select
location / *san francisco bay area*
status / *single*
age / *20 to 30*
sex / *male*
preference / *doesn't matter*
ethnicity / *doesn't matter*
just be as dark as me

cause www.downelink.com
exhausts all the same boys
i've already seen in
AOL's gam4gam / four years ago
in www.friendster.com / one year ago

my online search for a soul mate
desperately longs for
a 100 percent match
a *single* man to
send me a message
about *wanting to get to know me*
and when I
click the link back to his page

he'll
be a candid smile
a 5'7" to 5'10"
grad student and
reader of not just
FHM or
Maxim or
I don't like reading

so I can click and drag
to change my profile

to *in a relationship*

Jill Sobule and Four Other Torture Devices
by Ella Pye

One. French-Kissing for Girls.

I am five and Katie is six. Her birthday is in September. Mine is in
June. We are both in kindergarten, she in the p.m. class and me in
the a.m., but we go to day care together. We are best friends. We
both love New Kids on the Block. I like Jordan the best, and Katie
likes Donnie. Katie's parents are divorced, and she and her mother
move a lot. It seems exciting. I've lived in the same house since I
was two. Katie lives in apartments.

Today I am going to Katie's for a playdate. I have never had
playdates with anyone before Katie. We listen to the New Kids and
have concerts off the end of her bed. We like to pretend we're Paula
Abdul, even though I guess we can't both be Paula Abdul. That's
okay, though. We play Barbies, and hers have much better clothes
than mine.

Katie is wearing ugly blue shorts today. She is too tall and her
clothes always look weird on her. We go to her room. Her room is
round and the doors are double. It's really neat. You have to walk
through her mom's room to get to it, though, and it makes me feel
rude. We listen to Eagle 102.1 and talk about going to concerts. We
chew New Kids on the Block gum. I thought each piece would be
shaped like a New Kid face but they're not. Katie said they would
be, but she lied. They're just pink and yellow dots in a plastic case
with a New Kids sticker on the front.

Katie pulls her shorts off. She is wearing blue and white polka-dotted Hanes underwear, the kind that I have at home. They come in a three-pack with a matching blue pair and a matching white pair. She lies down on her floor and pulls her underwear off over her butt, and tells me to spank her because she's the baby and I'm the mommy. It seems kind of weird and she yells at me to do it. Then she makes me be the baby and she spanks me, too. She tells me that I should learn how to French-kiss because boys always do that, so she kisses me and puts her tongue in my mouth. I roll my tongue hot-dog style, because that is fun.

Her mommy drives me home, and in the backseat of her white car Katie Frenches me again.

We are in second grade now, and Katie still makes me practice Frenching her. It feels weird and kind of slimy. I am visiting Katie, and she has a new bike for her birthday. She is living in a new apartment and they don't have a good backyard. The whole thing is made out of cement and they share it with the house behind theirs. She rides her bike around the stones and falls. She breaks her wrist and tells everyone in our dance class that I did it. My mother says I can't talk to Katie anymore and I don't mind.

Two. Jill Sobule.

I am thirteen and my soul bleeds poetry. I hate the world and the world hates me. I want to start saving change so I can get my own apartment instead of living with my stupid parents. They think they know everything about me and can tell me what to do. I hate them.

My best friend is Nicole now. It used to be Kim, but she's so annoying. Nicole moved here last year. I sleep over at her house almost every weekend, because my dad doesn't let me have friends over. Sometimes we skip school. I'm really good at faking my mom's handwriting. Once I wrote a note saying that I had to get my wisdom teeth out that afternoon. They didn't even notice. Then I just walked over to Nicole's, and we flipped her couch upside down and watched her dad's porn, which was weird.

I overhear my dad screaming about me to my mom sometimes. He says that Nicole and I are dykes and that I shouldn't let the door hit me on the way out.

Nicole's dad has this friend named Chris. He's really cool. He's eighteen and he comes over to Nicole's house to play Magic: The Gathering and drink beers with Nicole's dad. He usually spends the night, because Nicole's dad doesn't want him to drive home. Kim is sort of dating him. She thinks they're engaged. Nicole and I sleep in the basement, and Chris sleeps upstairs in the living room. He picks on us sometimes. He rips the head off Nicole's stuffed buffalo, Bill, because he's a total asshole. Sometimes he picks us up and won't let us go. We both like him, so we don't mind. We hate Kim, though.

One night Chris kisses me in the dark on Nicole's living room floor. It's after five in the morning, which I know because I watch the clock the whole time. His mouth is huge. I've never kissed a boy before. It turns into a habit, and sometimes Nicole and I lie in sleeping bags on either side of him, pretending we don't know that he has one hand up each of our shirts. Once, Chris has his hand in my pants and asks me if I'm awake.

Kim has sex with Chris on her kitchen floor one night in December, and Nicole and I want her to die. I swear privately to starve myself until Chris calls me again. I last about three days.

Nicole turns fourteen, and at her birthday party we play a game called Suck and Blow. You take a business card and pass it down the line on each other's mouths, sucking in the air to hold it to your mouth, and then blowing it to get it on the other person's mouth. The card falls between Nicole and Kim and they touch mouths for a minute. Kim freaks out, probably because she saw a character in a movie act this way, and wipes her mouth and spits for like fifteen minutes. When we get back to school someone tells, and then the whole eighth grade knows, but they blame me instead of Kim and everyone calls Nicole and me dykes.

We have Language Arts during fifth period, and for almost a month, every time we come in the room a bunch of kids starts singing "I Kissed a Girl" by Jill Sobule. I start cutting my arms with a razor blade in the bathtub. No one understands me except Nicole, who cuts her arms, too. The kids who sing Jill Sobule at us start calling us Satanists as well as lesbos. The girls won't sit next to us because they think we're lesbians. This lasts for the rest of eighth grade. I hate myself.

I leave my schoolbooks on the table one afternoon, and my dad writes "Ella loves Nicole" on the covers of all of them.

The January after I turn fourteen, I am at Chris's house with my pants off and my sneakers on while the movie *Twister* is playing and I am losing my virginity. It hurts and it never gets better. When I get home there is blood in my underwear. I refuse to acknowledge that it hurt, because then I would be a wuss and sex isn't supposed to hurt, anyway. I tell no one. Chris talks to me on the phone for a few days afterward, but it is the last time I see him for a year. On Valentine's Day the next year, he invites me over and while we are having sex, another girl calls. He drops me off on a street corner and I walk two miles to Nicole's house to cry. Kim is there and I can say nothing. The next time I see Chris, passing him outside of the high school, where he has no right to be, he glares at me like I've done something to him. Later, he is arrested for molesting an eight-year-old boy.

Three. "Exile in Guyville," Track Ten.

I am going to be seventeen in three weeks. I am madly in love with Noah, and for the weekend we go to the beach with his best friend, a case of Heineken, and a lot of weed. I don't know where he got the Heineken. In the car on the way there, someone drives on our ass and I am afraid that we will get rear-ended. I imagine the beer spilling out onto the highway unceremoniously, bottles of Heineken spraying all over the asphalt. Noah seems unfazed, singing along to a song about a guy who finds out his girlfriend is a lesbian with such passion and dedication that you would think this happened to him frequently.

One night when we are drunk, Noah whispers, "I've got a con-dom, what do you say?"

I say yes. He hitches up my black skirt right there on the beach. It hurts and he doesn't kiss me, and I don't think it's good at all. There is something wrong with me. The next day we don't ex-change more than two sentences. We get so drunk and high that we pass out on the beach for seven hours and I get third-degree sunburns on my legs. Later, they turn blue and ooze pus from blis-ters that I pop with safety pins.

He drops me off at home when we get back, and I don't talk to him again. I write him a long letter. I apologize for being bad in bed, for being fat, and hope that he will understand my deep pain and speak to me again. Nicole and I egg his car.

He kills himself several years later, and I don't find out until he's long gone.

Four. Vermont.

I am twenty and she is twenty-eight. She is smarter than me, better-read than me, wittier than me, classier than me. Essentially, she's everything I'm not and everything I wish I was, and I want to crawl inside of her to be closer to her. Love doesn't even seem like an adequate word. We make grand and indecent plans to build log cabins in Vermont—twin cabins beside each other, with a crawl tunnel between so that we can access each other easily but still have our separate space. It's an odd fantasy, but we find it some-how perfect. I want to make blueprints.

She makes me feel beautiful, succeeding where no one else has tried.

We are nerds, and I am comfortable with that. We quote books and cult television shows together, saying how much we belong to each other. She is my best friend, and I feel like she is the only one that I have ever had.

At work, they ask me if I am seeing anyone, and I say yes. They ask if he lives with me. They ask his name. I make things up, because

I am a coward. I feel like I am punching her every time I do it. One day my supervisor says that another employee is "a little bit faggoty," and I don't feel nearly as guilty.

When I have loved her for more than a year, I write my mother a long letter. *She knows how to read the language from* The Lord of the Rings, I write. *She makes me feel beautiful.* I am terrified to give it to my mother. Finally, in a cop-out, I e-mail it to her. We agree to discuss things over dinner. I order chicken fajitas and a Long Island Iced Tea. The food takes forever to get there.

My mother and I sit across from each other at the table, and I fold and refold my straw wrapper. I sip my drink, and my mother bursts out with the oddball question that she has apparently been yearning to ask: "Does she like cats?"

It is okay, after that. My mother asks how she is every now and again, and although I will never be comfortable talking about it with my mother, she does not stop loving me. She does not tell me that it is a phase. She does not cry behind a closed door. She does not tell my father.

This is how my worst broken heart goes: She is smarter than me, better-read than me, wittier than me, classier than me. I start feeling stupid and inadequate. She doesn't want me to touch her anymore, and I feel like a rapist when I do. I am jealous, wildly, and I am immature. She quotes Shakespeare to me, and I am left feeling clueless as to what it means. I tell her that I feel stupid, and my nagging insecurities annoy her.

I am dumped seven months later, and I am too embarrassed to tell my mother that all of the things I wrote *(I know that you probably think I'm too young to know whether or not I'm in love. This is real)* were wrong.

Five. History.

It is 2004. Nicole is my best friend, and one night we go to one of the bars in our town. I mean to tell her about how my ex has a new girlfriend, imagining us gabbing like all girls do, though this has not happened once during the other few times I've talked about my ex. When we get to the bar, nearly everyone there is a boy we went to high school with, the boys who called us dykes and sang Jill Sobule in our faces. They are still friends, much as we are. Nicole lives with her boyfriend now, and is probably unaffected by their presence. I am terrified that they will laugh at me and declare that they were right all along. I wonder if I would have turned out this way if not for eighth grade. If it's like when someone calls you fat and you overeat in response.

In movies, the ones who were picked on forget about high school and go on to be successful. The nasty, popular kids are the ones who dwell upon their glory days, while the geeks they tortured have forgotten all of it in their newfound success. In the real world, the popular kids are still just as popular, just as lighthearted, and they don't recognize the geeks. The geeks recognize them, remember every name.

The guys at the bar don't even look at us. They have lost none of their confidence, and I have found none. I hightail it out of the bar and never go back.

Gaydar
by Jesse Bernstein

I saw Simon's profile on Gaydar, a popular international gay Web site, and immediately became excited. I was in Cape Town at the time, and had just learned that I would soon travel to Cairo to work for an organization that helps refugees with their asylum claims. Being a single gay man, I decided to check out the Egypt personals section of Gaydar, and it was there that I found Simon.

Simon is British, and under the *occupation* section he had written that he worked for a refugee-related NGO (non-governmental organization). Finally I had found a gay man who had interests similar to my own; refugees, human rights, and social change—all of these were mentioned in his profile. I immediately e-mailed him, telling him that I, too, was working for a refugee-related NGO. I asked what NGO he worked for, and just generally proclaimed myself. In an instant, I had it all planned out: We were going to meet, fall in love, and travel the world together doing refugee work. It was a wonderful thought to relish, a thought that surfaced without my even having talked to the guy. Simon returned my e-mail, and we continued an every-so-often correspondence until we eventually met in Cairo.

It turned out that he was working for a United Nations agency that decides asylum claims, and I was working for an organization that advocated for the rights of refugees to be respected. In essence, Simon was the judge, and I was the defense. There was an immediate conflict of interest, but I thought we would work through it. Our exchange of e-mails showed that Simon was warm and welcoming. He spoke of past work in Cairo helping gay prostitutes, and of knowing many gay Egyptian men. Most importantly, he suggested that upon my arrival I would meet all of his friends. I would have a community ready and waiting. I could not wait.

Upon arriving in Egypt, I met Simon at the fashionable Marriott Hotel, located in Zamelak, an island in the heart of Cairo that offers a quick getaway from the loud and bustling central downtown district. Zamelak has a large expatriate population, and many embassies, ambassador residences, Western-style food markets called Metro, a Pizza Hut, and even dry-cleaning delivery services. Elite restaurants and trendy bars are also located in Zamelak, all with English menus and signs, drunken Marines, and the occasional bewildered French cultural attaché.

As my taxi approached the hotel, I saw a beautiful Christmas tree that reminded me of the tree in Rockefeller Center. Though this one was smaller, for me it symbolized the West and Western comfort—which I desperately needed. Cairo is a city of around fifteen million people; the majority of Egyptians reside within the city proper. Cairo and Mexico City are the two most polluted cities in the world; I would blow my nose and brown gunk would come out. Everything I wore got dirty. I was told that when crossing the street, I should not look at the cars about to hit me on both sides. They would eventually stop. And don't worry about the honking—all drivers in Cairo drive with their fists poised over their horns, it's just the norm. At times I wanted to throw myself at the American embassy and plead for salvation from the madness that was everyday life.

The Marriott is a converted palace located right on the Nile. Once inside, I felt the grasp of Cairo slipping. The bar where I was supposed to meet Simon and some of his friends was on the other side of the property, necessitating a walk through the garden. It was wonderful to see green again, as everything in Cairo is brown: the sky, the streets, the buildings, the cars, the donkeys that pull vegetable carts—everything. This green garden had lighted trees, reminiscent of those around Tavern on the Green in New York City's Central Park. I would return here often, I thought.

I immediately noticed people's clothes. The men's long simple robes were replaced by fancy black suits. Many women remained in traditional Arab dress, with only their eyes showing through small slits cut in their black veils. Still, Gucci, Prada, and Chanel were everywhere: Handbags and scarves dappled the orthodox body coverings. Most designer goods had been bought abroad, likely at a recent fashion fête in Dubai. It wasn't uncommon to see a Saudi prince, a Moroccan sheik, or the U.S. ambassador having a meal at the hotel's restaurant. Why didn't I see these people on the street? I wondered. They didn't walk—they all had drivers, who drive black cars with black-tinted windows, like any other elite group. Except here in this hotel the elitism was magnified. This seemingly multinational, trans-border, designer-wearing, religious class had fused together so many elements that an anthropologist would have a field day. I was having trouble making sense of my thoughts, I was experiencing visual overload, and it was only my first week in Egypt.

I finally arrived at the terraced bar, which overlooked the warmly lit garden below. There was a lull, one that I would come to enjoy, an escape from the constant honking sound that I had become so used to. I looked around and saw raised bed-like benches covered with comfortable, colorful red Egyptian carpets. Men, mainly, sat around smoking flavored tobacco from hookahs. Every so often a Marriott employee would come around to replace the tobacco. He would also check the apparatus to make sure it was functioning correctly. I looked around for Simon and his friends and saw a group of men sitting in one corner. Although my gaydar was off due to this new cultural context, I suspected that Simon was amongst them due to their tight shirts, styled hair, and of course their stunning good looks. One of them was a short fellow with red hair and freckles. As I noticed him, he rose and approached me. "Jesse?" he said.

"Yes, that's me," I said in response. "You must be Simon?"

"Yup. It's nice to meet you," Simon said in a heavy British accent, maybe from the North. My colleagues at work were mostly British, so my ear was slowly acclimating to differing regional accents. We shook hands, and he invited me to meet the rest of his friends. Immediately I knew I wasn't attracted to him. He was short and stocky; I had imagined a tall, sexy, sleek, and cosmopolitan save-the-world type, but I told myself I could learn, that the attraction would come. As we walked to his table, I was excited—here was a group of men who liked men.

Simon and I sat down. "Guys, meet my friend Jesse," he said. The three looked at me and nodded. "Hi, I'm Ahmed," said one, who then introduced his two friends, Gamel and Farouk. They inhaled the hookah smoke slowly, eyeing me suspiciously. I was immediately drawn to Ahmed. He had shoulder-length brown hair, sharp brown eyes, and hazel skin. He was tall and had a wide chest. In a physical sense, compared to Simon, Ahmed was all the rage.

"So, what brings you to Cairo?" Ahmed asked.

"I'm here working with refugee—"

"Just like me," Simon said, interrupting. "Remember? I told you that, Ahmed."

"Ohh. I forgot, there are so many foreign boys here." Ahmed laughed together with his friends.

Ahmed might be a player, I thought; I should be wary. I asked him what he did. He told me he was a graphic designer, and lived in Heliopolis, an upscale suburb of Cairo. As Simon and Ahmed hadn't seen each other for a while, Simon asked Ahmed if he had met anyone. Ahmed responded: "Yes, I met someone. But it didn't work out. He was too small, and you know, I like them big." With this, Ahmed shot an impish glance in my direction, tilted back his head, and started to humbly chuckle. As the conversation continued, Ahmed continued to stare at me now and then, seeming to have a twinkle in his eye that said "fuck me." Or perhaps the hookah smoke was just obscuring my vision; I couldn't really tell what was going on. I took a couple drags on the hookah and began to feel at ease—a feeling I wished I could hold on to.

Ahmed and his friends had to leave; one of them had to catch a train to Alexandria. We shook hands, wished each other well, and said that we would see one another soon. Simon suggested we all go to hear a band playing at the Cairo Jazz Club in a couple days. Ahmed nodded and grinned with approval, and then took off. I eyed his figure desirously as he walked away; I guess it had been a while.

Simon and I were left alone—we spoke of work, refugees, the time he had spent in Uganda, and my time in South Africa. Although Simon interested me, he used phrases that were all too common with those who decide asylum claims, such as refugees "asylum-shopping" of "them" and "us." His strategy, and the strategy of most government immigration offices, was one of weeding through the masses of refugees to see which refugees were really genuine. For me, refugees were people, and regardless of their official legal title they all needed help. I was not impressed with Simon. In fact, I was disheartened by his views, though happy he had introduced me to Ahmed. My fantasy had busted, though another was brimming on the horizon.

Two days later, another gay friend, Richard, invited me to a party. Richard is a British diplomat, notorious amongst gay Egyptians as queen of the gay expats. He lived in a swanky British embassy apartment, which had heated tile floors, three bedrooms, and even included a live-in cleaning woman. He had organized many parties—making the best of a British salary in a third-world country.

I arrived at Richard's with some colleagues from work. As most of my colleagues had been in Cairo for much longer than I, they all knew Richard—everyone knew Richard. His parties were not to be missed, I was told. Walking in, I heard techno music. The lights were dimmed, and Richard's living room had been turned into a dance floor. In their Diesel and Armani jeans, two dozen or so olive- and white-skinned men moved in rhythmic motion as one, romping and rubbing their bodies together as if they were at a gay disco in London or New York. Richard's apartment was one of the only places in Cairo where gay men could really let loose. One of my friends from work who had been in Cairo for quite some time told me that this scene was similar to a famous incident that had occurred in May 2001. Egyptian police raided the Queen Boat, a gay nightclub on the Nile, and arrested fifty-two gay men, most of whom are still languishing in prison. Since these arrests, gay hangouts closed or mysteriously vanished. In Richard's apartment, the sexually charged atmosphere was a privilege to be a part of. I was lucky to have found these people, as well as the place. I was happy, and began to dance. I saw Simon and asked when Ahmed would be arriving. Ahmed was too fashionable to miss a gathering such as this.

Simon looked worried, wrinkles on his forehead rumpled together. "You didn't hear what happened?" Before I even answered, his stare dropped to the ground.

"No, what happened?" I responded.

Simon told me that the preceding night Ahmed had met someone off of Gaydar. But the person turned out to be a spy for the Egyptian secret police. Ahmed was arrested and put in jail.

"What? I don't understand. We used Gaydar to meet each other and we were fine."

"Don't be so ignorant, Jesse. This is Egypt; they don't tolerate anything. Ahmed is in jail, and he isn't the first."

My heart sank, my throat swelled. Ahmed, beautiful Ahmed—how could he be in jail? A million thoughts raced through my mind—I didn't know what to think. Madonna had come on—the gay boys screamed, rejoicing, and sang along as their romping intensified. Why weren't they doing anything to help Ahmed? I wondered. Their brother was in jail and all they did was dance. Didn't they know what was going on? What if they were in danger? Wait a second. *I* was in danger, I realized. I had a profile on Gaydar. What if Simon was a spy? If I was arrested, would the embassy save me? I had to get out, I had to leave. I felt like I was going to pass out.

The balcony. Air. I breathed in deep. I tried to feel the air circulate through my body. I saw dirty brown buildings, soldiers in the distance, guarding some embassy. I heard honking, yelling. Simon soon joined me. He told me that the next morning some people were going to Ahmed's trial. I could go too, if I wanted, to show support. I told him I would go. I took in another deep breath. Simon brought me a vodka and cranberry juice. I downed it in what seemed like two seconds. My friend and colleague Jackie had come looking for me. I told her what had happened—the whole situation. "Jesse, this is the norm here," she said. "This is what happens every day. Not only to gay men, but to political dissidents, refugees. Egypt is paranoid about everyone who might be the slightest bit different."

Three nights before Richard's party, Ahmed had arranged to meet a man in front of the McDonald's in Heliopolis, the area of Cairo where he lived. Ahmed arrived and waited. Two black sedans with tinted windows pulled up. Two men in black suits got out. They approached him. Before he knew it, he had been thrown in the car, which then zoomed off to central security headquarters.

Ahmed was interrogated for five hours. The officers accused him of whispering to men on the street, of walking like a girl, and prostituting himself. After five hours of being cursed at, of being told that he was evil, that he had a disease, Ahmed signed a confession saying that the security officers' accusations were true. Ahmed was officially charged with public debauchery, the usual charge issued against prostitutes.

A week before this incident, Ahmed's mother had confronted him, asking him if he was gay. She had screamed hysterically, saying that if he was gay, she would jump off the balcony. Ahmed had no choice other than to deny his true sexuality. At the time of the trial, Ahmed's mother was sure he had had been set up, that this was a big mistake. She even brought a friend along whose son had recently been arrested for smoking marijuana. Ahmed's mother thought this friend could help her through the court process as both of their sons were being charged with similar crimes. She didn't understand that Ahmed was seen as a social evil, a cancer that could spread.

• • •

Ahmed's boyfriend, Jim, an American, had organized Ahmed's supporters and brought us all together at the court. Jim worked for an American development organization, and he too had a profile on Gaydar. He and Ahmed must've had an open relationship, as they both had active online profiles. And, after all, Ahmed was planning on meeting another gay man on that fateful day in Heliopolis. The two didn't seem that compatible. Perhaps I was just jealous of Jim, although this was beside the point now. Ahmed was lucky to have Jim, who had contacted the only NGO in Cairo that helps people in Ahmed's situation. And that NGO provided a pro bono lawyer to defend Ahmed for committing the crime of being gay.

I met Jim outside of a Cairo courtroom, amongst a group of expatriates and Egyptians. Some of them had been at the party the night before, others were new faces. The Egyptians were friends of ours. Most of them spoke English and had spent time in the U.S. or at the American University in Cairo—they constituted Cairo's elite educated class. All the Egyptian men present were gay, and very brave. They could easily have been thrown in jail with Ahmed.

It was a brisk day; a little bit of blue sky could be seen through the brown smog that crowded the horizon. The courthouse resembled those in the U.S., with pillars and steps that people sat on. People were rushing in and out, in and out. Policemen were everywhere. Groups of huddled and fully covered women were also on the steps, holding their babies with gloved hands.

The pillars reminded me of the scales of justice—this was justice? I thought. A gay man being sentenced for being gay? Isn't that the same as a black being charged with being black, as a female being charged with being female? What was about to go on was wrong. Sadly, Egypt hadn't always been this repressive. It had been known as the gay capital of the Middle East, up until the Queen Boat incident. Since then, entrapments of gay men were regular occurrences. The Marriott Hotel, the hotel where I had met Ahmed, was a common place of arrest and entrapment. Egyptian undercover agents would plant themselves at the bar and try to pick up men. Or they would wait in the locker-room sauna, masturbating, and arrest anyone who joined in. Later that month, a friend of mine was lured into a conversation at the Marriott, and then led up to a room with waiting Egyptian police investigators. While he was questioned, the "entrapper" smoked a cigarette on the balcony. My friend was lucky. He was with a monitor from a major U.S. human-rights organization. The Egyptian police became scared by the United Nations identity document the monitor waved in front of them. Though my friend was freed, I decided I would stop going to the Marriott. Although the Marriott is an American franchise, it is still at the mercy of Egyptian despotism. If the police need a room, they get a room—questions are simply not asked.

Jim told us that it was time. As we walked into the courthouse, we entered chaos. People brushed by us, nudging us, as if our presence was undetectable. Guards were everywhere. The hallways were lined with covered bodies; all that could be seen were glimmering pupils. There didn't seem to be a central information point, just people screaming at each other, prisoners in chains being led from here to there.

In the actual courtroom, people were sleeping on benches. A stench of urine rose from the floor, and the ceiling was crumbling. Jim directed us to sit on a row of benches toward the back. Nearby there was a black metal cage that would hold the prisoners on trial. I felt a heaviness inside of me, my stomach tightening. In front of us was the judge's bench—though there was no judge to be found. Instead, the guards in the room had decided to have playtime. They were wrestling, tumbling over each other, like playing and scratching cats. Vendors came in selling tea and chips.

For about ten minutes we waited for the trial to begin, watching the soldiers roughhouse with each other. Then a man from the back rushed forward, shouting in Arabic. He was short, fat, balding, and dressed in a worn-out brown leather jacket and brown pants. Then another man appeared at the main entrance holding a chain to which three prisoners were handcuffed. The guards got off one another; the man who had shouted earlier from the rear was now screaming like a madman. In an instant, the prisoners were led into the cage, unhandcuffed, and locked in. There was so much tussle involved, I didn't get a good glimpse of Ahmed until he was in the cage. Two women rushed over, extending their hands and forearms into the cage in a feeble attempt to hug their imprisoned relative. The prisoner held their hands through the iron bars, trying to embrace them the best he could. A guard soon noticed and shooed the women away.

Ahmed looked like a different person. His beautiful hazel skin was pale. His hair was messy, but still attractive. He looked lost. His mother began to cry. We were nervous, not knowing what to do or what not to do. Two guards stood between us and him. At first we were afraid to talk, but when one of Ahmed's British friends spoke to him, the guards said nothing. They were stone-cold, and became surprisingly well behaved. Ahmed's stare went down our row. When his eyes reached mine, we nodded at each other, and I pointed to his hair. He raised his shoulders, as if to ask what was wrong. I whispered, "Your hair, it looks good." A slight smile emerged; he laughed. At least I could do something.

The man who had brought the prisoners entered the cage, re-cuffed them to the chain, and led them out. More shouting ensued. The prisoners were led to a room behind the bench. The first prisoner went in; the doors slammed shut, and five minutes later he was led out of the room. Then the second prisoner went in and came out, and then Ahmed went in. What was going on? Where was the judge? What were they doing with Ahmed back there? When Ahmed exited this mysterious room, all three prisoners were rushed out of the courtroom. Ahmed managed to turn to us and say, "Tell me." We were left clueless, as he was, it appeared. The courtroom became somewhat quiet again, and the guards resumed their game.

Our group left the courtroom, most of us wondering if our attendance had been worth anything. Jim went to go find the lawyer to find out what had happened. It turned out that Ahmed's case had been deemed a matter of state security. Thus his trial was held in the judge's chambers, behind closed doors. The judge's decision would be made public later in the day. Jim would wait. I had to go back to work. Jim told me and the others that he would let us know the outcome.

Later that day, Jim sent out an e-mail. Apparently, the judge had listened to the argument of Ahmed's lawyer and, without asking any questions, waved Ahmed and his lawyer out of the room. Ahmed was found guilty and sentenced to one and a half years in prison. After what I witnessed at the courtroom, I wasn't surprised. It had all seemed like a performance—like a skit that was acted for someone. I canceled my dinner plans for that evening, went home, ate, drank, and tried to forget. The language barrier, the distance—I felt I was in a place that defined helplessness. I tried to make sense of what had happened that day, though my logical thoughts lost strength as my emotions took over. In Cairo I felt as if I was in the heart of the dragon; I felt the breathing beast against my own skin. I saw what it destroyed, what it left in its wake. I tried to have hope, but it was hard.

The Short Version
by Grover Wehman

Part 1: Swanton, Ohio

Junior high felt like a constant bad day out at the tetherball court. You know, a ring of dirt with a pole and a string with a ball on it. The kids bigger than me would whip the ball around and it would smack me in the face, and then on the way back the cord would rope-burn the back of my neck. Most days felt like that. I walked up the stairs, the jock guys yelled, "Wehman's a MAN" and then laughed and pushed me against the wall as they ran past. The locker room was a whole lot of lotion application and gossip about bras; I had neither. At basketball games when the girls' team was forced to sit and watch the boys, some cool kid would come up to me and ask me to go out with his friend. "He REALLY likes you," he'd say. I'd ignore him until he finally bounded the bleachers away, laughing. When not being harassed at school, I took care of my brothers, read every book in the library, kicked the soccer ball against the garage, ran laps around the field. *Overachiever* is what my older brother said. He called me a resumé builder. Could you really blame me?

Jump forward to fifteen. Born-again Christian. Rural working-class farming and industrial community outside of Toledo, Ohio, the heartland of America. Spending my weekends praising Jesus and preventing adolescent drug use. I wore a button-down men's shirt and a sweater-vest to school every day. Men's carpenter pants. I was a threat, apparently. Backed into lockers. Threatened to be shot. Backed into corners by teachers, asking if I thought I was some kind of feminist man-hater. I would tug on my What Would Jesus Do bracelet, wait for the bell, and dash out. At homecoming while the rest of the girls were worrying about whether their nails were an even coat, I was trying and retrying on the same dress every year, hoping it would be just enough to get through the night without a whole lot of attention. Eventually the stress got overwhelming and I'd throw on a baseball hat as an accessory to the dress. My friends' boyfriends would squeeze my biceps and ask me to flex. There was no winning, and certainly no passing as that kind of a girl, even when I tried.

It all started to settle in and make sense when an older daughter of my drug-prevention group leader told me she was a lesbian. My friend and I stayed up late asking her questions. The next morning I woke up, looked at her, and thought, My God, she's beautiful. I prayed for three hours straight on the plane ride home for a sign that the boner I had for this girl wasn't real. I woke up the next morning and knew it was. I made my amends with God and busted out of the closet with flying rainbow wallet colors.

At sixteen, I found a program that allowed "bright" kids from underperforming public schools to take all their high school classes in college, paid by the state. My first semester, I walked into my freshman writing class, themed "Women in Writing," and who stood up front but a version of myself, only twenty years older. Carpenter pants. Men's shirt. Suit jacket. Long brown hair. A trace of a mustache. The pieces came tumbling down into place. I read the books, took a swan dive into women's studies. I cried and did extra homework every night.

I started telling my parents I was staying at a friend's house when I was going instead to the only gay dance club in town, Bretz. I'd stroll in with my college ID and a group of older sporty dykes that took me in. They'd all get quite drunk and dance and play out their dyke drama. Sober me would just lean up against the bar and smile and smile and make small talk and smile. They all knew I was really young, and kind of took care of me. It was the only time I really lied to my parents. I needed this sanctuary so badly, this place where I could just stand and be.

A feminine popular girl who I knew from childhood was out, identifying as bisexual, but we never really spoke too much. As I became out more and more publicly, she was on me like flies onto manure on that band bus, and I was on her as fast as our adolescent hands could travel. We were butch/femme to the extreme with extreme, extreme denial. The first out couple ever in our high school. Once we were together the harassment got much worse. One time when I was out running in my neighborhood, a car of guys sped by really fast and threw packets of mustard that exploded at my back. They yelled "DYKE" and sped away. Guys pushed into me when I picked her up from parties. Telling me they had something for her I could never give her. Shooting weapons into the air, looking at me with threatening eyes. Cars sped by me as I huddled on the curb at the side of the street, the cars so close I could feel the shape of the wind change when their side mirrors passed. Drunk and dangerous, the men and almost-men in my town. She didn't understand this. Not then. She was the object of their attention. She was gorgeous, fun, and flirty. She was their ex-girlfriend. Whenever she wasn't within two feet of me, it was open season. For our prom she wanted me to wear a tux. Begged me. I told her no tuxedo, knowing such a confident display of my masculinity just might be the last fight I ever got to fight. It was their territory and I was so, so close to finished with it. I wore a pantsuit that looked like a skirt when my legs were together, a baseball cap, and tennis shoes. A comfortable compromise. A halfway way of survival I had learned the hard and harassed way.

• • •

I wish I could say the biggest shock of my first year at NYU was the subway and all the gay people and the amazing time I had. But honestly, the biggest shock was an intense, dangerous class and regional difference between me and my East Coast peers that made my education in white male and middle-class privilege the real focus of my thirty-thousand-dollar scholarship education. I tried to find community at mixer after mixer and meeting after meeting. Fleeting, these connections. And frustrating. And fake. If this rich university is giving us ten thousand dollars to spend as we please, WHY is it important for you and ten of your closest ex-one-night-stands to watch *Queer As Folk* and eat pizza every night? Um . . . what about the queers our age getting rounded up by police every night three blocks away at the piers because they're not white and rich and don't have an entire floor of a building to do their flirting and communing in? What kind of community is this? And how should I know who Ani DiFranco is? Does she play on Clear Channel's radio stations? No? I thought not.

I was consistently confronted with the question: Are you butch? No, I would always answer without a second's lapse. I came out in rural Ohio. My girlfriend and I spent weekends cuddling safely in front of the women's bookstore on lesbian movie night. A very androgynous, anti-SM, anti-porn, Second Wave lesbian feminist bookstore. *Butch* was a bad word I couldn't unlearn for myself at first. I wore only men's clothes, I shaved my head, I had a feminine girlfriend, but I couldn't take that word as my own. In some way, I felt I hadn't earned it. The day I started reading *Stone Butch Blues,* kind of by accident, I didn't leave my bed for class and barely to go to the bathroom the entire day. I lay on my pink husband pillow and cried and cried and cried until at the end of the book I was curled underneath the toilet of the bathroom dry-heaving and bawling and talking nonsense. So much of her story I identified with, either by living through it myself or seeing my life in hers if I had been born even twenty years earlier. I was terrified for my life and my future and the fact that a way of being so despised in the world felt so right to me. So honestly true. I started drag-kinging and reading more about gender. I walked right up to my trans-girl friend who asked frequently if I identified as butch and said with hesitation, "I think I understand now why it was so important to you for me to be butch. I can't call myself butch because I feel like I haven't earned the badge, you know, been through enough yet to be butch, but I think it's the closest thing to me at this point." She smiled and hugged me. Said, "I knew you'd come around."

The first and only summer home in Ohio from college I had a smart crew cut and a baby face. I wanted to work a fast-paced high-paying waitressing job, lay low, mourn the loss of my first girl-friend, and get back to New York as soon as possible. I was more depressed that summer than I have ever been and I hope ever will be. I was fighting with my parents for the first time ever about my gender expression. My underwear, my body hair—anything that made it clear to my mom that I wasn't "outgrowing" that tough tomboy stage. I could NOT get a job, despite qualifications. People would look at me, furrow their eyebrows, and say sorry as I turned to walk past the *Help Wanted* sign to my car. I ended up working three part-time jobs that summer, two with people with mental retardation and developmental disabilities, and one at Steak-N-Shake making about two dollars and fifty cents an hour in tips. I was too rattled over whether or not I was passing or learning to weather the comments and reactions that now roll off me like rain. At that time in Toledo, Ohio, I was frighteningly convinced I was just one drunk angry asshole guy away from saying goodbye to this world in some fucked-up kind of queer martyrdom. And the saddest part was sometimes I thought I deserved it. I lost thirty-five pounds that summer. I sat up many a night just typing nonsense on my keyboard. My mom tried to get me to go to ther-apy, but I was petrified of having a homophobic therapist or a therapist who was going to diagnose me with Gender Identity

Disorder, put it permanently on my record, and have free rein in submitting me to homophobic, transphobic "therapies." This felt especially risky with the "wide range" of options my father's health insurance at the Dodge-Chrysler plant offered. Eventually, my mom said if I found a therapist I could trust she would pay the fees, even though my family really couldn't afford such luxuries. My ex-girlfriend's mom recommended a former college-buddy therapist who she knew was a lesbian. I went for two sessions. The first one she told me all about her breakup with her partner and how badly she needed me to stay in counseling for her financial security. Once we got down and dirty with my "problems," instead of diagnosing me with Gender Identity Disorder, she recommended I just go to the gay bar of my youth and a softball game that weekend and it would all be fine. She said I just needed to meet some "ladies." I sat with my mouth gaping. Did she just recommend— for my severe depression and anxiety over gender dysphoria and fear of queerbashing—that I go to a dyke bar and a softball game and meet some nice ladies? I knew in that moment that my time there was finished and I could not survive there anymore. She was not my people, and my own family, my people, could not be my people. I hitched a ride with a co-worker headed east a few weeks later, weeks earlier than my planned return to New York City. I promised myself to never look back—a promise I thankfully wasn't meant to keep.

Once back in New York, I began talking with my friends and my roommates about all this "gender" stuff. One friend and room-mate came out as trans within a few weeks of school starting back up. Two transguys had started school at NYU and had immediately become part of our crew of masculine people assigned female at birth. A week later, on my way to class, two towers full of thousands of people fell and burned fifteen blocks from my dorm. I covered my face with the football jersey I was wearing and stood in awe as blood-streaked people and my own soot-covered, terrified room-mates stumbled uptown and stumbled over bridges and into the deepest kind of hell I never could have imagined. We called it "the day the world ended." And really, it felt like the day my world ended and another began. A sad, confused state of privilege and disadvantage. Damage to a place that was not my own but was. A world of shock and sadness and losses too heavy for one body or one city to hold. My little genderqueer posse and I, banned from returning to our home, wandered the streets for days. We sat through *Hedwig and the Angry Inch* four times at the Union Square movie theater on day two. A cool, filtered-air place to be. A momentary distraction from ongoing confusion and sadness. A relief from dangerous, choking air. A sick, sick movie-mirrored metaphor for the beginning of a journey to find a gender, a class, a racial, and a political identity that held some kind of honor and truth in a world that had obviously lied too deeply to trust.

Once we had housing again, we began eating out of the Dumpster as our primary form of nourishment. We thought of it as a way to not consume in a world that depends on our consuming (even though our use of the waste depended on surplus creation for consumers). It was a way to balance out our racial privilege (even though not everyone in our posse was white, somehow this was consistently overlooked, as was how privileged it was to feel proud about eating out of the trash) and our class privilege (even though I and others were choking on the reality that we came from working-class and poor homes and attended a super-rich private school that depended on our silence about this fact). Our studying time suddenly centered around when Au Bon Pain dumped trash bags full of donuts, bagels, and pastries, or the fast-food sushi place put its sushi trash on the curb. Nights were spent sitting on a small kitchen floor, eating dry bagels and talking about gender and feminism and telling stories to laugh off the damaging pains of socialization and abuse as gender-variant kids and teens. One of the guys who was new to NYU said to me one night in private, "You know, I'm not really comfortable calling you *she*." And so, the *he* pronoun was born, and I adopted it, thankful to have an option and a relief from the question that had been trying on me so hard the months before and even more intensely following September 11. The name and pronoun change was sent through my classes to my teachers, and on and on.

I always knew I was gender-variant, but I also knew deep in my core that I was not a man, or male, a boy, nor was I meant to be. Being "he" gave me a relief and space from the damaging girlhood and teenage time when "she" and "girl" were consistently used as markers to reinforce how "off" I consistently was in hitting the gendered bull's-eye. I dove into the transmasculine community, hungry to find answers to how I, a young, white, working-class, gender-variant person attracted to women could survive safely and truthfully and honestly in this world. I heard and adopted and threw off all kinds of words and considered very seriously chest surgery and various hormonal options. Some days I thought I wanted to pass, but it was those few days out of the week when I'd walk behind a woman and she'd rush ahead and look frightened, or when I considered my relationship to my beloved in women's-only spaces, that I knew passing for the rest of my life as a boy or man was not right for me.

Eventually, as I healed from the abusive gender binary trauma of adolescence and girlhood and began healing from childhood sexual abuse, I felt more and more comfortable identifying as a woman. And the intense longing for my tits and hips and body to be invisible faded. I realized I didn't hate my tits, just how the world interacted with them. A kind of misogyny I learned about in my women's studies textbooks began jumping out at me in a mu-tated form, at first in slight, then monumental ways within the transmasculine community I was trying to call my own. Girls and femme women were props, markers in which to measure the con-trast of masculinity. It seemed the community had something in-vested in me being on "their team." Even when I requested that my friends add "she" into the mix of "he" they were calling me, I was still he, him, and one of the boys, time and time and time again. When at a queer or trans event, almost always upon meeting someone new, I would eventually be asked, "So, when are you transitioning?" The Second Wave feminist bookstore Saturday-night circle discussions came back to me and I began to wonder, What's so wrong with a woman being a woman like me? Why are we so terrified of things feminine we have to keep them at a distance and silenced? What other kind of oppressions does this look like? What other times in our queer histories does this look like?

I was homeless for a month in January in New York City. Standing on stoops of friends' houses late into the night, ringing the buzzer and hoping they'd answer so I would have a place to sleep that night. Crashing on couches until someone became so obviously overcrowded in their one-room studio that I knew it was time for me to leave. Friendships got damaged, and I became cynical and untrusting of a community that supposedly had my back. I was so ashamed that I had failed the American Dream. The wonder-daughter-makes-it-big-in-New-York-City-out-of-the-cornfield-auto-factory dreams all smashed into little broken bottle bits at the curb I sat on. There was nowhere to go to. No trust fund or a little cash Dad had set aside for the day when I didn't make it out okay. So I did what I do best—packed up my bags and ran away.

I left the city and followed love. I worked too many crappy underpaying jobs to mention. I didn't make it many more times, a few hungry and cold years. I always landed on my feet, and it seems I finally made it out of the downpour. I've created a life that has room for more than struggle. I've developed values that have room for more than guilt and rage. I'm twenty-three now, technically still a "queer youth." My skin weighs heavier and my heart and hands bear more scars in contrast to the bouncing sixteen-year-old with fast hands on the band bus. I'm finally calling myself a butch now. I guess I earned those patches. Like some sick genderqueer version of Girl Scouts. And this is only the short version.

All You Need Is Love
by Stefanie Davis

My sister is transgendered. There, I said it. It's strange that those words become so awkward any time I try to say them. I have recently been able to say out loud that she is gay, but that was with my GSA (Gay-Straight Alliance), so it doesn't count. I don't know why I can't say it—wait, I do know. I can't say it for fear of upsetting my parents.

My sister's birth certificate says Jessica on it; she likes to be called David. I am not fazed by the name nor am I fazed by other people calling her "him." It gets tricky when they call her my brother. I can't say I see her as a "girl," but she's not my brother. I guess in some ways it would be easier to say brother, but that would not go over well with my parents. They are accepting, for the most part. They love her partner and have no problem with the whole gay aspect, but when it comes to the transgendered part, it gets tricky. My mother has the most trouble with it. She worries that my sister was forced by other people to "label" herself as Trans. She blames herself by questioning how she raised my sister. Last but not least is her disapproval of the name choice, David. She hates it. She wanted her to choose a name that was more like the one they chose for her, such as Jess. This is where it gets tough for me because I get caught in the middle.

I can still remember this one fight my mom and sister had that happened around the time my sister was coming out. I was young at the time, maybe nine, and I didn't really know what was going on, but they were both crying and I wanted to comfort them, both of them, which was very hard to do when I only agreed with my sister. I went to my sister first and let her cry on me. Then, feeling guilty for not helping my mom, I wrote her a note explaining my opinion, but still trying to make her feel better. My mom rejected my letter, closed the door on me, and continued to cry.

I can understand how hard it is for my mom—I mean, she *is* the mother. My sister grew inside of her, but I wish that she would remember how hard it must be for her "daughter." My father is not much help either way; he doesn't like to talk things over, he would rather pretend that they don't exist. So here I am, the younger sister, trying to find a way to please everyone.

I call my sister Truffy, short for Trufflebeast, a character she made up as a way to not use Jessica and, I have a hunch, to tell me what was going on. I try to avoid pronouns but I tend to stick to female. I have heard from my sister's old advisor and from her that I was so great and supportive when she was really miserable coming out. All I can say is love. I don't care what gender—or sex, for that matter—Truffy is. I will always love her or him. The person who is my best friend and who I love unconditionally is always going to be there. I can't say it isn't hard, but I am never ashamed or angry with anyone but myself for not being able to say what I need to. I have gained many new friends through the Gay-Straight Alliance at my school who are not there to judge and are able to help me. I want to be there for Truffy no matter what, and I know that my mom will always love her even if she is never able to accept "David." Every time Truffy goes into the women's bathroom and is asked whether this is the women's room, my mom is there to stand up for her, and she's always ready to be a mom. It's never easy for anyone, especially not for Truffy, who has to put herself out there every day and believe in herself no matter what anyone says. But I have the easiest job—all I have to do is love, and that is more than enough. I hope that everyone will be able to do the same because it really is easier to love than to hate.

That Night
by Matthew Mayo

It's 1 a.m. when I finally arrive home.

For the past week now I have spent the nights with you, unable to leave your embrace. I don't know quite what it is about you that makes me feel this way, but I know that I never want it to go away.

At first you were afraid, and I understand. I don't think many people we know would understand this—that it is possible for two boys to say "I love you" to each other and mean it.

I think, though, that as long as we know what we mean to each other, it will be okay.

For the first time tonight, our bodies have touched. I never thought that something could be so . . . beyond words. I never thought that a moment in time could be so special that I would carry it with me for the rest of my life.

I never thought that I could ever be so in love with anyone.

You have brightened my world. And this I will never forget.

I reach the door. Unlocking it, a familiar odor fills the air, burning my nostrils.

Alcohol.

My father has been drinking again. This is nothing new. My father has been drinking for as long as I can remember.

I don't know or understand why. All it has ever done is tear my family apart, opening new wounds, deepening old ones.

I take off my shoes and place my dress shirt on the chair. I would make some dinner, but it is late and I want to go to bed.

I silently creep up the stairs, trying desperately to avoid waking my father. Unfortunately, I don't try hard enough, and he stirs when I reach the top of the landing. Instantly, he begins yelling, speech slurred by the poison flowing in his blood.

"Where have you been! It's one in the morning! Probably out with that faggot friend of yours again!"

I don't know why, but something inside me snaps this time. I have always been able to insulate myself from the homophobia, from the gay bashing, from the hatred.

But not this time. Not this day. The moments with you still linger in my mind, still hold in my memory. They, those moments, will not allow this. Will not allow something so beautiful to be tarnished by something this disgusting.

My mouth opens before I can stop myself.

"Don't ever call him that. Ever. Don't ever say things like that again. You don't even realize what he means to me, do you?"

My mother is awake now. She realizes what I have just said. She just stares at me from the bed.

My father breaks the silence, his voice booming. "You're one, too, then. Another queer."

A tear slides down my cheek as I run back down the stairs and grab my car keys. I should have known that something like this would happen.

That I couldn't hide it from my parents forever.

That sooner or later I would slip up.

I'm at your house before I realize that I have no shoes on. I dial your number on my cell phone and get no answer. I should have known you would be sleeping by now. I leave a message as I continue on to a friend's house.

As I park my car, I fall apart. Hot tears stream down my face, soaking my shirt. It is an hour before the sobs subside.

Andy lets me sleep on the couch for the night. Even if my father is gone, I can't go home again tonight. I can't face those stairs again tonight.

Being so up, then quickly dragged down.

I'm starting to drift to sleep when the phone rings.

I tell you everything.

You tell me everything will be okay.

I wish I could believe you, but right now I'm not so sure.

We spend the next two nights together, you doing your best to comfort and reassure me. I still don't go home.

I talk to my mom briefly on the phone. She tells me all I need to know.

"It's going to take your father some time."

It's three days before I realize that I can't avoid my life because someone can't accept who I am. I resolve. I talk to you quickly for reassurance, then step through the door.

My father stares at me from across the room. We say nothing to each other for some time.

I break the silence.

"It's who I am. I really don't care if you like it or not, it's who I am. I'm not going to change for anyone, and I'm not going to stop being me to make someone else feel better about themselves. If you can't deal with it, that's just too bad."

He says nothing, just continues to stare. Finally he stands and goes to the kitchen. I hear pans banging around, followed by the sound of butter sizzling. He has started to cook dinner.

It takes me a moment to realize that the hard part is past. It will be some time before I can have a real conversation about it, but for now they will let me be.

A week later you break my heart. You do it gently, but you don't do it in person. At first, I don't understand why you do it.

How can you say you love me and mean it? How can we share a moment like we have shared, and then in the next throw it all to the wind?

It takes me time, but I finally understand.

You are not yet ready to face what I have.

You are not ready to show the world who you really are yet. In all fairness, I wasn't either. But for some reason you have chosen to take this road alone, and there is nothing I can do to change your mind.

I move on slowly, to other crushes, other relationships, other heartbreaks. But I will never forget you.

Continuation of the Life
by Tyrell Pough

It's been a hard road for me. Here I am smiling when deep down inside I'm crying and begging for someone to rescue me.

When I was three years old, I lost my parents. My mother died of breast cancer and my father was shot. There isn't a day that goes by when I'm not thinking about them. I miss them so much from the bottom of my broken heart. I want to see them again. Losing parents as a baby is the worst experience a child can face.

I realized I was gay at five years old.

My foster mom abused me with anything she could get her hands on. She used bats, wire, cable cords, pots, hands, anything. She would bash my face in the refrigerator and my nose would bleed instantly. One day she punched my brother and gave him a black eye. I lost my mind and hit her; she picked me up and threw me down the stairs. Some nights when my brother and me would be sleeping, she would sneak and hit us with whips. My brother would be crying my name and asking me to help him but I was too scared.

There would be times when I would stay up all night and would have to memorize the Bible. She said that if I fell asleep while reading the Bible she would hit me. I would have to memorize a chapter every night and I didn't like that. She told me that I'd be nothing in life and she hoped I'd die. I wanted to die, too. That is the past and I want that to stay in the past. When I reached thirteen, I was sent to a group home in New Jersey; I thought this was a rescue from God. My brother was left behind, but he got sent to another place later. Although we were apart, we grew closer together and called each other every night.

I've been through it all, such as physical and verbal abuse, abusive relationships with guys in the group homes, and even suicide has crossed my mind.

I've been in three group homes. It was hard being the only gay kid in each; I remember the other kids in the home telling me that I was straight, but I knew I was 100 percent gay. I was never molested or raped. I was just born gay. Whenever men were around me, I felt safe and secure.

I didn't choose my sexuality, my sexuality chose me, and that's the truth. From my high-pitched voice to my flamboyant ways, like me swishing when I walk, it's all natural. I didn't wake up one day and say, "Hey, I wanna be gay!" I enjoyed wearing tight shirts and jeans and being in fashion shows. As a child I only hung around girls because they treated me just like them. They taught me hand games and how to dance.

The boys used to throw rocks at me because I was gay and flamboyant. They pushed me in a closet and put a dresser in front of it so I couldn't get out. It took hours to break myself out of there and when I told the staff they said, "What are we supposed to do?" and "That's your problem, not ours."

I recall dating this guy from one of my group homes. He told me that I would be happy with him, but he verbally abused me in public. At night, I would ask him why he would abuse me in public, but at night he'd want to be with me. He said, "If they see me being nice to you, they may think I'm gay." He said he still loved me and asked me to try to understand. I still wanted to be with him. He made me laugh and he made me cry. I just couldn't take the pain and suffering anymore. This wasn't my only relationship; I've hooked up with other boys in the group homes. There would be times when my partner would hit me because I said I wanted to leave; they would punch me in the face and push me around.

My friends kept me grounded; they love me endlessly. I did eventually have some good partners, who treated me like royalty.

As of right now I'm in a gay group home called Green Chimneys and I attend school at the Harvey Milk High School. I'm finally getting the respect I deserve. It's a dream come true; a long and painful past is overcome. For those who are in the struggle, hang in there and just believe. I never got left back in school and I am wiser and smarter than ever before. I'm growing up and I need to feel sure about the choices I make.

In life there are many obstacles that I still have to overcome. I believe in myself and I know deep down in my heart that everything is going to be okay. People may criticize me and judge me, but I will not let their words get the best of me. If I feel someone is trying to cross me and take advantage of me, I will talk to the person and try to solve the problem. I have never been a fighter; instead, I resolve conflicts with my mouth. I've been through a lot. It's by God's saving grace that I'm still here and have the ability to never give up.

When I become a father, I'll love my child dearly and I'll give him all the love that I was denied as a child. I identify as a gay male who's open-minded and believes that anything is possible.

Three Sunsets
by Robert Brittain

1.

I'm sitting on my patio.

Sky colors whisper commentary on the sun's movements behind the hills.

I vow to experience more sunsets.

I deceive myself into believing that certain experiences are limitless. If I tried, I could watch tens of thousands of sunsets in my lifetime, though I know the final tally will be closer to a few hundred. In terms of sunrises, I've only seen a mere handful, not to imply that those experiences were trivial enough to fit in the palm of my hand. No, I know they're very much beyond my grasp. And that's probably why I've seen so few.

I vow to experience more sunrises.

There's something about staring into a low-hanging sun that inspires introspection. I always want to talk with God during these times. And that's what I've done for the past six nights: lower my eyes with the sun.

My prayers always dwell on the same topic, the same boy: Devon.

I've never been big on intercession. It's probably because I don't know why I need to pray. Since God is sovereign, it seems like God already has a will . . . a plan . . . a purpose . . . not to be swayed by the requests of a twenty-something screwup in Oregon. But, like a good Christian, I pray. But, unlike a good Christian, I pray mostly for myself and the goofball situations I find myself in. Sometimes I see God answer my prayers, though I guess I'll never know if the answers came as a result of my requests or if they were God's intention all along. Perhaps it doesn't matter.

I've never been big on intercession. But lately I've found myself praying for Devon.

> Dear God . . . I don't even know what to ask for.
>
> I know so many spiritual people who pray for people they care about and yet their requests go unanswered. So I really don't know why you'd answer my prayers for Devon.
>
> I know you love him. . . . I know your heart breaks for him, and maybe that's why my heart breaks for him, too.
>
> God, I want him to experience love. That's all. That's all I want. I know he and I aren't right for each other, so I won't even bother praying for that. But, God, I just want him to know you love him. He's gone his entire life hearing the opposite. God, convince him you're absolutely crazy about him.
>
> Please put people in his life who will pray for him . . . who will love and care about him . . . who will reveal your love for him and what you're really about.
>
> Keep pursuing him, God. Overwhelm him with joy. Overwhelm him with love.

I'm overwhelmed with grief. I'm overwhelmed with despair.

I can't help but weep and I don't know why. My heart has never ached like this.

I watch the sky's first night-freckles reveal themselves. I find peace in their company.

I sit lost in thought . . . lost in feeling.

Yielding to reality, I stand, not really wanting to face the barrage of heart distractions I know are waiting for me inside. But I guess that's what yielding to reality is all about.

I vow to experience more sunsets. More sunsets for Devon.

2.

I'm leaning against my car waiting for him.

The parking lot is almost empty. The sun has just set and everything glows pink.

I want to look busy when he sees me. I check the locked doors to my car. *Locked.* I check the pressure of my rear tires. *Pressured.* I check my watch. *8:55.*

"Hey, Rob." I hear the playful voice behind me.

I turn and see Devon approaching. My heart yo-yos in my chest.

"Hey, friend." I hug him. He kisses me and I lose my balance.

"Whoa, there." He laughs, steadying me with an arm around my waist. "We better get to the movie." We start walking down Main Street, his arm still holding me.

"So how was your day?" I ask, interested.

"It was good, but I have the craziest story for you."

"Oh, yeah? What happened?"

"Well, it's kind of a long one. I was hanging out at Will's house before you got here. I used the bathroom to change clothes and when I came out, he said there were three girls at the door asking to talk with 'the blond-haired guy who just came in'—me. So I went outside. This one girl was like, 'I know this is going to sound weird, but have you ever been discouraged?' And I was like, 'Well, yeah, of course I've been discouraged.' And she said, 'Well, I just want to let you know that God has a plan for you, that something great is about to happen, that you should just hold on. Just hold on.' Then they left. Isn't that weird!?"

I don't know what to say. "It's definitely weird."

Street-witnessers have always weirded me out—mostly because I believe that God prefers spiritual revelation to come through relationships, not five-minute conversations with strangers. But who am I to put limits on God? It *is* uncanny. I remember praying that God would place people in Devon's life, that God's love would be revealed to Devon in profound ways. Was this God answering my prayers?

I'm skeptical.

"So what do you think about it?" I ask, trying to remain neutral.

"Well. It was awkward. They're Christian. Of course they believe God has a plan. And of course good things *will* happen in my future, good things along with the bad. I don't know. Seemed kind of vague. Will thinks they were just hitting on me in a really weird way."

"Could very well be." I leave it at that.

We arrive at the theater and he buys my ticket.

I wake to the feeling of cold plastic on my belly.

I wake to the sound of music playing through Devon's stereo.

I wake to see Devon walking toward the bed.

"Good morning, cute boy." He gets back into bed and kisses me with minty lips.

"Good morning." I speak through my hand, knowing that I don't have minty lips.

"I made you a mix CD." He grins. "So now you'll have a piece of me to listen to when you're at home."

I pick up the jewel case and open it, curious about the track listings. I read the title he gave the mix: *Afraid of Staying the Same.*

That's all it takes. Reading those words unlocks a beast within me. I quickly shut the case and feel an emptiness devour me from the inside out. I know I'm about to cry. *Since when did I become so emotional?*

Devon sees my sorrow. "Awww, Rob . . . you don't like it?"

"No, it's not that. . . . I'm just touched." I know it's not the complete truth, but I don't know what else to say. *Why am I sad?*

He kisses me, interlocking our lips, and grabs my hand, interlocking our fingers.

He holds me as we listen to each song on his soundtrack.

I want to cry through each refrain, but I refrain.

He explains why the songs are meaningful to him and begins to sing along with the final track, "Baby Mine," as if the words were meant just for me.

I close my eyes, more lost now than ever.

3.

I'm scooping ice cream at the coffee shop.

And I hear it.

I know her voice.

I know the lyrics.

"Baby Mine" plays through the store Muzak, resonating in my ears, resonating in my heart.

I sigh without thinking. An instant flood of memories drenches my lowland plains.

"Are you okay?" my co-worker Jamie asks.

"I'm fine. My friend burned me a mix CD with this song on it. It just reminds me of my friend, that's all." Jamie doesn't know I'm gay, so I'm careful not to tell her any more than this.

My managers had warned me about her—warned me not to talk to her about my orientation. When I asked why, they explained that Jamie's a "conservative Christian" who just graduated from a "conservative Christian high school" and would most likely "make the workplace awkward for everyone" if she knew.

"She must really like you," Jamie interjects.

"Who?"

"Your friend . . . who gave you this song."

"Oh, yeah. I hope so." I don't correct her pronoun.

I place the espresso milkshake on the blender and turn it on high, successfully ending our conversation.

The last hour of my shift always seems longer than the rest. My feet drag like the time.

I overhear Jamie talking to a customer. "I love the co-op grocer in Ashland. I always shop there, too. Well, you have a nice night."

"My friend lives right by the co-op," I offer, watching the customer leave the store.

"Oh yeah, what's your friend's name?" Jamie asks, volleying the conversation.

"Devon." *I'm safe. . . . I'm not giving away too much.*

"Devon?" She looks at me through the corner of her eye, suspicious. "Does he have bleached-blond hair?"

My heart skips a beat. "Um . . . yeah."

"Does he have a soul patch?"

I try to stay calm, but my innards are starting to go AWOL. "Yeah . . ."

"Oh my gosh!" She starts to laugh.

I grin to hide my growing discomfort. *Maybe I did give away too much.* "Why . . . do you know him?"

"I think so. Okay, it's kind of a long story."

I raise my eyebrows, prompting her for more.

"Last Tuesday I was walking through downtown Ashland with two of my friends. And I saw this guy go in a house. And I don't know why, Rob, but God was just telling me that I needed to talk to him. So I went and knocked on his door—"

I interrupt. "Oh. My. Lord. That was you?" I begin to have a breakdown. "I went to a movie with Devon that night, about an hour after you talked with him. He told me all about your conversation."

Jamie's eyes widen, as does her smile.

"After we close, we need to talk." She leaves to help some customers who just walked in, leaving me to melt like a summer snowman.

What's happening?

We sit on the curb behind the store. The sun is setting, which means we'll only have an hour to talk before it's dark.

"Okay, Jamie. Tell me everything."

"Well, I was in Ashland about two months ago shopping at the co-op. As I was leaving, I saw this guy who had the most haunting blue eyes I've ever seen and, I dunno . . . he looked so sad. I instantly felt like God wanted me to encourage him, but I couldn't. I mean, how awkward would that be? For me *and* for him.

"But I kept seeing him around town. . . . I saw him everywhere . . . and God kept prompting me to go say something. But I refused. What would I say? It was just too intrusive. I mean, I know what it'd be like if someone came up to me.

"So I shared the story with my best friend at church and we prayed together about it . . . about him. I prayed for him every night for weeks. Prayed that he'd have peace . . . that God would place people in his life to love him.

"I prayed and I cried for a complete stranger. My heart literally felt like it was breaking in my chest. I've had burdens for people before, but this was completely different." She begins to tear, confirming her sincerity.

I want to chime in, want to tell her that my story is similar, but I'm too overwhelmed to articulate anything coherent.

"Whenever I saw him around town, I'd get these visions . . . and I don't mean . . . y'know . . ." She wiggles her fingers dramatically. "I mean, I just saw things. Like him looking into a mirror and seeing a perfect reflection. Simple things like that. Weird, huh?"

She doesn't have a clue how weird it really is. When Devon and I were waiting in line to see the latest summer blockbuster, he shared with me that he had a recurring nightmare as a kid where he'd look into a mirror and see a distorted, twisted reflection. I contemplate telling her this, but she continues before I have the chance.

"So last Tuesday, when I was walking downtown and saw him, I just broke down . . . started crying. I sat on the curb with my two friends and we just prayed. I had no clue what I was going to say to him, I just knew I had to say something. So we followed him . . . knocked on his door . . . asked this guy if we could talk with him.

"He came out and my mouth just started going. I asked him if he'd ever been discouraged or hurt. He said he had, like anyone would. So I just told him to hold on . . . to not let go because God had a plan for him. That things were going to get better, that something great was about to happen. 'Just hold, just hold on,' I kept telling him.

"I really don't know how he took it. His eyes kept shifting. I could tell it was awkward for him. I mean, it was awkward for me, too. I can't imagine what he was thinking."

"Well, he told me what he thought about it," I offer.

"What did he say?"

I repeat what Devon told me.

"He thought I was hitting on him?" She looks devastated.

"Well, he thought it was a possibility. I really didn't know what to say to him. I felt so divided."

"Maybe I should have said more. I don't know. It *was* kind of vague."

We both sit in silence.

"So how do you know Devon?" Jamie asks.

I stare at her, unsure of how much I should say. I figure the whole situation is too bizarre for me to hold anything back, so I jump into the water, knowing full well that the temperature is going to sting.

"Jamie, remember when you asked me about a rumor you heard—maybe two months ago—and I just brushed it off?" Her expression tells me she doesn't remember. "Well, the rumor is true. I'm gay. I wanted to tell you, I was just nervous, I guess . . . of how you'd react."

I keep talking. I don't let her get a word in for fear she'd start condemning me. I talk about scripture and theology. I talk about the two years I spent in ex-gay counseling. I talk about the wonderful things I've seen God do in and through me as a result of my orientation, once I embraced it.

I realize that I've avoided eye contact through my entire rant. So, mustering the mustard seed of courage within me, I look back, preparing for the worst.

Her eyes are soft and watery. Her smile is muted, but genuine.

"Rob. I want to tell you that from the very first day you started working here, I knew you were a man of compassion. I could see how much love was in you. And it saddens me that you'd feel scared to talk with me." She starts crying. "I want it to be obvious that *I'm* a person of compassion. That I'm safe to talk to. It's all about loving people. That's all . . . loving people. Rob, I'd never judge you. Never."

I want to cry, but I have no tears. I want to thank her, but I have no breath. I mouth a silent thank-you.

Silence.

"Rob, this is so weird."

What an understatement.

I tell Jamie about my prayers for Devon . . . about how I've felt a unique burden for him, too.

This is heavy. Too heavy for me.

I have absolutely no clue what my role is in Devon's life.

None.

No clue.

What once seemed like a happy romance now seems like a divine conspiracy . . . a conspiracy so big and so obvious that it doesn't even seem real. I second-guess everything.

I'm petrified I'm going to screw things up.

Maybe I already have.

4.

I'm walking to my car in the dark, but I can tell the sun is rising.

Sky colors again whisper commentary on the sun's movements behind the hills, but this time in reverse.

Everything feels alive and fresh at dawn. I'm a fan of beginnings.

I start my car and turn onto the roads that will take me to the coffee shop. I remember vowing to experience more sunrises months ago, and thanks to my new work schedule, I get to experience a new sunrise each morning of the week. I smile at the irony.

Waking before dawn makes me feel like an adult, like reading the newspaper with my legs crossed or writing a check to pay for health insurance. I must be growing up.

I've grown up a lot this year.

I've grown up a lot in the past three months.

I've learned that there's purpose behind everything, if one stops to look for it. The people I meet, work with, date, or bump into at the grocery store all play integral roles in my dramedy of a life. I owe a lot to these friends, these co-workers, crushes, and strangers, for without their contribution to my life, I'd be without one—at least one worth sharing.

I think back on the next night, eating dinner with Jamie before she left for an internship in Los Angeles. It's marvelous how we came together. She will always be special to me.

Our dinner conversation naturally drifted to Devon. I told her that he and I were no longer dating, that he was dating someone else. I told her I wasn't disappointed, that it was better this way. Things-That-Should-Be always have a way of changing into Things-That-Are. I no longer question my role in his life, for at last it has been defined by our new circumstance. I will be Devon's friend and confidant. I will continue to invest in him, continue to hope for him.

I will continue to love him.

I know that something good always comes from love.

I roll down my window, allowing the morning air to chill my cheeks.

Everything feels alive and fresh at dawn.

I'm a fan of beginnings.

Acknowledgments

We gratefully acknowledge the following for permission to use their work in this book.

"O.K." copyright © 2006 by Courtney Gillette. • "A Gay Grammar" copyright © 2006 by Gabe Bloomfield. • "It's Not Confidential, I've Got Potential" copyright © 2006 by Eugenides Fico. • "Snow and Hot Asphalt" copyright © 2006 by Benjamin Zumsteg. • "When You're a Gay Boy in America" copyright © 2006 by Danny Zaccagnino. • "I Smell the Gas of My Father's Fishing Boat" copyright © 2006 by Adam K. Boehmer. • "Fourth of July" copyright © 2006 by Lauren Rile Smith. • "MY DIARY: DOCUMENTED. DONE." copyright © 2006 by L. Canale. • "Crying Wolfe" copyright © 2006 by Jack Lienke. • "Trans-ventures of an F2M" copyright © 2006 by Alexzander Colin Rasmussen. • "Queer: Five Letters" copyright © 2006 by Kat Wilson. • "Falling Off My Bike and Riding into the Sunset" copyright © 2006 by Christopher Wilcox. • "The Night Marc Hall Went to the Prom" copyright © 2006 by J. J. Deogracias. • "Don't Tell Me That I'm Overly Sensitive and Paranoid" copyright © 2006 by Alex Weissman. • "My poems" copyright © 2006 by Isaac Oliver. • "Sacagawea" copyright © 2006 by Laura Heston. • "A Fairy's Tale" copyright © 2006 by Travis Stanton. • "A Boy in the Girls' Bathroom" copyright © 2006 by Dylan Forest. • "Our Space" copyright © 2006 by Jovencio de la Paz. • "Four Photos" copyright © 2006 by Justin Levesque. • "Break-up in Slow Motion" copyright © 2006 by Joshua Dalton. • "A Story Called 'Her'" copyright © 2006 by Alison Young. • "Moment: This Could've Been Me" copyright © 2006 by Evin Hunter. • "A Quietly Queer Revolution" copyright © 2006 by Laci Lee Adams. • "Hatchback" copyright © 2006 by Kaitlyn Tierney Duggan. • "Walking the Tracks" copyright © 2006 by Eric Knudsen. • "The Most Important Letter of Our Life" copyright © 2006 by JoSelle Vanderhooft. • "Without a Trace" copyright © 2006 by Anthony Rella. • "body isn't this" copyright © 2006 by Zara Iris. • "Nice Ass" copyright © 2006 by Jesse Cameron Alick. • "Girl + Faggots" copyright © 2006 by Caspian Gray. • "Something for the Ladies" copyright © 2006 by Danny Thanh. • "Click and Drag" copyright © 2006 by Joel de Vera Moncada. • "Jill Sobule and Four Other Torture Devices" copyright © 2006 by Ella Pye. • "Gaydar" copyright © 2006 by Jesse Bernstein. • "The Short Version" copyright © 2006 by Grover Wehman. • "All You Need Is Love" copyright © 2006 by Stefanie Davis. • "That Night" copyright © 2006 by Matthew Mayo. • "Continuation of the Life" copyright © 2006 by Tyrell Pough. • "Three Sunsets" copyright © 2006 by Robert Brittain.

About GLSEN

GLSEN, or the Gay, Lesbian & Straight Education Network, is the leading national education organization focused on ensuring safe schools for *all* students. GLSEN envisions a future in which every child learns to respect and accept all people, regardless of sexual orientation or gender identity/expression. For more information on GLSEN's research, educational resources, public-policy agenda, student-organizing programs, or development initiatives, visit www.glsen.org.

According to David Levithan, **Billy Merrell** is the sweet and talented author of *Talking in the Dark,* a poetry memoir he completed when he was twenty-one. In 2006 he will turn twenty-four, marking the first year he would have been ineligible to be in this collection. He is a graduate of the University of Florida and the MFA program at Columbia University. He currently lives in New York City with his boyfriend, Nico; their pug-child, Paisley; and some guy named Nick who has nice hair. He is not the heir to the Merrell shoe fortune.

To find out what Billy's *really* like, visit www.talkinginthedark.com.

According to Billy Merrell, **David Levithan** is the new green, which was the new black. This is perhaps how he managed to write five books (*Boy Meets Boy, The Realm of Possibility, Are We There Yet?, Marly's Ghost,* and *Nick & Norah's Infinite Playlist,* written with Rachel Cohn) in the time it took Billy to finish school. He lives in Hoboken, New Jersey, because it has the best view of the city. He loves his viewfinder because it is the best way to look at his life.

To get an approximation of the full David Levithan experience, check out his imaginatively titled www.davidlevithan.com.

For more information about the contributors in this anthology, as well as other writing on the young LGTBQ experience, go to www.queerthology.com.